The Architecture of
Frederick Clarke Withers

Frontispiece. Frederick Clarke Withers, c. 1861. From
American Architectural Archive.

THE ARCHITECTURE OF
Frederick Clarke Withers
AND THE PROGRESS
OF THE GOTHIC REVIVAL
IN AMERICA AFTER 1850

Francis R. Kowsky

WESLEYAN UNIVERSITY PRESS

MIDDLETOWN, CONNECTICUT

Library of Congress Cataloging in Publication Data

Kowsky, Francis R 1943–
      The architecture of Frederick Clarke Withers and
the progress of the Gothic revival in America after
1850.

      Bibliography: p.
      Includes index.
      1. Withers, Frederick Clarke, 1828–1901.
2. Gothic revival (Architecture)—United States.
I. Title.
NA737.W57K68   720′.92′4   79–25005
ISBN 0–8195–5041–8

  Distributed by Columbia University Press
136 South Broadway, Irvington, N.Y. 10533

Manufactured in the United States of America
First edition

To My Father

❧CONTENTS❧

❧ILLUSTRATIONS❧

❧ACKNOWLEDGMENTS❧

THE SCARCITY of readily available material on the life and work of Frederick Withers has placed the author under obligation to many institutions and individuals. Lack of space precludes thanking all of those persons who have taken the time and trouble to reply to my letters and inquiries. Without their help, much of the material in this book would never have come to light.

This study could not have been made without the assistance of the staffs of many historical societies, museums, and libraries. I owe a special debt to the following institutions: the Library of Congress, the Avery Architectural Library of Columbia University, the American Architectural Archive, the New York Public Library, the Peabody Institute Library, the Edward Miner Gallaudet Memorial Library of Gallaudet College, the New York Historical Society, the Fine Arts Library of the University of Pennsylvania, the library of the Royal Institute of British Architects, the library of the American Institute of Architects, the National Archives, the Historic American Building Survey, and the Buffalo and Erie County Public Library.

Of the many individuals who assisted me in a variety of ways, I am especially grateful to George Tatum, former H. Rodney Sharp Professor of Art History, University of Delaware; Adolf K. Placzek, Avery Librarian, Columbia University; Charles McLaughlin, editor-in-chief of the Frederick Law Olmsted Papers; Charles Beveridge, associate editor of the Frederick Law Olmsted Papers; Lucille Pendell, former librarian of the Edward Miner Gallaudet Memorial Library of Gallaudet College; Giorgio Cavaglieri, FAIA; Wilcomb Washburn, director of the American Studies Division of the Smithsonian Institution; Mrs. Peter Merrill, wife of the president of Gallaudet College; Rose Cline, former recorder of the Parish of Trinity Church, New York City; and Mr. and Mrs. Peter Cantline of Newburgh, New York.

Others who generously provided help include Ronald Andrews, Phyllis Barr, Barry Benepe, Sydney Billin, T. Robins Brown, Catherine

Dembsky, Arthur Channing Downs, Jr., Nancy Ferguson, Margot Gayle, Larry Gobrecht, Peter Goss, Elsa Hasbrouck, Rev. Harold H. Hayes, Robert Heidrich, Corine Hilton, Melancthon W. Jacobus, Terry Karschner, Garret B. Linderman, Jerry Long, Flora MacNemar, Stewart Manville, George H. Moss, Jr., Edna Nichols, Leonard Peluso, Charles Profitt, Judith Schiff, Mrs. Oliver Shipp, Jonathan Slocum, Michael Sulman, Ruth Wilcox, and Annette I. Young.

Finally, I am most deeply indebted to Alan Burnham, FAIA, former director of research, New York City Landmarks Preservation Commission and holder of the American Architectural Archive, Greenwich, Connecticut, for many valuable references and illustrations and especially for his encouragement of my work and for sharing with me his knowledge of American architecture, in general, and that of Withers, in particular; to Helen Ver Nooy Gearn, historian of the City of Newburgh, New York, for material on the career of Withers in Newburgh; to Dennis Francis for his valuable assistance on many important details, especially those surrounding Withers's relationship to Calvert Vaux, and for sharing with me his unbounded enthusiasm for Victorian studies; to Sarah Landau, associate professor of art history at New York University, whose work on the Potter brothers parallels mine on Withers; to Phoebe Stanton, William R. Kenan Professor, Department of the History of Art, Johns Hopkins University, for her expert guidance and criticism; and to my wife Hélène for her unfailing assistance at every stage in the preparation of this study.

The Architecture of
Frederick Clarke Withers

❧ 1 ❧

INTRODUCTION

In 1852, the year Frederick Clarke Withers emigrated from England to the United States, the tide of British influence on American architecture was steadily mounting. To be sure, there was nothing new about Americans looking to England for guidance in matters of architectural design. Nearly all Colonial and post-Colonial building styles in the eastern states derived from English custom. But beginning with Benjamin Latrobe (1764–1820), who settled in America in 1795, professionally trained architects began arriving from Great Britain to practice here. During the second and third quarters of the nineteenth century this trans-Atlantic movement, aided by worshipful natives like Andrew Jackson Downing (1815–52), gained considerable momentum.

What distinguished the later and larger group of immigrant architects from those of Latrobe's generation was their allegiance to the Gothic Revival of Pugin and Ruskin rather than to the Neo-Classicism of Wren and Soane. Augustus W. N. Pugin (1812–52) and his tacit ally the Ecclesiological Society (earlier known as the Cambridge Camden Society) succeeded during the 1840s in making the church the most thought-about building type in England. In Pugin's hands, the Gothic style, which before his time had been imperfectly understood, became the epitome of noble construction. He forged a holy alliance between recrudescent English Gothic and modern Christianity that became one of the enduring characteristics of Victorian culture. First represented in America by Richard Upjohn's Trinity Episcopal Church (1841–46) in New York City, correct ecclesiology, as the new science of church building came to be called, remained an active principle — an article of faith in some circles — throughout the nineteenth century.[1]

It may be assumed that the Gothic Revival would have stayed primarily an ecclesiastical endeavor with an archaeological bias if it had not been for the intervention of John Ruskin (1819–1900). This doctrinaire critic of Victorian taste brought to manhood the cloistered child of Pugin and the ecclesiologists. Under the spell of his lavish thinking the Gothic Revival moved beyond the bounds of English precedent and gained a sharpened sense of moral integrity. Furthermore, the disciples of Ruskin in America and Europe championed the new style for all forms of secular as well as religious architecture. Through the medium of his widely read books and articles, Ruskin's notions came to be more prevalent than those of Pugin had been. This was especially true in America where the persuasive author found an enthusiastic audience.[2]

In recognition of the influential role that Ruskin played, wittingly or unwittingly, in its creation, the style was known even in its own day as "Ruskinian"; although today the more precise term "High Victorian Gothic" prevails. In his works, *Seven Lamps of Architecture* (1849) and *The Stones of Venice* (1853), Ruskin celebrated the warmth, richness, and color of Italian Romanesque and Gothic, which became major components of the new style. He also defined its fundamental architectural philosophy — its moral imperatives — when he extoled the ideals of "truth" and "reality," words which frequently appeared in his writings. Essentially these terms meant that the design of a building must declare its purpose, the logic of its plan, the nature of its construction, and the qualities of its materials.

Although Ruskin, who never actually sought to lead an architectural movement and who generally held unfavorable opinions on contemporary building, gained recognition as the theoretician emeritus of the architectural style that bore his name, it was the English architects William Butterfield (1814–1900), George Edmund Street (1834–81), and George Gilbert Scott (1811–78) who implemented and exemplified the spirit of Ruskin's teachings. Butterfield in 1849 drew the plans for the brick church of All Saints, Margaret Street, London (Figure 1), the first and most famous monument of the new style. Arches, many of them pointed, were constructed of alternating dark and light voussoirs. Together with walls decorated with varied patterns of black brick, they enlivened the exterior of the tower and parish buildings and prepared the visitor for the riotous variegation of the interior. There, colored tiles, glazed bricks, mosaics, paintings, and stained glass kindled an atmosphere more evocative of Ruskin's Italy than of Pugin's England.

Street and Scott, in addition to their buildings, contributed books that became manuals of the new style, although they were not practical pattern books. Street's *Brick and Marble in the Middle Ages: Notes of a Tour*

1. William Butterfield. All Saints, Margaret Street, London, 1849.

in the North of Italy (1855) and Scott's *Remarks on Secular and Domestic Architecture Present and Future* (1857) provided concrete suggestions and examples for architects and the public. They sought to awaken an appreciation of the new ideals of symbolic appropriateness, color, and functionalism, qualities that their authors considered lacking in building up to that time. Street developed the principle of "constructional polychromy,"[3] which was especially influential on a generation seeking escape from the drab urbanization associated with the Industrial Revolution. Derived from the colorful medieval buildings of northern Italy, Street's idea translated the rich beauty of marble into more prosaic and pragmatic materials, such as brick, granite, and tile. He recommended that they be used liberally and imaginatively in the fabric of modern buildings. Street had been ultimately inspired by Ruskin's theory that decoration be organic, that is, consistent with the structural realities of architecture, not merely applied to its surface. Constructional polychromy described what Butterfield had done at All Saints and what Ruskin admired in Venetian architecture.[4] (It would have a strong impact on Withers, who always kept abreast of developments in his homeland.)

Less clearly understood than its English origins is the role French architecture played in the evolution of High Victorian Gothic. While English and American Gothicists were not attracted to the grandiose Classicism of the Parisian Second Empire style — although they did borrow the mansard roof, which became a common feature of High Victorian Gothic — they found other things to interest them in French architectural practice. The French had long been fond of polychrome decoration. Since the 1830s, when Jakob Hittorf (1792–1867) aired his theories of the bright colors that were applied to Greek temples, color had played an ever-increasing role in French design. Ornament based on natural forms was also a serious concern in France, where *Flore Ornementale* (1876) by Victor Ruprich-Robert (1820–87) — whose work apparently strongly influenced Louis Sullivan[5] — was the counterpart to such English handbooks as Owen Jones's *Grammar of Ornament* (1856) and James K. Colling's *Art Foliage* (1865). The Neo-Grec movement, of which Henri Labrouste (1801–75) was a prime representative, and the theoretical writings of Eugène-Emmanuel Viollet-le-Duc (1814–79) also appealed to the followers of Ruskin. The rationalism and structuralism of Viollet-le-Duc and the Neo-Grecs were values sympathetic to those held by the Gothic Revivalists.

Stimulated by writers such as Viollet-le-Duc and Ruskin and by events such as the competition for Lille cathedral (1855), which was won by English competitors, British church architects began in the 1850s to look seriously at French Gothic buildings. There they discovered new forms and motifs to enrich their Gothic vocabulary, notably the apse and the twin-towered facade. Furthermore, in the eyes of Charles Eastlake (1836–1906), the contemporary historian of the Gothic Revival in England, a result of the study of French medieval works was that British "modern Gothic might be said to approach a more archaic type than previously. From a constructive point of view they were pronounced in the professional slang of the day, more 'muscular.' "[6] This austere quality, which was particularly strong in the rural churches of Street and John L. Pearson (1817–97), appears in Withers's church architecture, in such buildings as the First Presbyterian Church at Highland Falls, New York (Figure 50), and the Chapel of the Good Shepherd, Roosevelt Island, New York City (Figure 85).

In the 1860s, Americans became increasingly aware of the comprehensive genius of Viollet-le-Duc, whose influence was to endure well beyond the period of High Victorian Gothic. In 1869 Russell Sturgis (1836–1909) wrote for *The Nation* a highly favorable review of Viollet's *Dictionaire raisonné de l'architecture française du XIe au XVIe siècle* (1867–68).[7] Sturgis revealed that the Ruskinian wing of the American architectural profession, of which he was a leading member, was thoroughly familiar with this and other writings by the French author. After 1870, Viollet's books appeared in American editions, notably *Discourses on Architecture* (1875) — translated by Henry Van Brunt (1832–1903), a prominent High Victorian Gothic architect — and *Rational Building* (1895) — translated by George Martin Huss (dates unknown), a student of Withers.[8] From its beginnings in 1876, *The American Architect and Building News* published excerpts (in English) from Viollet's writings and often informed readers of his activities as a restorer of medieval buildings.

The influence exerted on American post–Civil War building by French architecture, in general, and Viollet's theories, in particular, has yet to be studied. All indications are, however, that it was widespread. Jacob Wrey Mould (1825–86), an English-trained colleague of Withers, clearly modeled the interior of his Presbyterian Church (1874) in Bath, New York, with its broad semicircular arches resting on stubby columns, on "Maçonnerie," plate XIX, in Viollet's *Entretiens* (1864). In addition,

2. Richard Morris Hunt. Music
room wing, Tioronda, Beacon,
N.Y., 1872.

James O'Gorman has shown that the architecture of Frank Furness
(1838–1912), the most original High Victorian Gothic architect in America, would not have taken the form it did had Furness not been familiar
with Viollet's writings.[9] He was introduced to French theories during his
student days in the New York City atelier of Richard Morris Hunt
(1827–95), the first American to study architecture in Paris at the Ecole
des Beaux Arts. Hunt himself designed several medieval-style buildings,
notably the Presbyterian Hospital (1872, destroyed) in New York City
and the music room addition (1872) (Figure 2) to Withers's Tioronda
(Figure 13). There the main body of the house (designed by Withers in
1859) and the music room afford an instructive comparison of the
French and English backgrounds of the American High Victorian Gothic
movement.

More than any other American, Andrew Jackson Downing paved the
way for the influx of British Ruskinian architects and ideals after 1850.
Downing made Gothic a legitimate style for domestic architecture in
America. From his home, Highland Garden, in Newburgh, New
York — America's Strawberry Hill — he waged war on Classicism and
the Greek Revival.

Downing was not an architect but a proselytizer of new ideas in landscape design and domestic architecture. At Newburgh he wrote the popular books *Landscape Gardening* (1841), *Cottage Residences* (1842), and *The Architecture of Country Houses* (1850) and edited the influential journal of rural living, *The Horticulturist*. In these publications he presented the drawings of professional architects, especially those of Alexander Jackson Davis (1803–92) who worked closely with him until 1850. Written descriptions along with explanatory texts accompanied perspective views and ground plans of modest cottages and extensive mansions. Although Downing was not entirely passive in his relationship with Davis, for he often made suggestions that Davis crystallized in architectural form,[10] his chief contribution was the missionary zeal with which he sought to convert the American public to the virtues of common-sense practicality and picturesqueness that buildings might possess. So pervasive was Downing's influence that he was and continues to be recognized as an arbiter of American taste in his time,[11] a major prophet of the "cult of domesticity" that flourished in mid-Victorian and High Victorian America.

Downing's preference for informal arrangements of interior space, his desire that exteriors possess a homelike expression of shelter and comfort — achieved, in part, by accentuating constructional elements such as brackets and battens[12] — as well as his belief that dwellings should harmonize with the character of both their owners and their natural surroundings, had their roots in earlier doctrines of the Picturesque and separated him from the formalistic Greek Revival and lingering Federal styles. His own home, Highland Garden (Figure 3), illustrated the innovative character of many of his ideas.[13] Designed in 1838 (it is no longer standing), the house was Elizabethan, which, according to Ruskin, was "the only style of villa architecture which can be called English."[14] The historical dressing gown was important, for through the associations it conjured up, it conveyed notions of the personal tastes of the occupant and the appropriateness of the dwelling for its setting.

Of equal significance to the style of Downing's villa was the irregular configuration of its ground plan (Figure 3). Even though the main entrance, marked by an enclosed porch and twin turrets, was centered in the facade, the main rooms, which varied in size, conformed to no system of monumental symmetry, but were arranged for privacy and convenience. The stairway, the focal point of the traditional American house, in which it generally occupied a central position, was consigned to a less

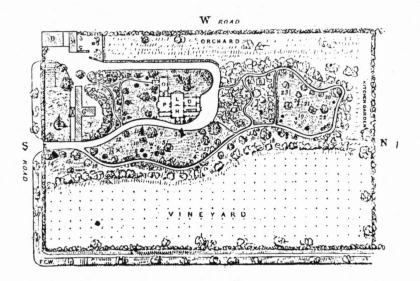

3. A. J. Downing, "Highland Garden," Newburgh, N.Y., 1838,
view and plan (demolished).

important area to the right of the entrance. Cleared of the stairs, the hall was functionally pivotal rather than ceremonially axial and afforded more privacy to the individual rooms than houses built with a central hall.

The elevations of Downing's villa also breached the rules of Classical formality and self-containment. Steep gables and dormers invaded the roof, towers and chimneys animated the skyline, and expansive oriel and bay windows courted the landscape. Low, informal porches, rather than a single imposing portico, further relaxed the tension between the exterior and man-made worlds. The quality of naturalness that Downing sought in his landscape designs appeared also in the planning of the house.

A number of young English Gothic Revivalists took advantage of the favorable climate Downing had created in America. Downing himself fostered the trans-Atlantic migration by turning to England to recruit architects. The first was Calvert Vaux (1824–95),[15] who arrived in 1850, and then came Frederick Withers in 1852. Others who emigrated, though not at Downing's request, and whose careers bear examination by modern architectural historians were Jacob Wrey Mould, Thomas Wisedell (died 1884), Arthur Crooks (1837–88), George B. Pelham (d. 1889), Charles Duggin (1830–1916), Henry Parfitt (d. 1888), Thomas Fuller (1822–98), Thomas Stent (ac. before 1870–c. 1891), and George Kent Radford (ac. 1860–92), who was reputed to have been a student of Pugin. In addition, there were many native architects "under the sign of Ruskin," as George Santayana characterized them. Notable among the American Ruskinians were Peter Bonnet Wight (1838–1925), John H. Sturgis (1834–88), Russell Sturgis, Frank Furness, William R. Ware (1832–1915), Henry Van Brunt, Francis H. Kimball (1845–1919), J. C. Cady (1837–1919), Robert H. Robertson (1849–1919), Edward T. Potter (1831–1904), William A. Potter (1842–1909), and Richard M. Upjohn (1828–1903). When one adds to these the names of men trained on the Continent who in varying degrees shared ideals and companionship with the Ruskinians in the 1860s, such as Richard Morris Hunt, Leopold Eidlitz (1823–1908), and Henry Hobson Richardson (1838–86), one comes to recognize the truth of Henry Van Brunt's statement that "The Gothic revival of that time was a universal cult among all English-speaking people."[16]

Among his contemporaries, Frederick C. Withers's reputation rested primarily on his ecclesiastical buildings. During his early years in America, the English parish church revival, a thorough knowledge of which Withers brought with him, appeared to be a reforming movement. Withers, however, arrived in the United States close to the end of the struggle between the temple and the church. Pugin died in 1852. This was also only three years before the dissolution, in 1855, of the New York Ecclesiological Society whose members thought, somewhat optimistically, that their mission of converting the nation to the propriety of the Gothic style had been fulfilled, at least in the Protestant Episcopal Church.[17] Before Withers published his book *Church Architecture* in 1873, *The Ecclesiologist,* the leading British journal of the Gothic church revival, had ceased publication. Withers therefore broke no new ground. The battle for the English medieval parish church was nearly over, even in America, when he came on the scene.

Throughout his career, in the majority of his church designs, Withers lovingly refined the mature ecclesiological Gothic that he carried with him from England. Unlike his British counterparts, Scott and Street, who expanded the limits of "correct" ecclesiology by the addition of foreign Gothic elements, Withers generally remained closely tied to the Anglo-Saxon purity of Pugin and the Revivalists of the 1830s and 1840s. As late as 1893, he designed a church that would have been equally at home in the early 1850s. He was almost alone in this country in the tenacity with which he held onto the principles and spirit of the parish church style. His contemporaries noted this commitment and implied that the reasons were deeper than artistic. One obituary remarked:

> Mr. Withers was a churchman as well as a church architect, and he was uncompromising. He had his ideas as to what a church should look like . . . and there was no power that could have moved him from his convictions as to what was proper to be done.[18]

Withers's accurate yet inventive manipulation of Gothic forms won him the respect of his American colleagues and endeared him to conservative churchmen. Admirable though it was, however, most of his church architecture seemed more accomplished and original in the midst of nineteenth-century America than it would have in contemporary England. Nonetheless, Withers's authoritative example confirmed in America the spirit and principles of Anglican ecclesiology, which in the twentieth century have produced such monumentally authentic medieval recreations as the Cathedral of St. Peter and St. Paul in Washington

(1907 by Vaughan and Bodley with revisions by Frohman, Robb, and Little after 1917) and the Cathedral of St. John the Divine in New York (1889 by Heins and LaFarge with revisions by Ralph Adams Cram after 1911), both of which have yet to be finished.

Had Withers's achievements been confined to ecclesiastical architecture, we in the twentieth century would have limited interest in him. He became involved, however, in a variety of secular projects in which he demonstrated initiative and imagination. The dichotomy between his religious and secular architecture is one that defines two artistic personalities within the same man. The first was static and conservative, the second dynamic and progressive. As a church architect, he scrupulously adhered to the ecclesiological past; as a designer of domestic, commercial, and public buildings, he espoused new ideas.

The decades of the 1860s and 1870s were the fertile period of Withers's career in secular building. A spirit of experimentation attended his conversion to the "Ruskinian" Gothic. Constituting a sort of baroque phase of the Gothic Revival, this virile, heterogeneous style enjoyed a good deal of success in America. "Ruskinian," of course, is not a descriptive term. It does not convey the essence of the architecture associated with it. Venetian Gothic, alternately used to characterize the same buildings, is perhaps more appropriate but still inadequate. High Victorian Gothic or Victorian Gothic is perhaps a more useful synonym.[19]

The vocabulary of High Victorian Gothic was not self-contained. Its repertoire was derived from the forms of the older medieval ecclesiastical revival, onto which generous quantities of northern Italian and Continental details were grafted. Such a generalization is, however, subject to revision as soon as one examines individual buildings. Accessories from Byzantine, Norman, and other periods, as well as from nature itself, were present. Simple plate tracery in tall pointed-arch windows — which were often clustered together and frequently were divided by a thin colonnette into two lights — colorful polished granite columns with ornate foliage capitals, and banded arches were the chief elements derived from Italy. Elegant *flèches* — generally used to disguise ventilation flues — decorative courses of black brick, bartizans, and semicircular pavilions constituted the most easily recognizable borrowings from the Continent. The inventory of materials included the much favored red brick for exterior walls with white freestone details, lintels, and door frames — hence the derisive name, "Lean Bacon Style." Roofs were steep and inevitably covered with bands or diamond patterns of gray and red slate tiles; ridges were accentuated by spikey iron crestings. Stained glass filled important windows, and even the most economical examples sported carved details in the form of foliated capitals, diapered patterns in gables and under windows, and sculpted decorations on stone lintels. The character of the ornaments varied from naturalistic to conventional, although there was a preference for the former and especially for motifs derived from common leafy plants.

Beneath the diversity of forms, High Victorian Gothic was a complex, additive architecture that expressed itself through multifaceted units. The Ruskinian desire for "truth" led to compartmentalization, which was simple or intricate as the requirements of the structure dictated. Complicated ground plans gave rise to tortuous elevations, such as that of the Royal Courts of Justice (1867) in London by G. E. Street. Simpler buildings had more reserved exteriors, on the premise that an edifice should express externally its internal arrangement of space. Each component was defined in some way on the surface, by a projecting wall, a turret, a taller roofline, or an eccentric fenestration, as the architect endeavored to explicate the mechanics of the building. The structures that resulted were the picturesque sum of their parts.

To naturalistic ornament and functional planning should be added another major characteristic of High Victorian Gothic design: planarity. "As regards abstract power and awfulness," wrote Ruskin in *Seven Lamps,* "there is no question; without breadth of surface it is vain to seek them. . . ."[20] High Victorian Gothic architects treated the wall as a continuous surface enveloping the building and kept buttresses and other elements that might have disturbed the sheerness of the wall plane to a minimum. Towers, for example, often rise flush with the facade and seem to grow from the mass of the building, as in Withers's Tioronda School (Figure 28) and Chapel Hall (Figure 38). Horizontal bands of stone or brick emphasized the wall plane and, by extending uninterrupted around corners and across broad stretches of facade, stressed the continuity of the surface.

Emphatic lines of division derived from this predilection for flat surfaces and went hand-in-hand with the unitary theory of design. Angles and corners were crisp and clean, and openings were given only shallow external moldings or none at all. The parts, whether large or small, always retained their particular identity. The High Victorian

4. P. B. Wight. National Academy of Design, New York, N.Y., 1862.

Gothic architects seem to have sought an architectural equivalent to the sharp focused naturalism and sense of reality of the Pre-Raphaelite painters.

The popularity of High Victorian Gothic in America grew during the 1850s and endured roughly until the centennial year. In England, All Saints, the seminal building, would have been partially familiar to Withers before he left in 1852, for the exterior had been completed by that time. The close attention he paid to the British architectural press, especially *The Builder* and *The Building News,* and his ties with his brother Robert, who established his reputation as an architect in London during the 1850s, brought Withers the information that made him one of the first architects in the United States to absorb the style. As early as 1859, the influence of the polychromatic idiom was evident in his work.

In America, High Victorian Gothic always had the air of a transplanted hybrid. Its monuments were usually grandiose in conception as well as in scale and execution. An enumeration of some of the leading examples, exclusive of the works of Withers, reveals its exalted character: the National Academy of Design (1864, now destroyed) in New York City by Peter B. Wight (Figure 4); Harvard University's Memorial Hall (1866)

5. Ware and Van Brunt. Memorial Hall, Harvard University, 1866.

by William R. Ware and Henry Van Brunt (Figure 5); the old Boston Museum of Fine Arts (1871, destroyed) by John H. Sturgis; and the State Capitol (1873) at Hartford, Connecticut, by Richard M. Upjohn. As the names and locations of these buildings indicate, the style was closely associated with the wealth and sophistication of urban centers in the East; it did not necessarily answer the pressing practical building needs of the new, fast-growing communities in the West. The expense and time involved in the erection of buildings that required large amounts of face brick, dressed stone, ornamental terra-cotta, and hand carving placed it within the reach of only well-do-do patrons. For this reason, it tended generally to become an institutional and commercial rather than a popular style, a fact that, in addition to its connection with England, may have made it seem special to the American layman.

The association with wealth and corporate structure identified High Victorian Gothic in the United States with the spirited culture of the Reconstruction period. The validity of this connection rests on the near chronological coincidence between the duration of the political era and the maturity of the style. In addition, however, High Victorian Gothic eloquently represented the affluence, opulence, and aggressiveness of those years. The flamboyance of Beriah Sellers and the confident drive of Philip Sterling in the novel that is synonymous with the epoch, Mark Twain's *The Gilded Age* (1873), found their physical embodiment in the buildings of the Ruskinian architects. The inflated masculinity of Samuel Clemens himself could not have been more appropriately accommodated than in the Victorian Gothic house designed for him in Hartford by Edward T. Potter in 1874. The daring Gothicists reflected the mood of the age as accurately as the quiet elegance of Augustus Saint-Gaudens and Stanford White mirrored the refinement and quest for stability of the decade of the 1890s.

A significant reason for the extinction of High Victorian Gothic was economic, for the Panic of 1873 put the country into a decade of recession. The affluence that had sustained the expensive architectural projects disappeared, leaving Ruskinian idealism without financial foundations. When, in the 1880s, the situation brightened the caesura had been dramatic enough to preclude any attempt at resuscitation. Compared with the somber and massive Romanesque that had become popular, Victorian Gothic appeared garish and unrestrained.

The demise of Reconstruction in the South and the national return to political patterns of the pre–Civil War years brought to an end a volatile period in American history. The centennial year and the grand exhibition commemorating it in Philadelphia, aroused nostalgia for the apparently simple, unpretentious life of revolutionary America and at the same time turned the nation's attention toward the future and to the frontier of industrialization. In architecture, both of these impulses were felt. Domestic architecture, inspired by the sentimental fascination with the American past, revived early American building forms. The interest in the products and problems of industry and an industrialized society led eventually to the era of the skyscraper.

These conflicting tendencies confused and disoriented Withers, who was not drawn to experimentation with new structural systems and the materials that preoccupied several of his fellow Gothicists, such as Peter B. Wight, who broke new ground in the area of fireproof construction. Nor was it possible for him to become excited about colonial architecture. His experience with Downing, the leader of the departure from the eighteenth-century heritage, would have instilled in Withers a reluctance to work in this tradition.

Isolated by these developments, after 1880 Withers disassociated himself from the most vital currents of American architecture. He took the path offered by the picturesque English Queen Anne style, which he practiced with precision and craftsmanship. Viewed individually, his works from this period continue to display the values of functional spatial organization and architectonic composition. Nonetheless, they also indicate that his esthetic vision had dimmed — or rather that cirumstances had deprived him of it.

In addition to Withers's standing in the architectural profession, the respectable social status he easily attained in his adopted country bears mention. English citizenship and education were fashionable assets. The prestige of connection with Downing brought Withers and the other men who had been confreres at Newburgh further assurances of distinction. His two marriages also enhanced his station: Withers's first wife was descended from John Quincy Adams, and his second was a grandniece of Martha Washington.[21] Withers's background, gentlemanly personality, and devotion to Episcopalianism earned him the friendship and esteem of his colleagues and patrons. Among the latter were: the Reverend Morgan Dix, rector of Trinity Church in New York City; Andrew Haswell Green, reformist city controller of New York; George Bliss, banker and financier; the Reverend Henry Field, popular writer, historian, and world traveler; and Edward Miner Gallaudet, president of the Columbia Institution for the Deaf in Washington. Withers's membership in the Century Club,[22] to which his associates Frederick Law Olmsted (1822–1903) and Calvert Vaux also belonged, and in the Church Club[23] undoubtedly provided a number of contacts from whom came important commissions.

2

EARLY YEARS IN ENGLAND AND AMERICA (1828–1853)

FREDERICK CLARKE WITHERS was born on 4 February 1828 in the quiet English market town of Shepton Mallet in Somersetshire.[1] The facts of his early life, prior to his embarkation for America in 1852, are obscure, and only the briefest biographical outline can be reconstructed. His father, John Alexander Withers (1788–1863), was a solicitor's clerk, but other details of his background are unknown. However, Withers's daughter described her grandmother, Maria Jewell Withers (1790–1865), as a woman of superior intelligence and education who took a direct interest in her children's intellectual development. She personally instructed them at an early age. Before her marriage in 1822, she is said to have been a tutor "in private families and schools of the first respectability."[2] In 1830 she opened at Shepton Mallet an academy for "young gentlemen from five to ten years of age."[3] Maria Withers must have encouraged attention to the arts, for two of her sons, Frederick and Robert, became architects.[4]

In 1839 the Withers family moved from Shepton Mallet to the Dorsetshire town of Sherborne, where they remained until Frederick left for America. In Sherborne he received a traditional education at venerable King Edward's School, where his name first appeared on the register in 1839.[5] In 1844, after the completion of his formal schooling, Withers embarked upon his architectural career. On 15 April 1844, his father signed a certificate of indentureship for his son with a little-known Dorchester "builder and architect" named Edward Mondey.[6] It stipulated that Frederick would work as an apprentice in Mondey's office for five years. The lengthy document, which has a strong medieval flavor, enumerated in detail the obligations of the master, who was required to train his pupil as well as provide "the said Frederick Clarke Withers good, proper, and sufficient clothes, Pocket Money, Medicines, and Medical Attendance in the case of sickness and all other necessaries." The indenture agreement is all that is known of the relationship between Withers and his first instructor. Nor are there records of the buildings Mondey may have erected at that time in or around Dorchester.[7] In any event, Withers's tutelage familiarized him with the principles of construction and the techniques of drawing, if not the finer points of architectural style.

Soon after the completion of his indentureship, probably in 1849, Withers entered the highly regarded office of Thomas Henry Wyatt (1807–80) in London. He stayed there as an assistant until late in 1851, when he accepted a position with Andrew Jackson Downing, who was working something of a revolution in American architectural taste in Newburgh, New York. Leaving England early the next year, Withers began his professional career in America.

No more is known of Withers's activity in London than of his earlier life in Dorchester. In later years, however, in a letter to a client, Withers discussed the position of office assistant. He was undoubtedly describing his own experience:

> To be an architectural draughtsman requires at least three years of office routine, during the first two years of which time the learner is practically valueless. In taking a pupil without any premium it is generally calculated that his third year's services will repay for his tuition on the previous ones — but even this in many cases cannot be reckoned upon. In England five years is considered none too great a time to devote to the study of the art, and no one is considered an assistant until he has spent that time in his studies.[8]

The solid discipline that Withers received under Wyatt, who was described as a "scholarly worker,"[9] was of considerable value in America where such training was difficult, if not impossible, to obtain. Above all, Withers acquired an intimate knowledge of the intricacies of Gothic church design, for Wyatt and his partner David Brandon (1813–97) were prominent ecclesiastical architects. Wyatt, a committed Gothicist, had been one of the four men honored in the dedication of Pugin's *Examples of Gothic Architecture* (1836).[10] He communicated his enthusiasm to Withers, who sustained a love for the Middle Ages and competence in Gothic design throughout his long career.

Like his contemporary G. E. Street, Withers developed as the Gothic
Revival in England was reaching a comfortable plateau; both men inher-
ited its lessons without participation in its struggles. Even Wyatt's Gothic
fervency had cooled somewhat by the time Withers knew him. In 1846 he
and Brandon had experimented with the Italian Romanesque in their
design for St. Mary's, Wilton.[11] By the time Withers entered their office,
the Gothic style was secure in its position as an established standard of
architectural design and was no longer avant-garde. From the first, Withers's churches possessed an easy competence and confident correctness;
they bear no evidence of the striving and searching that characterized the
work of the revivalists of the 1830s.

In America, however, the principles of the Gothic Revival were less
perfectly assimilated than in England. Withers's designs were faithfully
medieval and so were successful here where such historical accuracy was
unusual. In his adopted country, he quickly assumed a place among the
leaders of ecclesiastical architecture along with such men as Henry Dudley (dates unknown), Frank Wills (died 1856), John Notman (1810–65),
Richard Upjohn (1802–78), and John Weller Priest (1825–59).

The prologue to Withers's immigration to America occurred when
Downing visited London in the summer of 1850. At that time he engaged
Calvert Vaux,[12] who had worked in the office of Lewis N. Cottingham
(1787–1847), as the first professional collaborator for his newly formed
"Bureau of Architecture,"[13] as Downing called his workshop and office at
Highland Garden. Through his publications, Downing's reputation had
risen steadily in the 1840s and was at its zenith by mid-century, when he
established his own agency for the preparation of architectural and landscape plans. In 1851, Downing turned to England for a second professional assistant. He entered an employment proposal in a London paper
and Withers responded, fully expecting to be turned down because of his
youth and inexperience.[14] Surprised and flattered when he was invited
to come to America, he accepted enthusiastically. He could have obtained
no more promising position than an association with Downing, whose
eminence was confirmed in 1851 by the distinguished commission to
landscape the grounds between the United States Capitol and the White
House.[15]

Sailing from England in February 1852, Withers wrote that the
American steamer *Atlantic,* even though its engines broke down twice
during the crossing, provided "luxurious accommodations." There were
five meals a day, all "in the first rate style."[16] His chronicle of the journey,

a letter to his mother that is his longest extant personal document, contains observations and commentaries that reveal an alert and engaging personality. The several American passengers favorably impressed him and he described them as "very agreeable." One, who knew Downing, assured Withers that in deciding to leave England for America he "could not have done better as . . . there is such an opening for architects there that a man with a little energy is sure to succeed." Statements like this prompted Withers to call his new acquaintances "the greatest braggadocios I have ever met with."[17]

Withers's arrival in New York was more auspicious than that of most immigrants. He lodged at the Astor House, where Downing promised to meet him. One of his shipboard acquaintances, a congressman from Florida, introduced him to Daniel Webster, who "welcomed us to America and shook us heartily by the hand." Withers had time to tour part of the city. He was impressed with its "beautiful houses, 'Stores' as the shops are called, fine carriages, beautiful women promenading in Broadway . . . the real 'Broadway Swells' . . . and the Railway Trains in the middle of many streets." He also delivered letters of introduction to a number of influential people, all of whom received him warmly and promised to remember him.[18]

Instead of Downing, Vaux arrived to greet the new assistant and Withers recognized him "from his likeness which had been shown to me by his mother in Croydon."[19] Thus it appears that the two young men had not known one another in London. Before Withers left for Newburgh, Downing stopped at the Astor House on his way to Washington and dined with him. Withers journeyed the final sixty miles north to Newburgh alone by train. He arrived late at night at Fishkill Landing, where he stopped at the home of John P. DeWint, Downing's father-in-law.[20] There he must have met for the first time the youngest daughter of the family, Emily, who became his bride four years later.

Despite the advanced hour and the extreme cold, Withers crossed the Hudson to Newburgh that evening. The magic of the river enchanted him as it had Downing, Cole, and Bryant. The scenery was "awefully grand," he thought, as he sleighed across the frozen surface in the moonlight. In Newburgh he was lodged at a boarding house[21] and the next day sipped tea at Highland Garden with Mrs. Downing, who "highly delighted" him.

Fragmentary written and visual accounts permit a partial recreation of the genteel surroundings and hard-working atmosphere of the Downing office. The Downing home provided a unique and idyllic setting for an office of this type, a nineteenth-century forerunner of Frank Lloyd Wright's Taliesin. It was briefly described following Downing's death when the house and grounds were offered for sale, as being

> in keeping with the principles of the art he practiced. . . . It is situated on the northern border of the village, on an eminence which overlooks the Hudson and commands a fine prospect in every direction. The house is in the Elizabethan style, and wears the quiet, unobtrusive air of a gentleman's residence. . . . The grounds, comprising about six acres are all planted in the most tasteful manner and so disposed as to give the most pleasant effect to the shrubbery, lawn and flowers, which blend in a harmonious picture. The collection of fruits, plants, and flowers is very choice and in the best cultivation.[22]

A prodigious amount of work was underway when Withers entered this tranquil retreat. Shortly after his arrival, Downing wrote John Jay Smith in Philadelphia that he was

> really a man of no leisure — except after dinner at home. I wish I could show you my 'Bureau of Architecture'; in my new wing of my residence — full of commissions, and young architects, and planning for all parts of the country.[23]

A writer in *The New York Evening Post* corroborated this statement several months later when he noted that Downing had been engaged on commissions for "a large number of gentlemen about to construct private residences, to prepare the designs and lay out of the grounds," and that even though the office had existed only for a short time, "evidence of his fine professional accomplishments now meets us in all parts of the country."[24]

A more personal account of the office comes from Frederika Bremer, the Swedish feminist and traveler who visited Highland Garden in September 1851. In *Homes of the New World,* she portrayed the industrious environment she had encountered:

> I rejoice to see the development of life and activity which has taken place in Downing. His outward sphere of activity is now very wide and effective. President Fillmore has it in contemplation to lay out

extensive grounds around the Capitol at Washington, and there are here two young architects from England who, under Downing's direction, are preparing plans for houses which he is commissioned to erect for private persons, who in their villas and cottages desire to combine the beautiful with the useful. Downing's engagements and correspondence is at this time incredibly great, and extends over the whole Union, but then he does all so easily, so *con amore*, as Jenny Lind seems to sing.[25]

Miss Bremer also felt she perceived in Downing a growth of democratic spirit, for she quoted his editorial in *The Horticulturist* calling for a pleasure ground in New York, the genesis of Central Park.[26] His budding populist attitude had a positive influence at Highland Garden, for in his essay "Should a Republic Encourage the Arts" Calvert Vaux proposed government assistance to the arts for the benefit of all the people.[27] Vaux also became instrumental in fulfilling Downing's vision of Central Park. Although Withers never proclaimed republicanism, his actions and works in later life demonstrated that he was sympathetic to the views of both Downing and Vaux.

Clarence Cook (1828–1900), the art critic, furnished the most complete and authoritative description of the Newburgh office. After graduating from Harvard, Cook attracted Downing's attention and was employed at Highland Garden as an assistant. In 1853 he wrote an article for *The Horticulturist* entitled "A Visit to the House and Garden of the Late A. J. Downing,"[28] for which Vaux and Withers provided the illustrations. Withers, whose gift for graphics had been recognized, prepared a view of Downing's home and a plan of the estate (Figure 3). Vaux drew several vignettes of the grounds, including the only known picture of the office extension of Downing's house. Concerning the workshop, Cook related that "Mr. Downing's office was the upper south chamber in his house, but increasing business and the frequency of calls made it necessary to construct a room which could be entered from without." He described in detail the wing where he and Withers worked:

An addition was built to the house entered from the garden by a porch, and from the library by one of the book-cases, which, set into the wall, was made into a door, and when shut could not be distinguished from the others in the room. The office is divided by a partition into two rooms; one was Mr. Downing's private study, the other the place where the architectural business was carried on. No place could be more delightful than this room to work in. On one side the southern windows let in warm and cheerful sunlight, on another the rows of books give a grace and charm to the apartment, and opposite them the bright wood fire warms body and soul with its crackling flames. The room is no merely whitewashed parallelogram, but, though inexpensive in its construction, is agreeable in color and proportion. The walls are divided into panels, and the wood-work is stained; some fine architectural prints adorn the western end; and the whole air of the place is that of taste and refinement.[29]

The names and locations of many of the commissions executed by Downing's firm are lost, but Matthew Vassar's "Springside" at Poughkeepsie, the Daniel Parrish estate at Newport, and the government grounds at Washington all date from these years.[30] Withers could not have worked on the Vassar assignment, for as Tatum has indicated, all of the surviving drawings are dated 1851.[31] Nor is it evident that he contributed to the design of the Parrish villa, which was in progress after his arrival. Withers did, however, furnish *The Horticulturist* with a perspective drawing of the house, which was labeled "A Marine Villa by Downing and Vaux, Architects, Newburgh, 1852."[32] The Washington project involved primarily landscape design rather than architecture, and while there is reason to believe that it was Vaux who prepared the sketch for a triumphal arch entrance to the White House grounds,[33] no existing document links Withers to the plan for the capital. At this stage, he apparently functioned as a draftsman, not as a junior partner.

A design for a church is the first positive indication of Withers's presence in Newburgh. In the August 1852 edition of *The Horticulturist* — the last issue prepared by Downing before his death — the frontispiece was a "Church in the Lombard Style" by Wyatt and Brandon, "eminent architects in London," where it had been erected.[34] Withers had undoubtedly brought the drawing with him. Downing, who previously had attacked classically inspired church architecture, reiterated in a brief commentary on the illustration his condemnation of the simple meeting house that had been associated with American piety for over a century. He allied himself with the reformers who preached the authenticity of the Gothic Revival:

> The uncouth wooden buildings with frightful steeples, which deformed so many of our country towns, are gradually being displaced by tasteful and convenient churches of stone and brick, built in more

correct proportions, and the interiors of which are really calculated to raise devotional feelings in the minds of the congregations.[35]

This statement assured a sympathetic relationship between Withers and Downing.

The convivial community at Highland Garden was unfortunately doomed to be short-lived. In late July 1852, Downing, who was thirty-six years old and at the height of his career, perished in the explosion of the steamboat *Henry Clay.* The tragedy, the worst of its kind on the Hudson, was widely lamented. Memorials from friends and admirers appeared in the pages of *The Horticulturist,* but Clarence Cook, casting Downing as "The Immortal," expressed the feelings of those who had been with him at Newburgh:

> Somewhere in silent starry lands,
> Forlorn with cold or faint with heat,
> He folds his ever active hands,
> and rests his never-resting feet.[36]

Downing's death jeopardized the future of the enterprise at Highland Garden. In October, *The Horticulturist,* which had been taken over by the publisher Luther Tucker, printed a notice that Downing's home would be auctioned on the seventh of that month.[37] In the following issue, Downing's friend N. P. Willis reported that two Newburgh businessmen had purchased the estate and planned, for Mrs. Downing's benefit,[38] to market it at a more favorable price. The house eventually passed, in 1853, into the hands of A. C. Alger, who employed Downing's former achitectural consultant, A. J. Davis, to remodel it.[39]

As late as March 1853, the architectural office continued to function in the studio Downing had built, for in that month Vaux announced in *The Horticulturist* that:

> In consequence of the death of Mr. Downing, the business of this firm is now carried on by the surviving partner, Mr. Calvert Vaux, and the necessary arrangements having been made with the purchaser of Mr. Downing's residence, Mr. Vaux' office will remain, for the present, in connection therewith.[40]

The notice also requested that those who had respected Downing should place the same trust in his successor, for "Mr. Vaux has been in close professional connection with Mr. Downing from the commencement of his architectural practice, and trusts for a continuance of the confidence which has been extended to the firm." By June 1853, the office had been removed from the former Downing house; a statement on the inside cover of *The Horticulturist* read: "In consequence of the death of Mr. Downing, the business of this firm is now carried on by the surviving partner, Calvert Vaux. Offices removed to Crawford's Hall, Newburgh."[41]

With the demise of romantic Highland Garden, a new phase began in the careers of Vaux and Withers, one forced upon them by the tragedy of the *Henry Clay*. Yet Withers salvaged at least two important assets from his brief time in the Downing circle: his friendship with Vaux, which produced a successful business partnership, and the association of his name with Downing's domestic architecture, which benefited him for a long time afterward.

❧3❧

THE DOWNING TRADITION
AND ENGLISH ECCLESIOLOGY
(1854–1863)

In the introduction to his book *Villas and Cottages,* published in 1857, Vaux stated that "some of the designs . . . are marked "V&W"; these have been prepared during my three years partnership with Mr. F. C. Withers."[1] The partnership began with the architects' move from Highland Garden after Downing's death and lasted until 1856 when Vaux left Newburgh for New York City[2] to join Frederick Law Olmsted in the preparation of the "Greensward" plan for Central Park. The number of large-scale designs in *Villas and Cottages* shows that during these years the two British architects were in demand as Downing's heirs and young successors.

Villas and Cottages summarized the early careers of Vaux and Withers, but it also included plans on which Downing too had worked. Of the total of forty-nine buildings represented, eleven were by Vaux in partnership with Withers, thirteen were by Downing and Vaux, and twenty-five were by Vaux alone. The self-serving character of the book was criticized by an English reviewer who noted that "on an otherwise blank page at the end of the volume, we find in large capitals the significant inscription, which renders it impossible for anyone who reads the book, to say he does not know where to find Mr. Vaux when he wants him."[3] The "inscription," framed by entwined branches, recorded Vaux's office address and schedule of charges.

Downing's spirit pervaded the designs in *Villas and Cottages* and many of the houses that survive in Newburgh are locally called "Downing houses." Vaux and Withers had united Downing's feeling for rusticity with their own professional sophistication. Generally, the proportions of their buildings are larger, heavier, and taller, and ornamentation is more

6. Vaux and Withers. Halsey Stevens House, Newburgh, N.Y., 1855.

aggressive than in the examples that had appeared in Downing's books. Brick predominates over wood, which Downing had preferred toward the end of his life. Downing's ingenious board-and-batten Bracketed Cottage is conspicuously absent. Where wood is called for, traditional clapboards are used. In addition to the steeply pitched saddle-back roofs that hover protectively over Downing's houses, the elegant curved mansard appears in Vaux's book, possibly for the first time in American architectural literature.[4]

The precise nature of Withers's contribution to *Villas and Cottages* is difficult to establish, for no hand other than that of Vaux is clearly ascertainable. It is apparent that even after Downing's death, Withers continued as an assistant to Vaux, rather than to have assumed the role of equal. Withers, who drew most of the illustrations in *Villas and Cottages,* went unacknowledged when a substantial portion of the book appeared in *Harper's New Monthly Magazine* in 1855 under the title "Hints to Those About to Build in the Country,"[5] even though several of the houses that were afterward labeled "V&W" appeared in the article.

Several buildings with the "V&W" designation nonetheless suggest Withers's cooperation. These are the Halsey Stevens house (Design No.

XX) (Figure 6), the Nathan Reeve house (Design No. XXII), and the E. J. O'Reilly house (Design No. V), all of which are distinguished by surface simplicity that is especially noticeable in the character of the bay windows. Purely decorative details, such as paneled ornament, Moorish balconies, and fancy verge boards, which flavor many of the Vaux designs, are absent. Such sobriety was to be characteristic of Withers's designs after his separation from Vaux.

Likewise, the restrained Gothic details on the Stevens House also point to Withers. The entrance is accentuated by thin buttresses and colonnettes, and at the corners, curved Gothic drain spouts descend gracefully under the eaves. Resembling a sign bracket from the George Inn at Glastonbury that had been illustrated in Pugin's *Examples*,[6] these drains anticipate the accurate derivations from Gothic that distinguished much of Withers's later work.

Vaux concluded the first part of *Villas and Cottages* with a rural church. One is inclined to agree with the English reviewer who said of it that he could not "after the deepest meditation . . . guess whether Mr. Vaux intends his church to be Gothic or Grecian. The truth is, Mr. Vaux knows no more how to design a church than I do to find the longitude."[7] Nothing in the meager building indicated the competent Gothic designs that would shortly emerge in Withers's church architecture. However, the final illustration, signed "V&W," surely was a Withers design. A tombstone in the form of a simple medieval cross graced with a reverent Biblical inscription, it forecast the character and mood of his religious architecture. The marker was a rebuke to the church that preceded it in the book and suggests why Withers moved into ecclesiastical architecture and Vaux did not.[8]

A year prior to the publication of *Villas and Cottages,* in 1856, Withers had married Emily DeWint and initiated his independent career in Newburgh. Professional recognition came in 1857, when the founders of the American Institute of Architects invited him to join the newly formed organization. For the next seven years he enjoyed a happy marriage and a successful practice. He had earlier become a member of the venerable parish of St. George,[9] and in 1859 he was instrumental in organizing another Episcopal congregation in Newburgh, St. Paul's.[10] His formal association with Vaux temporarily ended. The two kept in touch, however, and Withers seems to have assisted, after 1860, in the work at Central Park.[11]

Withers opened his first office on bustling Third Street in New-burgh's waterfront business district.[12] His decision to remain in New-burgh after Vaux had left proved to be financially sound, for he was favored with remunerative commissions from well-to-do businessmen whose prosperity fortuitously escaped the national recession brought on by the 1857 Panic. Before the Civil War, Withers had designed one major church and several important residences and required the help of at least three assistants.[13] The sole representative in the city of the dismembered fraternity of Highland Garden, [14] his practice clearly benefited from the afterglow of Downing's fame.

The link with Downing's memory was strengthened by the curious book *Dr. Oldham at Greystones and His Talk There,* which appeared in 1860. It was written by the Reverend Caleb S. Henry, the transcendentalist minister who had been associated with the New York Ecclesiological Society.[15] Greystones and Dr. Oldham were imaginary creations of Henry, who, speaking through the garrulous doctor, "dashed through" the fields of theology, metaphysics, philosophy, and politics with "charming sangfroid."[16] For the book, Withers, who had designed a house for Henry in Newburgh, furnished an elevation and plan of Greystones, which Dr. Oldham extolled as exemplifying the ideals of the lamented Downing; it was a

> sensible, unpretending house; a convenient and judicious disposition of rooms. Nothing appears to be wanting to the accommodation and comfort of the inmates, who are evidently persons of refinement and culture. The size of the library shows the predominance of in-tellectual tastes in the family, and the general appearance of the interior — its disposition and arrangement — indicates a love for domestic life, for refined pleasures and the simple enjoyments of a quiet country home in the midst of a beautiful nature.[17]

The plan (which is not unlike those of the Clarkson and St. John houses discussed below) provided a great deal of semienclosed space in the form of verandas and a conservatory and makes one think that Frank Lloyd Wright's feeling for spacious interiors extending into the landscape had deep roots in American Victorian architecture.[18] To the reviewer who called the book to the attention of the architectural profession, Grey-stones was the most worthwhile feature of Henry's volume. "If Dr. Old-ham," he concluded, "by writing another book, which he threatens to do,

7. "Glenbrook," the David M. Clarkson House, Balmville, N.Y., 1856.
Architect's watercolor drawing.

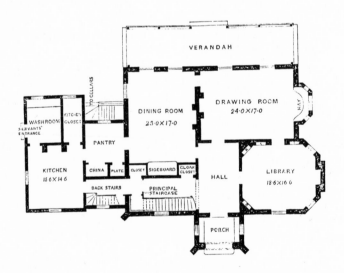

8. "Glenbrook," plan.

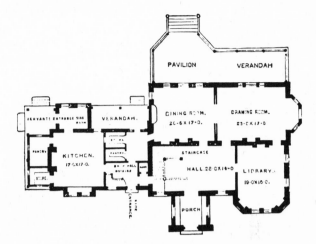

9. Vaux and Withers. Nathan Reeve House, New-burgh, N.Y., c. 1855, plan.

will elicit from the brains of Mr. F. C. Withers another plan as admirable as this, we will be willing to endure the infliction of more of his talk."[19]

Glenbrook, the David M. Clarkson house (Figure 7) on Grand Avenue in Balmville, a northern suburb of Newburgh, was actually the first of Withers's buildings to be published. Dated 1856 and described in *The Horticulturist* as built of brick laid with darkened mortar in order to "avoid the white lines which give so cold and disagreeable an appearance to ordinary brick work,"[20] it too reveals the strong influence of Downing. The hallway preceded by a porch, the separate stair hall, the subordinate service wing, and the careful orientation of the rooms for the best views,[21] all reflected Downing's inspiration. Precedents for these features could even be found in Highland Garden.

Externally, a nice balance exists between the extended horizontality of the main section and service wing and the syncopated verticality of the entrance bay, hooded gables, and chimneys. The calm planarity of the walls, uncomplicated by window hoods, balconies, or labels, invests the design with greater clarity and strength than the more decorated houses in *Villas and Cottages*. The balanced fenestration of the main segment of the facade and the solid proportions also contribute to this impression. Withers composed his volumes and designed his details to insure that substantiality underlay picturesqueness.

The Clarkson house bears comparison to the similar Nathan Reeve house, the most noteworthy design in *Villas and Cottages* and one labeled

10. Daniel B. St. John House, Balmville, N.Y., 1856.
Architect's watercolor drawing.

"V&W." The ground plans of the two residences (Figures 8 and 9) are fairly close. The Clarkson plan modifies that of the earlier Reeve house by the expansion of the dining room into the area of the stair hall, the shift in position of several fireplaces, and the rotation of the beveled end of the library from the front to the side of the house. Otherwise, the plans are alike, even to the dimensions of the rooms. It is plausible that Withers was rethinking a scheme on which he had collaborated or possibly formulated himself.

Another early house by Withers that shows kinship with the Reeve house is the one he designed for Daniel B. St. John, a state legislator, merchant, and banker who purchased twelve acres of ground at Balmville in 1856 and soon established himself there on a gentlemanly estate.[22] The large dark-colored brick house Withers designed for him (Figure 10) rests majestically on the highland ridge overlooking the Hudson.[23] For all its picturesqueness, the design is strictly controlled by the balanced rhythm of the openings, the symmetry of the main block, and the compactness of the outline. This penchant for simplicity, a fundamental quality of the Withers style, is eloquently expressed in the long veranda that stretches across the main part of the house on the river front. The wooden supports, which vaguely suggest the curved braces of a framed timber roof, are light yet sturdy. Flimsy gingerbread details, so prevalent at the time, are notably lacking.

The plan of the St. John house is so directly related to those of the Clarkson and Reeve houses that it substantiates the probability that Withers had a prominent role in planning the latter. In discussing the Reeve house in *Villas and Cottages,* Vaux had stated that "no contracts have at present been made,"[24] indicating that it existed only on paper. Nathan Reeve, a Newburgh lawyer, never built the house; his name disappeared from the city directory the year after *Villas and Cottages* was published and no further record of him has been found. Comparison of the description of the site for the proposed house furnished by Vaux — "a very agreeable site commanding an extensive view of the Hudson River"[25] — with the location of the St. John house, as well as the ground plans of the two buildings, indicate that they share location and design. It may well be that St. John acquired the site of the Reeve house before the building of Reeve's house began and then asked Withers to erect a residence modeled on the one envisioned for the former owner.

The large entrance hall, which was repaneled after Withers's time, assumes the character of a separate room and is the notable feature of the St. John house. The idea for it came from the Reeve house (Figure 9) and was given more monumental expression in the house Withers designed in 1871 for James S. Goodwin in Hartford. The way the wide stairway descends into it anticipates the halls and living rooms common in American houses two decades later. The low scale and tight delineation of space, however, are definitively antebellum and not Shingle Style, nor is there a fireplace, a requisite of the later period. Nonetheless, the hall in the St. John house predates by several years the publication of Robert Kerr's *The Gentleman's House* (1864), which has been considered a likely source for this element in postwar works.[26]

Another important house from Withers's early period, the Walter Vail house of 1859 (Figure 11), is more modest than the previous residences,[27] but it still qualifies as a "villa" rather than a "cottage." The elevation — the most severe yet by the architect — displays the typical pattern Withers used, with modifications, for the next decade. The two-story dark red brick building rises from a low, red sandstone water table to a steeply pitched roof pierced by dormers and capped by massive brick

11. Walter Vail House, Balmville, N.Y. 1859.

chimneys. A tall entrance bay marked by a gable divides the facade into two nearly equal portions. The mellow materials create a warm tonality and banish harsh contrasts. The careful rhythm of the openings and the equation of three vertical elements with three horizontal ones reinforces the cohesiveness created by the materials. The proportional relationship between the walls and roof and the diminution in size of the windows from the ground floor upward compress the design and convey subtle strength. In keeping with the Spartan quality of the materials and design, Withers reduced ornamentation to a minimum, confining it to pierced quatrefoils in the verge boards and carved brackets under the eaves. Only the balcony over the doorway, which has since been removed, made a concession to the frivolous. For the most part, the shapes of the roof, chimneys, bay windows, and dormers provide variety and relieve austerity.

Inside, the principal rooms line both sides of a long hall. There is no spacious entrance hall, as there is in the St. John house, nor is there the easy communication between rooms found in the Clarkson house. The

12. Frederick Deming House, Balmville, N.Y., 1859.

rooms are, however, placed in relation to the landscape, one of Downing's admonitions. The dining room, for example, faces east so that it is
protected from the direct rays of the sun at the dinner hour, and the
parlor is on the west side to benefit from the evening light.

A more secluded site in Balmville was chosen for the home of Frederick Deming (Figure 12), the president of the Union Bank of New York
and a man who was described as "rich by virtue of the laws of inheritance."[28] Subsequently known as the Forsyth-Wickes house, the Deming
house dates from 1859.[29] Possibly as a concession to his client's wishes,
Withers graced the building with more ornate details than his restrained
taste generally allowed. Boldly curving verge boards front the tall gable
of the projecting entrance bay; a delicate balcony stands above the doorway; and stone quoins neatly trim the angles of the red Philadelphia face
brick exterior. "Harmonious and pleasing" were the words used by *The
Architects' and Mechanics' Journal* to characterize the design.[30] Over the
windows of the main facade banded, pointed arches of brick and stone
voussoirs are early signs of the pervasive influence Ruskin's writings on
Italian Gothic came to have on American Victorian architecture.

The Deming house bears evidence of having been finely finished, although years of neglect have left it all but an empty shell. Fortunately, the Metropolitan Museum of Art has removed the library with its handsome Gothic woodwork and ornamental plaster ceiling and will reconstruct the room in its American wing. There it will exemplify High Victorian Gothic taste in the decorative arts.

The grandest house Withers designed during his years in Newburgh is Tioronda, the home of General Joseph Howland in Matteawan (now Beacon), New York[31] (Figure 13). Bearing the date 1859, the imposing brick villa is more sternly monumental than any of the Balmville houses. Juxtaposition with the spikey picturesqueness of Richard Morris Hunt's 1872 ballroom addition accentuates its quietude. An anonymous critic writing in *The Architects' and Mechanics' Journal* about the watercolor drawing (now lost) of the building Withers exhibited at the National Academy of Design in 1860, revealed just how unsympathetic mid-century taste was to such understatement. Especially dismayed at the lack of window hoods, of which Vaux had shown himself so fond in *Villas and Cottages,* the writer complained that "the general impression conveyed by the whole composition is a feeling of uneasiness on account of the absence of those salient features which give the shadow and sentiment so essential to the expression of household comfort. The broad brick facade stares redly and hotly into the face of the sun, and we think of eyes without eyebrows."[32]

Yet Tioronda is not lacking in decorative appeal. Around the doorway and on the porte cochere, banded patterns of stone and brick testify to a nascent interest in colored materials. Withers was, in fact, one of the earliest architects in America to be attuned to the charm of polychromy, which by 1859 had become a major force in the architecture of England and France.

In these early houses Withers expressed his philosophy of domestic architecture. His artistic conservatism led him to select new elements carefully and to assimilate them cautiously into his well-ordered system of design. His work retained a single-mindedness of vision based upon a commitment to the constructive and functional ideals of Downing[33] and the Gothic Revival. He emerged as a designer with a predilection for plain surfaces, clear volumes, and quiet rhythms. These qualities separated his work from that of many of his contemporaries. They also led Montgomery Schuyler to characterize Withers among Downing's fol-

13. "Tioronda," the Joseph Howland House, N.Y. 1859.

lowers as an architect "who was much more thoroughly trained than any of the others in the architectonic as distinguished from the picturesque side of architecture."[34]

In 1858, *The Horticulturist* published an article by Withers entitled "A Few Hints on Church Building."[35] A concise essay offering general principles and practical suggestions on church architecture, it marked the debut of his career as an ecclesiastical architect. Withers's discourse, the title of which was similar to that of a pamphlet published by the Ecclesiological Society in 1841, acknowledged his debt to the English literature of the Gothic Revival, particularly the writings of Pugin. Not wishing to isolate himself from the majority of American Protestants who were still somewhat suspicious of High Church ritualism, Withers adopted a conciliatory tone. He avoided the rancor and condescension of *The Ecclesiologist* in Britain and *The Churchman* in America. Nonetheless, he emerged as an apostle of High Church philosophy and professed ecclesiological principles, which sustained him throughout his career as a church architect.

Reflecting Downing's opinion, Withers began by criticizing Neo-Classical religious buildings. He sternly condemned them as impossible "to recognize as churches from the fact that so little attention has been paid to their characteristic features . . . a court house or a private dwelling, all being after the same model."[36] To remedy this, Withers enumerated the necessary appendages of a proper church: "its heaven-pointed spire, or less pretentious bell-cot . . . its mullioned windows and open porch." These were the requisite historical references that brought to mind the golden days of Christianity, the sacrosanct Middle Ages.

Having pointed out the associational shortcomings of the Classical style, Withers explained the practical case against it:

> It seems to have been the prevailing idea that the ancient Heathen Temples are the best models for our churches, instead of which they are really the worst; for, in the first place, The Portico, with its monotonous repetition of columns — copied perhaps from the Parthenon — made of wood and painted white, is inconvenient; it neither affords protection from the sun, nor the pitiless blast of a winter storm; and, in the next place, to reach the church it is necessary to climb some eight or ten steep steps, rendering it extremely difficult for the old and infirm (for whom it should be the first duty of the church to care) to ascend. On reaching the platform, one sees

doors apparently of enormous size, but which on inspection are
found to open only half the way down, because perchance the gallery
for the "colored population" interferes. The windows are long and
wide, so much so, that if the light, even in the darkest days, were not
obstructed by the green blinds, it would be impossible to sit in the
church with any degree of comfort.[37]

Paraphrasing Pugin, Withers added that "it is the desire of Grecian architecture to hide"[38] what was necessary to construction, a situation that
was often at variance with the practical facts of building in North America. In particular, the steep medieval roof was "more adapted to the
climate in shedding the rain and snow, than a roof of a low pitch."
Furthermore, he said, "there is no doubt that Gothic architecture is the
most suited for churches for this style has the advantage over every other
in its application to all sites and requirements." He concluded the essay by
affirming that the Gothic "is a far more picturesque style than any other,
and if properly built cannot fail to impart some feeling of respect and
awe." Withers presented to his American audience the spiritual, practical,
and esthetic argument that had been offered earlier in England for the
revival of Gothic.

His premises established, Withers explained how to build a suitable
church. Again his close reading of Pugin is evident. He affirmed, for
example, as had Pugin in *True Principles,* that church architecture was an
architecture of unconcealed masonry. Withers advised that "stone for
walls is the best, but where this cannot be procured, then let brick be
used, with no attempt at a disguise."[39] As Pugin had done, Withers also
warned against the use of cheap materials in imitation of costlier ones.[40]
He stated that "no paint, no cement, colored and blocked off in imitation
of stone" should be employed, for "if we attempt to do this we shall
undoubtedly fail . . . for of what benefit is it that we put up our windows
in iron or wood, and paint them in imitation of stone?" Withers then
added a reworded statement of Pugin's — which Ruskin had developed
in the "Lamp of Sacrifice" — that to resort to imitation "must be to deceive man, for God it cannot deceive."[41] Withers concluded this advice
with a Ruskinian postscript that admonished: "If we would that our
works should live after us, and in succeeding generations be looked upon
with interest, we must work with TRUTH; we must let this be our motto,
ignoring all shams whatever."[42]

The model church at the end of the article (Figure 14) was further

14. Model Church. From "A Few Hints on Church Building," 1858.

tacit acknowledgment of Withers's attachment to the English ecclesiological movement. Although he avoided any mention of the historical categories of Gothic architecture or the need for stylistic consistency in church design, he offered a building that was in the "Middle Pointed" (fourteenth-century English Gothic, also known as Decorated) style favored by the English ecclesiologists. His description of the accommodations afforded by the plan (Figure 15) read like a condensation of High Church architectural requirements; he need not have remarked that the church was intended for an Episcopal parish because the liturgical necessities of a nave, chancel, south porch, robing room, chancel arch, and baptismal font were included.

Typologically, the building resembled St. James the Less in Philadelphia (1846), the plans of which had been sent to this country by the editors of *The Ecclesiologist*.[43] Like that church, Withers's example was based on St. Michael's, Long Stanton, Cambridgeshire, a medieval building he would have known from the Brandon brothers' book *Parish*

Churches, one of the text books of the Revival.[44] Although the plan of Withers's church lacked aisles, which the fourteenth-century model possessed, the position of the porch, the arrangement of the chancel, and the eccentric buttresses on the north side and at the southeast corner revealed the debt to St. Michael's. Withers undoubtedly committed himself to the Long Stanton church from his knowledge of its connection with *The Ecclesiologist.* In effect, the Anglican religious community had sanctioned it as an exemplar for American church architecture.[45]

When "A Few Hints" appeared, Withers was already involved with his first religious commission. He was not working, however, for an Episcopal church, but for the congregation of the First Presbyterian Church in Newburgh.[46] The church (Figure 16) he designed nevertheless was draped in full High Church regalia, which included a mock chancel that served as a lecture room. It was one of the first American Presbyterian churches, if not the first, to be designed in the spirit of correct ecclesiology.[47]

Building began in the summer of 1857 when the trustees approved Withers's plan.[48] The congregation had purchased a splendid site, commanding a vista of the Hudson on Grand Street at the corner of South Street. On the north and west sides lay the venerable Newburgh Cemetery, which contained graves from the earliest days of the city's history and provided an ideal romantic setting for Withers's building.

Withers practiced what he had preached in "A Few Hints" and limited himself to the early "Geometrical Middle Pointed," recreating an English parish church of the early fourteenth century. Using scrap pieces

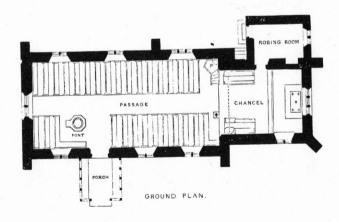

15. Model Church, plan. From "A Few Hints on Church Building," *The Horticulturist* 13(1858).

16. First Presbyterian Church, Newburgh, N.Y., 1857.
Old lithograph probably after the architect's drawing.

17. First Presbyterian
Church, interior.

of stone from flag quarries, the walls were laid in random rubble and dressed with sandstone. Details were drawn from the examples available in various Gothic Revival source books: the nave arcading, for example, has alternate round and polygonal piers and simply molded soffits that resemble the interior of St. Michael's, Long Stanton (Figures 17 and 18); the clerestory windows, which consist of foiled circles set within deep reveals, recall those in the nave of Filby Church, Norfolk (illustrated a few pages beyond St. Michael's in *Parish Churches*);[49] the design of the aisle windows seems to have been drawn from the manual of the Middle Pointed period, Edmund Sharpe's *A Series of Illustrations of the Tracery of the Decorated Style of Ecclesiastical Architecture* (1849); the central window in the facade repeats Sharpe's window from the church at Oundle, Northamptonshire, "in which cusps are used in the circle, but omitted in the heads of the lights";[50] the window at the end of the south aisle follows Sharpe's Plate No. 3, a detail from the church of Sts. Peter and Paul at Bourne, Lincolnshire;[51] the design of the aisle windows derives from the chancel window of Eton Church, Northamptonshire (Sharpe's Plate No. 1), which the author distinguished as transitional because the tracery was not perforated in the head but merely sculpted on the exterior, a peculiarity that Withers imitated.[52]

18. St. Michael's, Long Stanton, Cambridgeshire, fourteenth century.

Inside, attention is focused on the pulpit at the end of the nave, the evangelical center of the church (Figure 17). All details are regularized to suit the taste of the American congregation as well as the esthetic inclination of the architect. The capitals of the nave arcades, for example, have rather shallow profiles that emphasize the continuity of the shafts and arches. The capitals of St. Michael's (and St. James the Less) flared considerably more. Likewise, no unexpected vistas or personal mannerisms detract from the structure's unity. Diversity results primarily from the different window patterns rather than from eccentric details, surfaces, or spaces. The structure radiates order, refinement, and poise.

The First Presbyterian Church quickly attracted favorable attention. Vaux included an illustration of it in the second edition of *Villas and Cottages,* where he singled out the subtly diversified coloration of the materials for special comment: "the work is constructed of grayish bluestone, the dressings and the spire are of a slight olive freestone, and the roof is covered with two tints of slate."[53] Earlier, in 1859, *The Crayon,* the country's foremost art journal, had described the church in detail.[54]

The Crayon had increased its coverage of architectural topics after the formation of the American Institute of Architects, the proceedings of which the monthly periodical reported regularly. The journal also printed architectural criticism, such as the strongly worded attack on Dr. Gardiner Spring's new Presbyterian church in New York City (designed by the firm of Thomas and Sons). In 1858, the magazine castigated Dr. Spring's Neo-Classical building, then under construction at the corner of Fifth Avenue and 37th Street. The critic, who was probably the young Ruskinian, John Stillman, asked: "Why is it modeled after a Roman temple, if it be a Presbyterian Church? or if it be a temple, why has it a spire?" Furthermore, the proportions reminded him of "the Dutchman who built his stone fence six feet thick and four feet high 'that it might answer just as well when it tumbled over.' "[55]

The later lengthy description of Withers's correct Gothic church without any editorial comment was obviously intended as a rebuke to the inappropriateness of the design for Dr. Spring. It was also an admonition to Presbyterians to follow the enlightened example of the Newburgh congregation.

In addition to the article in *The Crayon,* a heartening notice of the building appeared in the April 1859 issue of the journal of the Ecclesiological Society, *The Ecclesiologist,*[56] which since the early 1850s had

19. St. Michael's Germantown, Pennsylvania.

generally ignored American church architecture. The high regard in which the work of Robert Withers was held may have accounted for the attention they bestowed upon the Newburgh church and subsequent buildings of the American Withers. Only on technical points did the British reviewer criticize the Newburgh edifice. He was especially puzzled by the inadequate size of the lecture room at the back, which he mistook for a chancel. Yet he admitted that "Mr. F. C. Withers . . . has built a fair church" and concluded on a characteristically partisan note by saying that while "the building was intended for the Presbyterian community, . . . it is hoped that ere long it may pass into other hands."

Withers's second ecclesiastical commission, a new church for the parish of St. Michael's in Germantown, Pennsylvania (Figure 19), arrived in 1858 while the First Presbyterian Church was under construction. Though still standing, St. Michael's has been greatly altered.[57] Fortunately, illustrations in Withers's book *Church Architecture* provide a clear picture of his first Episcopal commission.

The Germantown church was more modest than the one in Newburgh. Constructed of local, dark gray stone, it was distinguished on the western end by a slender buttress supporting a projecting bell turret. A chimney reminiscent of that on nearby St. James the Less provided a secondary vertical accent on the south side and helped balance the horizontal masses of the organ chamber and entrance porch on the north. As correct ecclesiology dictated, the chancel was fully developed and clearly expressed and enjoyed a more pleasing proportional relationship to the nave than had the lecture room annexed to the back of the Newburgh church.

St. Michael's repeated the plan of the church described in "A Few Hints," with the addition of an organ chamber adjoining the robing room and several feet in length to the nave. The elevation was Early English (the thirteenth-century style) rather than the costlier Decorated of *The Horticulturist* church, for the latter mode would have been beyond the resources of the parish. Such small but important concessions showed that Withers regarded proper accommodation as more important than the charm of style. The idea that the plainer Gothic styles should be employed to meet the requirements of a parish with a small construction budget was an implicit point in his book *Church Architecture,* published fifteen years later. Here was evidence of Withers's desire to compromise neither quality nor principles in less expensive commissions. The democratic spirit implied in "A Few Hints," that tasteful and inventive architecture was the right of every parish, regardless of its size or wealth, was fulfilled. During the remainder of his career, Withers continued to concern himself with secondary church buildings, despite his association with some of the nation's most prosperous parishes. His sympathy for the modest congregation was a legacy of his experience with Downing, who, as Miss Bremer remarked, had been as interested in creating beautiful cottages as in designing elegant villas.

St. Michael's, described by one critic as "cool and pastoral in effect,"[58] was a charming church that conformed strictly to ecclesiological principles, except for a fresh variation in the treatment of the walls. Calling the design "so good an architectural work among our Trans-Atlantic cousins,"[59] *The Ecclesiologist* commented that "brick dressings and horizontal bands of red brick were to be mingled with black brick."[60] The introduction of these materials clearly reflected the interest in polychromy that had preoccupied English architects since the advent of Butterfield's All Saints. Yet, Germantown was far from London, and the parishioners of St. Michael's mistrusted this High Victorian innovation.

In an unusually long account of an American building, the English journal *The Building News* of November 1859 reported:

> The walls were originally designed to be built of blue stone, with dressings, etc., of brick, not only for the sake of contrast, but also on account of the saving in expense. It is, however, to be regretted that the brick was omitted, and stone (the same as the walls) substituted. The change was probably made on account of the novelty of brick dressings, and the uncertainty (in the eyes of the Committee) of its effect.[61]

The most original church of Withers's Newburgh years was the Dutch Reformed Church of Fishkill Landing (modern Beacon), New York (Figure 20). The congregation was under the pastorship of young Rev. John Howard Suydam,[62] who later became a well-known novelist. On 2 June 1858, the parishioners voted to replace their dilapidated and stylistically old-fashioned Greek Revival building.[63] John DeWint's prominence in the parish may have led to the hiring of his son-in-law, Withers, who completed his design for a new church by October 1859.[64] It was dedicated with an ecumenical ceremony on 9 January 1861.[65]

Situated on Ferry Street, atop the bluff that borders the eastern bank of the Hudson River, the church was described by the architect as "a specimen of a very economical building."[66] Constructed of red Croton brick, the large rectangular hall, which held only a raised platform at one end for the elders and a wide loft over the vestibule for the choir, was loosely clothed in Gothic dress.[67] The accurate historicism that characterized the First Presbyterian Church and St. Michael's was lacking. The Low Church denomination and innovative materials seem to have freed Withers from the restraints imposed by Anglican ecclesiology. "It is not impossible," wrote *The Architects' and Mechanics' Journal*, "that the building committee has warned him from the ceremonial Gothic he is so fond of, and so he expresses a simple service with what he can make up out of a puritanical brick wall and very proper lancets."[68]

Only a shadowy resemblance exists between Dr. Suydam's church and an English medieval parish church. The central gable with its arched belfry,[69] borrowed from the parish church repertoire, is flanked by broad gallery roofs. Below, the symmetrical balance of the simple fenestration, the alternating voussoirs, and the barnlike proportions reveal that

20. Dutch Reformed Church, Beacon, N.Y., 1859.

Withers was looking to that Victorian brick architectural paradigm, the Gothic of northern Italy. In its secluded site on the Hudson, the church evoked G. E. Street's description of Cisalpine Gothic:

> The first view of an Italian Pointed Church, whatever its date, is startlingly unlike anything that we are accustomed to in our buildings. It is usually a long, broad, rather low building, lighted with but few windows, with a small clerestory, if any, and with scarcely any irregularity in shape or plan.[70]

The predominance of Italian Gothic characteristics, especially the decorative bands of light and dark brick, qualifies Withers's design as one of the earliest Ruskinian buildings in the United States. It predates, by at least three years, P. B. Wight's National Academy of Design building, which is generally considered the first monument of the style in America. Along with J. W. Mould's All Souls Unitarian Church in New York of 1853, it is one of the first American ecclesiastical buildings to be designed in this manner.[71] Most indicative of the advanced taste embodied in the design was the architect's comment that "when the church was built it was impossible to obtain black bricks, therefore it was necessary, in order to get some contrast of color, to use those of a buff tint."[72]

The modernity of the design confused an anonymous American critic who, in an article in *The Christian Intelligencer,* described the Beacon church as "of a somewhat peculiar, rather Gothic style of architecture."[73] In particular, the facade caused him to remark that "some exceptions may be taken to the exterior." Yet this Ruskinian pioneer won a favorable reception, for the writer saluted the church as a "monument of the munificence and liberality of the Congregation."

Behind Withers's conception of the Dutch Reformed Church stood Butterfield's All Saints, which had established a new architectural language for brick. G. E. Street's *Brick and Marble* (1855) and G. G. Scott's *Remarks* (1857) had been responsible for popularizing the new idiom in England. In *Brick and Marble,* Street defended the correctness of brick for religious buildings and won the approval of the autocratic *Ecclesiologist,*[74] which seconded his statement that:

> As to the question whether it be desirable or not to introduce brick at all in ecclesiastical edifices, or generally in public buildings, one might, a few years ago, have been anxious to say somewhat. I trust, however, that the ignorant prejudice which made many good people

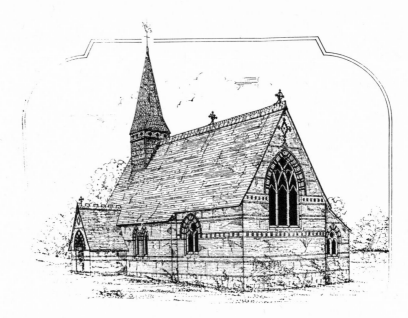

21. Robert J. Withers. St. Helen, Little Cawthorpe, Lincolnshire, 1858.

regard stone as a sort of sacred material, and red brick as one fit only for the commonest and meanest purposes, is fast wearing out, and that what now mainly remains to be done is to show how it may most effectively be used not only in external, but also in internal work.[75]

Two years later, in *Remarks,* Scott noted that All Saints and *Brick and Marble* had aroused much enthusiasm for brick and that "the merits of brick having been much underrated, a reaction has recently taken place, which for the time almost amounts to a mania."[76] Despite his isolation in Newburgh, Withers was aware of the current taste in England — "mania," as Scott called it — for red and black brick; he had also remarked about the beauty of the brick buildings of northern Italy in "A Few Hints."[77]

In addition to the secondhand knowledge of these developments he gathered from books and periodicals, Withers undoubtedly maintained through his brother Robert a direct link with the most progressive English thought on ecclesiastical architecture. Robert's work was frequently discussed in the pages of *The Ecclesiologist* during the 1850s and 1860s. Of direct importance for the Dutch Reformed Church was the publication, in April 1859, of Robert Withers's design for the parish church of St. Helen, Little Cawthorpe, Lincolnshire (Figure 21).[78] It was the first

22. St. Mark's, Shreveport, La., 1859.

patterned-brick rural church illustrated in the British review. The editors described it as a "truly excellent design" for a parish short of building funds and proffered it "in hope of procuring some help from such as may be able to offer it."

Frederick Withers was obviously influenced by his brother's design and, indeed, may have seen the drawing before it was published. Not only were identical materials specified for both the British and American churches, but the American also imitated the distinctive band of alternating vertical red and black bricks set between courses of black brick. The careful spacing of the bands in relation to the size of the windows in the Dutch Reformed Church shows that the immigrant kinsman was as fluent in the new idiom as his brother; the Italianate mood of the American church more openly asserted the source of this new style. The praise afforded St. Helen's by *The Ecclesiologist* unequivocally confirmed multicolored brick as a laudable material for modern rural churches. Withers's Dutch Reformed Church transplanted this axiom, together with its Italian Gothic corollary, to the United States and thus rooted a new architectural species in the soil of the American Gothic Revival.

Contemporary with the Dutch Reformed Church design was Withers's plan for a new building for St. Mark's Church in Shreveport, Louisiana (Figure 22).[79] Why Withers was hired by this obscure parish — in 1856 it was described as "destitute" — is unknown. Nevertheless, the project offered him the opportunity to design an Episcopal church in brick polychromy. As with St. Michael's and the Dutch Reformed Church, however, the architect's plans were not carried out as he had proposed. Once again the choice of materials disturbed the congregation, which rejected Withers's red and black brick fabric for stone.[80]

The volumetric appearance of St. Mark's Church, in general, and the cubistic nature of the details further demonstrated Withers's understanding of the architectonic sympathy between brick and planar forms. The chaste elevation sported a prismatic belfry mounted like a gem between pronglike buttresses at the southwest corner. It was a stroke of complexity that had as its antecedent the central buttress and belfry of St. Michael's. The ground plan and side elevations were nearly identical to those of St. Michael's, except for the porch and organ chamber, which were placed on the more ecclesiologically correct southern side rather than on the northern side as they had been, because of the nature of the site, in the Germantown church.

Clearly, in St. Mark's, Withers sought to combine new materials with the ecclesiological tradition. But strangely, neither the Dutch Reformed Church nor St. Mark's was the beginning of a line of development for Withers. In his post–Civil War church architecture, he returned to standard ecclesiology and reserve Ruskinianism for his secular architecture.

Soon after the Civil War began, Withers, thirty-three years old and head of a young family, volunteered for service in the Union Army. Why he did so remains a mystery, since he never became an American citizen.[81] Of the small circle of men who had been close to Downing, including Vaux, who had acquired American citizenship in 1856,[82] Withers alone volunteered for military service. Possibly his association with the Reverend Mr. Sprole of the First Presbyterian Church and the Reverend Mr. Suydam of the Dutch Reformed Church swayed him, for both men were outspoken abolitionists.[83] Perhaps he simply became caught up in the rousing spirit of the times, which stirred his brother-in-law, Clarence Cook, to write: "But nothing is talked about now — nothing but 'war.' . . . Never have I seen such enthusiasm, such devotion, such generous feeling prompting to sacrifice, the kindly feeling among all classes, to the healing of old feuds and differences as is rife today."[84]

Withers responded to the call for volunteers to serve three years issued by President Lincoln after the disastrous first battle of Bull Run. Immediately after signing up in New York City on 16 August 1861,[85] he received a commission as lieutenant in Company B of the First New York Engineers. His unit became a contingent of the Port Royal, South Carolina, Expeditionary Corps, which was charged with the enforcement of the Union blockade of the southern coast in South Carolina, Georgia, and northern Florida.

The siege of Fort Pulaski, Georgia, was the most important operation in which Withers participated. The painstaking preparations for the investment of the fort began in January 1862 and entailed engineering efforts that the indomitable General Quincy Gillmore, the officer in charge, described as "herculean."[86] Heavy Parrot guns had to be hauled furtively into position through unwholesome swamps under the cover of darkness. The arduous groundwork proved worthwhile, and the reduction of the fort, which was a victory of engineering and weaponry, figured as one of the significant episodes of the war and of seaboard warfare in general.[87]

The investment of Fort Pulaski was successfully concluded on 11 April 1862. Three days later Withers applied for a leave of absence. The "Miasmic" conditions of the wetlands had seriously impaired his health.[88] He was granted an extended leave and returned North, where he remained until 6 June, when he rejoined his company at Legareville on St. John's Island, South Carolina, where they were preparing to take Secessionville. Lingering illness incapacitated him, however, and on the tenth of August he tendered his resignation. The regimental surgeon pointed out that Withers's condition had worsened since his leave of absence in April. "He never can endure the effects of this climate," he wrote, "I consider a change of climate necessary to prevent permanent disability."[89]

His military avocation ended and his health undermined, Withers returned home to Newburgh to recuperate. There he suffered a deeper misfortune in the death of his wife in July 1863.[90] The time was right for a change. He left the Hudson River community for New York City. As he had done twelve years before, after the death of Downing when tragedy had closed a period of his career, he entered into partnership with Vaux.[91] With Withers's departure, the final vestige of Downing's memory disappeared from Newburgh, a town that, since the 1840s, had been identified with horticulture, rural life, and the architecture of country houses.

4

MODERNISM
AND CONSERVATISM
(1864–1870)

MARRIAGE in 1864 to Beulah Alice Higbee,[1] the daughter of the Reverend Edward Young Higbee, popular assistant minister of New York City's Trinity Church, marked the beginning of the most successful period of Withers's career. He became a leader among those Eastern architects who were endeavoring to draw the Gothic Revival out of the quiet sanctuary of ecclesiastical architecture and into the bustling world of commercial and institutional building.[2] During the decade after the Civil War, Withers helped establish the riches and beauties of the English High Victorian Gothic style in America. He was one of the "younger American architects of the early 1860's," as Montgomery Schuyler described them, who "betook themselves more and more to Italy for the motives and treatment of their secular designs in Gothic"[3] and constituted part of the international Gothic movement associated with Ruskin in England and Viollet-le-Duc in France.

At the same time, Withers sustained his reputation as a church architect who adhered to the traditional forms of the Gothic Revival. His renown as a craftsman in church design flourished alongside his fame as an adventurous secular architect. His attachment to Gothic, a commitment that Dr. Morgan Dix of Trinity Church described as "devout religious purpose,"[4] was admired. It brought him important commissions, although it eventually relegated him to the second rank of ecclesiastical architects.

After recuperating from his wartime illness, Withers immediately resumed his mission as a churchman and religious architect. His first church design was for his own parish, St. Paul's in Newburgh (Figure 23). The cornerstone was laid on 1 June 1865,[5] but the large structure was

23. St. Paul's, Newburgh, N.Y., 1864.

too extravagant for the young flock, which had separated from St. George Church in 1857,[6] and was never finished. The building stands half completed even today.[7]

The stolid Early English cruciform church with squared rubble walls and brownstone dressings was designed with a tower clustered with an organ chamber, north and south transepts, robing room, and chancel on the Grand Street side of the churchyard. This arrangement, which relegated the front of the building to a secondary position at the rear of the narrow lot, assured proper orientation with the chancel in the eastern end. The disposition of St. Paul's would have afforded an instructive contrast with Withers's First Presbyterian Church (Figure 16), several doors south on the same side of Grand Street. Built without regard for ecclesiological orientation, the ceremonial end and mock chancel of the earlier church faced west, although its tower, like that of St. Paul's, climaxed the composition on Grand Street. Illustrating the flexibility that was an attribute of the medieval idiom and that he had espoused in "A Few Hints,"[8] St. Paul's and the First Presbyterian Church together would have exemplified Withers' ability to reconcile physical and esthetic demands with religious imperatives.

24. Robert J. Withers. St. Llandgwydd Church, Cardigan, Wales, 1862.

St. Paul's owed its conception to the recently completed Anglican church of St. Llandgwydd in Cardigan, Wales, a design of Robert Withers (Figure 24) that had been published by *The Building News* in August 1862.[9] Because the Welsh church displayed correct orientation under circumstances similar to those of the Newburgh church, Withers had appropriated his brother's building as a model for St. Paul's. Not only did St. Llandgwydd's tower inspire that of St. Paul's, but its composition — tower on the south and chancel bordering the road — was echoed by the plan of the American church.

Even before the close of the Civil War, Withers attempted to broaden the scope of the Gothic Revival beyond the limits of church architecture. In 1864 he designed the Quassaick Bank of Newburgh[10] (Figure 25) in the High Victorian Gothic style, which was almost as unique then for commercial as it had been for ecclesiastical architecture when Withers drew the plans for the Dutch Reformed Church in 1859. In 1862, P. B. Wight built the Middletown Bank in nearby Middletown, New York, in incipient High Victorian Gothic. It displayed Italianate

25. Quassaick Bank, Newburgh, N.Y., 1864 (project). Architect's elevation drawing.

details only on the ground floor.[11] Withers's mature handling of the style in the Quassaick Bank facade far surpassed Wight's example. Throughout its elevation the Newburgh bank exhibited a developed High Victorian vocabulary of forms, including pointed arches, alternating voussoirs, stone bands, and roundels.

Withers regarded the Quassaick Bank design as significant. When the Boston architect William R. Ware traveled to London in 1867 to address the Royal Institute of British Architects on the condition of American architecture, Withers gave him a copy of the Quassaick Bank drawing to present to the Institute.[12] Ware offered Withers's sketch to his English audience as an example of advanced design in the United States. He had no need to apologize for American provincialism; Withers's lively building would have been more at home on Fleet Street than in Newburgh.

26. Eugene Brewster House, Newburgh, N.Y., 1865.

Commercial structures such as the Quassaick Bank permitted Withers to develop fully his High Victorian preferences. In domestic architecture, however, he continued to perpetuate the Downing legacy. What at Tioronda and the Deming house had been first steps toward reconciling Ruskinian modernism with his well-established mode of domestic design, by 1865 had become a commitment. The Eugene Brewster house erected that year in Newburgh[13] boldly features a banded entranceway in the form of a "Florentine" arch — the intrados is round, the extrados pointed (Figure 26). Another fine brick villa, Eustasia, which is closely related to the Brewster house, also makes use of polychromatic enrichment (Figure 27). Built for Withers's friend Judge John Monell on a magnificent site overlooking the Hudson at Beacon (formerly Fishkill Landing), New York,[14] the house bears the date 1867, two years after Monell had married Downing's widow, Caroline. In addition to a banded entrance arch, Eustasia has "Milwaukee brick, of a soft buff color . . . over the windows of the upper story, and as a moulding around the summit of the simple, clustered chimneys."[15] The yellow brick recalls the nearby

27. "Eustasia," Judge John Monell House, Beacon, N.Y., 1867.

Dutch Reformed Church, where it had been substituted for black brick, which was unobtainable in 1859. The local building situation had apparently not changed in six years, and Withers was again compelled to employ contrasts tamer than he would have liked. Nevertheless, patterns of mixed materials were a standard element of Withers's domestic architecture from then on. Otherwise he maintained the tradition established in his prewar houses, which owed so much to Downing. During the ensuing years, he brought to maturity this uniquely American product of the High Victorian Gothic movement.

In 1865 Withers was called back to Tioronda by General Howland, who wished to erect a schoolhouse on his estate. The Tioronda School (Figure 28), as it came to be known, was a gift to the children of the neighborhood from the philanthropic general, who asked only that he be allowed to conduct Sunday school classes in the building.[16] Idyllically placed in a dale near a babbling brook, the charming schoolhouse is built of red brick with courses of dark blue stone and primitive impost blocks of white sandstone. A massive chimney, which Withers felt presented "a

28. Tioronda School, Beacon, N.Y., 1865.

bold appearance,"[17] projects on stepped corbels from the south side and answers the engaged tower on the west.

The commission for the Tioronda School proved an important one for Withers's growing reputation. *The New Path,* the radical Ruskinian magazine published by the Society for the Advancement of Truth in Art,[18] warmly endorsed the design.[19] Commenting on the watercolor rendering Withers exhibited at the National Academy of Design in 1866, the journal commended the building for its outstanding virtue of "truth" and its undisguised statement of function:

> No. 150 is a "Design for a Schoolhouse" . . . a quaint and massy little building, and a very intelligible and sensible development of what may be supposed to be a very satisfactory plan. It means no mask, does not meekly ape some building of greater dimension and elaboration, or of different purpose, but rejoices in character and expression of its own, of which it has no reason to be ashamed.

The honesty of the design is at once apparent; free from needless features, the essential ones have been treated with such frankness and good sense that both the judgment and taste are gratified. The well-marked entrance, the groups of windows with their unique but simple voussoirs, the quaint and quiet bell-turret, the bold chimney, the large dormer, together with the handsome masses of brickwork and slate, are the attractive features of this building, the whole expressing well its character and purpose.[20]

Withers, so to speak, had earned his accreditation as a qualified modern Gothic architect.

The Tioronda School was but a modest prelude to the ripe High Victorianism of Withers's Newburgh Savings Bank of 1866[21] (Figure 29), which, unfortunately, has been destroyed. Constructed of hard red-face brick laid in places in herringbone courses, the building was arrayed with voussoirs, bands, quoins, and window frames of white freestone. A flourish of carved flowers, leaves, birds, and abstract designs decorated these details, and thick pink granite columns supported the stone porch that announced the entrance to the banking rooms.

This portal (Figure 30), a simplified version of the Lombard Gothic *motif* of an arched canopy resting on twin columns, was the most monumental detail Withers had produced so far. The robustness of the components, especially the dissimilar capitals consisting of luxuriant bunches of naturalistic aquatic leaves and flowers, contrasted markedly with the otherwise planar facade.[22] The massive strength of the bank entrance was a Victorian Gothic metaphor for durability and soundness.

The Newburgh Savings Bank and the esthetic that brought it into being were far removed from the elegant Renaissance style Bank of New York in New York City designed by Vaux in 1856.[23] Although the symbolic appropriateness of the palazzo style for banks seemed indisputable and established, Withers disregarded Vaux's example and instead followed the thinking of George Gilbert Scott, who, in *Remarks*, had provided the rationale for Gothicizing contemporary mercantile buildings:

Is the fact that a commercial system, certain political institutions, or a particular phase of social civilization which originated in Europe during what are called the middle ages, or whose origin may be termed "Gothic," have happened so to have developed themselves in modern times as to require structures of a somewhat new kind for the carrying out of their purposes, — is this fact, I would ask, any

29. Newburgh Savings Bank, Newburgh, N.Y., 1866 (demolished).

reason why the architecture of such structures, instead of being itself
also a development, to be copied from that of ancient Rome, with
which those institutions have no historical association, or from the
works of certain Italian architects of the fifteenth and sixteenth centuries, who saw fit to revive the architecture of a former world?
Reason would point to a course the very reverse of this, and claim for
such buildings a link of connection with the history of that family of
nations whose institutions they originated.[24]

In the Newburgh bank, Withers emulated the diverse "palatial style"
Scott had outlined in his book. It was an extravagant salmagundi of
Italian and Northern Gothic:

To go into more particulars, I think . . . we should adopt the horizontal cornice, and give it considerable importance though designing

30. Newburgh Savings Bank, entrance.

it with Gothic rather than classic details. We should have uniform ranges of windows subdivided into lights of considerable width by columns rather than mullions, the tracery, if any, being of the boldest and simplest form, — a mere circle being sufficient. We may give to these windows projecting sills or balconies at pleasure, and the central windows may be grouped on the Venetian principle, if desired. I should decidedly give the windows pointed arches if there is height for them. I am uncertain how far it may be consistent to accentuate the angles by projecting quoins, but I would certainly do so in some instances by shafts.

The details I would not make in any degree like Italian. It is not necessary that because we borrow ideas from Italy for a specific purpose, we should feel bound to borrow others which do not aid that purpose. The mouldings should be founded rather on Northern than Southern Gothic; or, more properly they should be designed to suit the case independently of either. The capitals, even if they resemble Corinthian in any degree in outline, should be founded on natural foliage of familiar type. No conventionalism either of classic or medieval origin should be admitted, all should be fresh and genuine, and as far as possible independent of precedent; and every feature and arrangement should appear the natural result of its position and its object.

While relinquishing *gabled* fronts, I should not feel bound to avoid high roofs. I have before advocated liberty in this respect, but there is no question that a high roof adds greatly to the dignity of a building and is more consistent with Northern architecture. A low roof to a building facing a street is, architecturally equivalent to no roof at all, inasmuch as it is utterly invisible. A lofty roof . . . will give individuality to our buildings.

A palatial street front, such as I am imagining, should have a certain degree of preciousness given to it by the choiceness of its sculptures and the richness of its materials.[25]

This virulent style was made architectonic by a system of articulation Scott termed the "columnar style of decoration."[26] Derived from Italy, it prescribed the liberal use of polished granite columns with foliated capitals at doorways, at corners, and in windows. The Newburgh Savings Bank windows (Figure 31), enriched with column mullions and crisply carved capitals, were excellent specimens of Withers's appreciation of Scott's advice. The granite colonnettes, along with the precisely ruled freestone window frames and the jagged brick and chamfered stone voussoirs, enlivened the exterior as Scott had predicted they would; they reinforced the building's sense of brittle hardness and assembled tightness.[27]

Sculptural embellishment of a different sort was planned for the

31. Newburgh Savings Bank, window.

32. Memorial Chapel, Yale
University, 1866 (project).

Civil War memorial building at Yale University (Figure 32). Eager to
immortalize the men who had led the armies of the Republic, New England's intellectuals moved quickly after the war to erect imposing buildings to the memory of their fallen comrades.[28] In 1865 Harvard commissioned Memorial Hall by Ware and Van Brunt (Figure 5); in 1866 Yale
University adopted Withers's design for its commemorative structure.[29]
Unlike Memorial Hall, which contained a theatre and dining hall as well
as a chapel, Withers's program combined the functions of a large university chapel with a hall for memorial plaques.

Memorial buildings of this kind were new to the American university
campus, a fact noted by Charles Eliott Norton in a July 1867 article in *The
Nation*.[30] Norton, who has been called "the only friend of Ruskin,"[31]
discussed the hallowed nature of this building type as idealistically as
Ruskin had spoken of church architecture in "Lamp of Sacrifice," the
source from which Norton surely derived his ideas. Asserting that the

inspirational content of the new buildings was more important than their utilitarian value, Norton wrote:

> Every stone of a memorial hall should bear evidence of its purpose of honor; every stone should be the object of solicitous care, and should receive every desirable adornment. There should be no expense spared neither in the material nor in the use made of the materials so the building should show that patient, inventive, and imaginative thought had been bestowed upon it, and that all the labor needed for its beauty or its strength had been given to it. The buildings to be worthy of commemorating the men whom they are designed to honor, and of celebrating the cause for which these fought and fell — to be worthy of the freedom and the arts of America, and of the great institutions of learning of which they are to be the central edifices — must take rank with the noblest buildings in the world, with those in which other people in other times have expressed their faith, their aspirations, and their highest character.

While acknowledging that both the Harvard and Yale designs were works by "skillful and educated architects" and examples of "the highest level of architectural art in our country," Norton expressed a mild preference for the Yale building. Unlike Ware and Van Brunt's hall, it possessed "the merits of unity of motives and simplicity of organization. Its parts combine to make a tolerably harmonious whole." But Norton also found Withers's scheme wanting:

> The design lacks in variety and abundance of thought and imagination. There is little to distinguish it as a work of original creative power. It is a careful and elaborate construction — a work of intelligence rather than of genius. It has no place in history as showing the development of the art of architecture. It is like most of the best Gothic churches of the present day, an ingenious adaptation of old forms to modern uses and requirements.[32]

Norton was correct in his estimate of what was Withers's most conservative High Victorian Gothic building.[33] Too closely related to ecclesiastical architecture, the design showed Withers a more reticent Ruskinian than both the Quassaick Bank and Newburgh Savings Bank indicated. The Yale memorial was poised between brave originality and conservative finesse, yet achieved neither. While Withers employed polychromatic embellishments, bronze friezes, and an unconventional modification of the ground plan, he failed to distinguish the building as anything more than a large church.

The unusual plan of the building was its outstanding feature. A long nave with wide transepts, intended to accommodate the university student body for religious services, formed the larger part of Withers's scheme. The memorial portion of the structure — two apsidal anterooms on either side of the vestibule and two screened aisles flanking the nave — embraced the nave like a horseshoe. This interlocking plan preserved the integrity of the public and private sections by keeping each of them distinct. It showed as well that Withers could conceive fresh solutions to uncommon architectural requirements with the same sense of functional efficiency that distinguished his smaller domestic designs.

Withers's Yale project and Harvard's Memorial Hall equated Victorian Gothic with the memorial building type. The conclusion of the Civil War coincided with the period of Ruskin's greatest influence on American thought. Association of the memorial building with the architectural style connected with his name was inevitable. A shrine of antique columns and porticos would no longer have satisfied the romantic sensibilities of the age. The moral uprightness of Gothic, an idea that Ruskin encouraged, commended the modern Gothic style for buildings honoring men considered latter-day Crusaders. The numerous "Old Mains" that arose on American campuses after 1866 were more than interesting architectural specimens, they were, as John Burchard and Albert Bush-Brown have said, "graceful reminders of our enchanting interlude with Ruskin."[34]

After Withers moved his office to New York City, he broadened his practice in domestic architecture to include city residences as well as suburban villas. In 1866, he exhibited at the National Academy of Design a watercolor drawing of his first design for an urban dwelling, the Charles S. Kimball house (designed in 1865), which once stood on Columbia Street in Brooklyn (Figure 33).[35] The three-bay stone row house had an arcade of tall pointed arches on the first floor and relieving arches of similar profile above the windows of the second story. The openings of the third level were capped by oversized keystones decorated, as were the window heads of the other stories, with incised floral designs. A sloping roof and bulky gable crowned the spirited elevation, and a lateral stepped buttress extended the wall plane at the side.

As though to illustrate the difference between the high fashion of

33. Charles Kimball Town House, Brooklyn, N.Y., 1865.
Watercolor perspective drawing. Attributed to Vaux and Withers. M. and M.
Karolik Collection.

this facade and the comparative dullness of the usual New York brownstone, Withers conspicuously included part of the adjacent house in his watercolor sketch. By rejecting traditional lintels and replacing them with banded pointed arches and by boldly expressing the roof rather than hiding it behind a heavy cornice, Withers divorced the Kimball house from its Renaissance neighbors. Accentuating the perpendicular dimension, he broke a rule of town-house design that had prevailed since the coming of the Greek Revival in the 1820s: that horizontality be stressed to mitigate the intrinsic steepness in facades confined by narrow city lots. Withers instead tendered Ruskinian "truth" through Gothic verticality.

In the Kimball house Withers adapted the High Victorian Gothic to yet another kind of building, one heretofore barely within the pale of the Gothic Revival. With the possible exception of David Arnot, who, in his book *Gothic Architecture Applied to Modern Residences* (1849),[36] had attempted to dress up the urban house with an assortment of Gothic drain spouts, railings, and doorways, American architects, in general, had clung to Neo-Classical norms in designs for city dwellings. Even Vaux had turned to the Renaissance style when he designed the A. C. Gray house on Fifth Avenue in 1856. Although hailed as a departure from the ordinary New York house because of its high mansard roof,[37] Vaux's design harmonized politely with its stolid brownstone neighbors. In designing city residences, as in his bank building, Withers refused to follow the lead of Vaux. He displayed a stubborn preference for Victorian Gothic in secular architecture that was as durable as his attachment to ecclesiological canons for church architecture.

Withers's professional reputation came to maturity when he received the commission to design the Hudson River State Hospital for the Insane at Poughkeepsie,[38] an institution founded in 1866 by the New York legislature (Figure 34). In 1867, the building committee, which included General Howland,[39] selected Withers as architect; by June of that year, Dr. Joseph Cleveland, the new superintendent, had approved his plans.[40] Construction began in the spring of 1868, but the huge project was not finished until ten years later.

From the nature of the plan (Figure 35) of the Hudson River Hospital, it is evident that Dr. Cleveland and the "eminent men" who acted as his advisors had instructed Withers to design the building according to the principles established by the American Association of Superintendents.[41] These tenets of asylum construction, which had been formulated

34. Hudson River State Hospital, Poughkeepsie, N.Y., 1866.

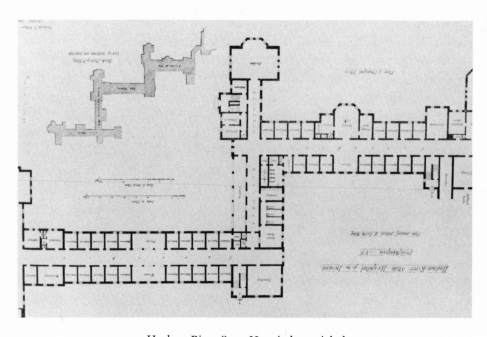

35. Hudson River State Hospital, partial plan.

36. Hudson River State Hospital, south pavilion, detail.

in a series of twenty-six "propositions" by Dr. Thomas Kirkbride of the Pennsylvania Hospital,[42] prescribed that narrow pavilions for patients should extend from either side of a central administration building. Joined at right angles to each other, the pavilions contained living quarters and rehabilitation facilities. The extended plan of Withers's Hudson River Hospital, which "from one end to the other was more than half a mile,"[43] was a factor that aroused serious opposition to the completion of the project in the 1870s. It had become clear by then that the cost of construction would be exorbitant.[44]

Generous amenities provided for the patients also made the Poughkeepsie hospital expensive. Not only were "living rooms" and "parlors" dispersed throughout the long stretches of bedrooms, but libraries and billiard rooms were made accessible to the quieter patients housed near the administration building. For exercise and recreation, Withers introduced "Ombra spaces," large, airy galleries on each floor of the transverse service pavilions[45] (Figure 36). Composed of a series of arcaded openings in the otherwise barrackslike exterior, the sweeping arches demonstrated the High Victorian Gothic style's potential for grace as well as utility.

37. Church of the Holy Innocents, Hartford, Conn., 1867 (project).

The plan of the Hudson River Hospital followed the dictates of the Association, but Withers's elevations were the first significant example in the United States of the application of High Victorian Gothic design to hospital construction. The disparate elements and loosely knit plan lent themselves to the variety and picturesqueness fundamental to Withers's esthetic sensibility. When the asylum was completed in 1878, however, the hard linearity and lively polychromy of its red brick and white sandstone walls summed up a style rather than introduced one. By then, in the same state, H. H. Richardson had already installed the powerful Romanesque in the repertory of asylum architecture; the brooding towers of his Buffalo State Hospital (1871) set the mood that characterized institutional architecture in the 1880s.[46]

Together with his successes in the secular sphere, Withers's activity as a religious architect continued to draw attention. In the spring of 1867, *The Ecclesiologist*[47] discussed his unaccepted design for the present Church of the Good Shepherd in Hartford, Connecticut, a memorial erected by Mrs. Samuel Colt to her husband and their two children[48] (Figure 37). (The dedication was initially to have been the Church of the Holy Innocents.) Why Withers's drawing, which he revised at least once,[49] was passed over is not known, but the fact that he was seriously considered for the prominent commission bespeaks his position, in the mid-1860s, as an architect in favor with eastern society.

The cruciform Hartford church that Withers proposed to be built of Connecticut brownstone had one dominant feature: a mighty tower that rose over the north transept where it marked the location of a small tomb chapel in the eastern portion of the transept. The tower arches descended into the interior and, on the east, formed the entrance to the memorial chapel, an arrangement that emphasized the commemorative room on the exterior and reverently isolated it on the interior. It also left the center of the transept clear to assure, as Withers noted, that "the view of the fine two-light window towards the north would be unobstructed."[50]

Despite the cleverness that Withers displayed in the arrangement of the north transept, the church belonged to the family of works that included his First Presbyterian Church in Newburgh designed ten years earlier. The virtue of the design for the Church of the Holy Innocents was not its originality but the craftsmanship demonstrated in design and details. *The Ecclesiologist,* now less sympathetic to such meticulous authenticity, noted that "the design very much resembles an average specimen of an English church of fifteen years ago." Its conventionality may have been a cause for Mrs. Colt's rejection; E. T. Potter's church, which she ultimately chose, was an adventurous High Victorian Gothic building.

More suggestive than either the Poughkeepsie hospital or the Hartford church was Withers's architectural contribution to the realization of a new campus for the Columbia Institution for the Deaf and Dumb, now known as Gallaudet College, in Washington, D.C.[51] Founded as a primary school in 1857 by Amos Kendall, postmaster general under Andrew Jackson, the institution earned its college charter in 1864. Kendall, an astute politician, had succeeded in making the institution a ward of the federal government. Even today, it depends for maintenance on appropriations from Congress.

Late in 1865, Edward Miner Gallaudet, the young president of the new college, asked Olmsted and Vaux to prepare a master plan for the campus.[52] From 1866 to 1885, he employed Withers to erect the institution's new structures.[53] These included a chapel building, a house for the

38. Chapel Hall, Gallaudet College, Washington, D.C., 1868.

president, an administration building, and three houses for professors, all of which were placed in locations established by the plan that Olmsted and Vaux had drawn up by November 1866. Two of the buildings, Chapel Hall and College Hall, are among Withers's most important works.

By the spring of 1867, construction had begun on the unique refectory and chapel building known as Chapel Hall[54] (Figure 38). It departed radically from the multipurpose pattern of the few buildings that had risen on the campus since the 1850s.[55] The idea to erect a large central building may have been conditioned by Charles Barry's plans for Dulwich College in London (and, perhaps, by German educational planning), yet the desire for an edifice in which grand appearance outweighed usefulness was surely prompted by the example of the memorial buildings proposed for Harvard and Yale. Although the commemorative

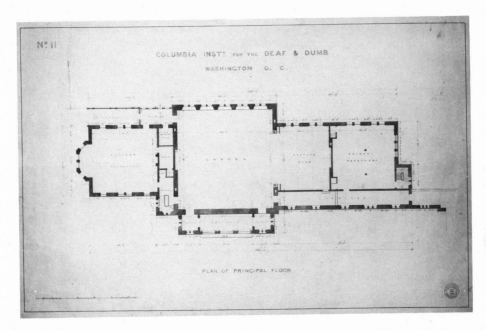

39. Chapel Hall, plan.

character of the New England structures was not appropriate to Gallaudet College, the well-being of the school was intimately tied to the national government, which had sustained it with funds and honored it with a college charter even as the Civil War threatened the existence of the nation. Such support warranted a monument to the triumphant Union, the benevolent patron of the deaf. The eagle and shield prominent over the central pediment of the porch of Chapel Hall announces the honorary character of the building,[56] which faces the United States Capitol visible in the distance.[57]

Chapel Hall's design clearly shows the influence of Ware and Van Brunt's Memorial Hall (Figure 5) in both function and form. Like Memorial Hall, and unlike Withers's own Yale memorial building, Chapel Hall served as an assembly and dining hall. Moreover, the Washington and Cambridge buildings each consisted of three basic units — a navelike extension, a tall transeptlike center, and a chancellike smaller section — and both contained arched portals on one of the lateral sides rather than entrances at the end of the long axis of the structure. Heeding the example of Ware and Van Brunt, Withers far surpassed his Yale Memorial design.

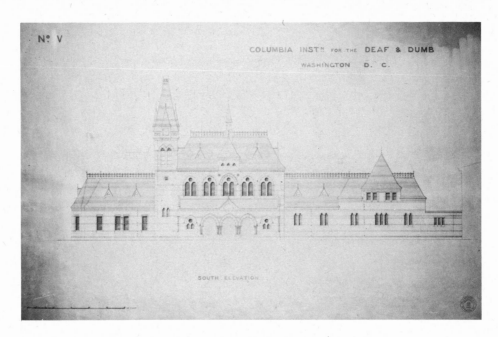

40. Chapel Hall. Architect's elevation drawing.

The plan of Chapel Hall (Figure 39) was a methodical adaptation to the requirements of the campus. The primary school dining hall was on the east end of the plan near the primary school building, which had been constructed in 1863. The college dining room was placed on the western end, close to the college building erected on the western side of the campus in 1865. Hence, both groups of students could reach their dining rooms without going through any other part of the building. In addition, from the primary school side of the campus, a corridor on the front of the long eastern section provided direct access to the central assembly room, as did a porch at the rear of the western section from the college side.[58] By this arrangement, the two departments were also linked to each other, since by going through the chapel room, the symbolic focal point of the institution, the members of each department could reach the opposite division. Thus, the ground plan of Chapel Hall coordinated the institution's unusual dual requirements of separation and communication.

The Connecticut brownstone facade of Chapel Hall (Figure 40) demonstrated the composite character of its interior. Withers's elevation neatly reflects the Ruskinian notion that a work of art must be "truthful."

41. Chapel Hall, porch capitals.

This requirement dictated that the functions of the building should be defined by emphasizing the volumes that housed them and that the character of these significant masses should be annotated by their minor elements. In Chapel Hall the larger size of the central room compared to the smaller low dining halls announces the main purpose of the building as an assembly hall. Subtly, the windows of each of the three sections of the facade suggest the nature of the spaces behind them: those in the chapel room are larger and more elaborate; those in the college dining room are smaller and utilitarian; and those in the eastern passageway are smaller still and repetitive. The position of the white sandstone belts also was determined by this feeling for distinctness; they answer not to the overall facade but to the height of the windows in each segment of the building. Equating different exterior forms and details with different interior uses, Withers brought the logic he exhibited in the creation of the ground plan to bear on the realization of the elevations.

In addition to this articulation, the facade of Chapel Hall was ornamented with details that concretely linked it to the English Ruskinian movement. The twin capitals of the entrance portal (Figure 41) repeated a lectern capital (Figure 42, D) that was illustrated by the British Gothic

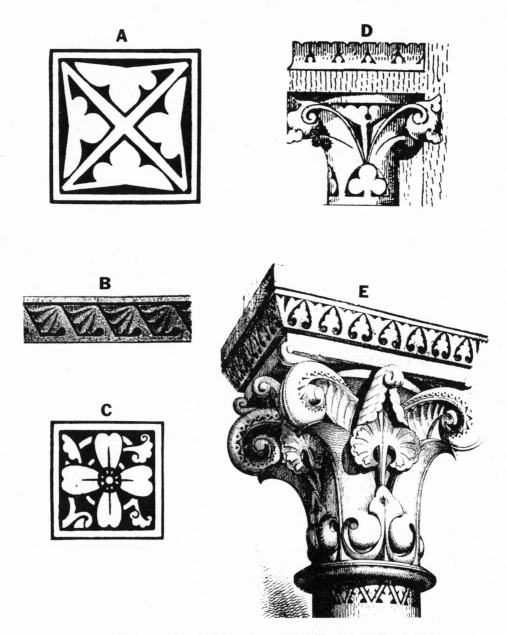

42. Ornamental designs and capitals from James K. Colling's *Art Foliage* (1865). (a) No. 12 of Plate 9; (b) No. 16 of Plate 9; (c) No. 9 of Plate 9; (d) lectern bracket, detail of capital; (e) stone capital, Plate 49.

43. Chapel Hall, detail of porch.

Revivalist, James K. Colling (1820–90) in his book *Art Foliage*[59] (1865).
Quotations from *Art Foliage* also adorn the buff-colored stone bands of
the porch (Figure 43). The alternating squares were derived from examples of center ornaments. The floral panel was from No. 12 of Colling's
plate 9 (Figure 42, A), and its abstract partner from No. 9 of the same
plate (Figure 42, C). The continuous band beneath this row copied a
Byzantine border design of "buds arranged upon a diamond form or
double triangle," which was No. 16 of plate 9[60] (Figure 42, B). Withers
generally disregarded Colling's admonition to use the book, which was an
extensive collection of ornamental designs based on flowers and leafy
plants, only for inspiration. In the case of the capitals, however, he com-
pressed and broadened their profile to make them more responsive to
the massive arches they cushioned. In comparison with what Withers
devised, the original model from *Art Foliage* seems stiff and lifeless.

 The ornamentation did not obscure the fact that Chapel Hall possessed the same "unity of motive and simplicity of organization"[61] for
which Norton had praised Withers's Yale building. Joining these qualities
with the cathedral character of Harvard's Memorial Hall, Withers
interpreted the ecclesiastical format much more broadly than had Ware

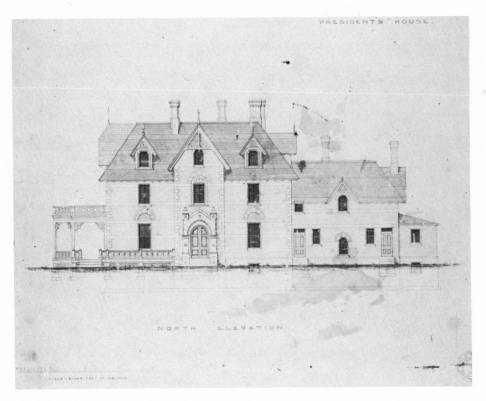

NORTH ELEVATION

44. President's House, Gallaudet College, 1867. Architect's elevation drawing.

and Van Brunt. He gave precedence to the clarified expression of function and in so doing, he avoided the overelaborate surfaces of Memorial Hall and based Chapel Hall's esthetic appeal on simple masses, a restrained outline, and subtlety of ornament and materials.

While Chapel Hall, which is a National Historic Landmark, was being built, a brick residence for the president of the college was erected in the southwest corner of the grounds (Figure 44).[62] Withers rejected urban standards in its design and returned to the conventions of his Newburgh villas. Characteristics of the Downing style persisted, but contrasting stone bands, voussoirs, and quoins, along with an arched stone entrance and Florentine relieving arches over the first-story windows, expanded the Ruskinian revisions Withers had introduced in the Brewster and Monell houses.[63]

The brownstone doorway is the finest entrance Withers ever designed for a house. Like Chapel Hall, this handsome High Victorian feature bears ornaments transcribed from *Art Foliage:* the medallions, best seen in the architect's drawing (Figure 45), repeated details from

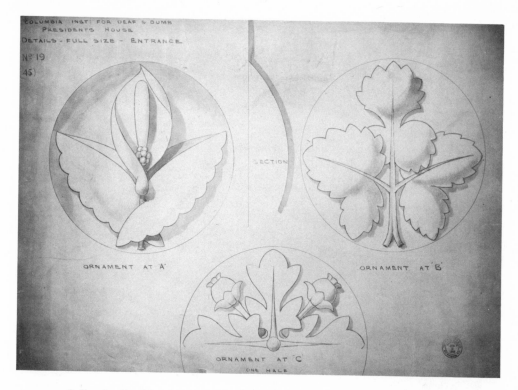

45. Gallaudet President's House. Architect's drawing for ornament of doorway.

46. Gallaudet President's House, detail of pier capital at entrance.

47. Gallaudet President's House, hall with glass partition of plant cabinet.

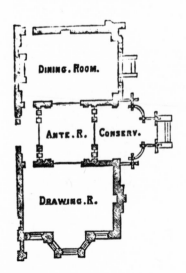

48. Robert Kerr. Dunsdale, detail of plan.

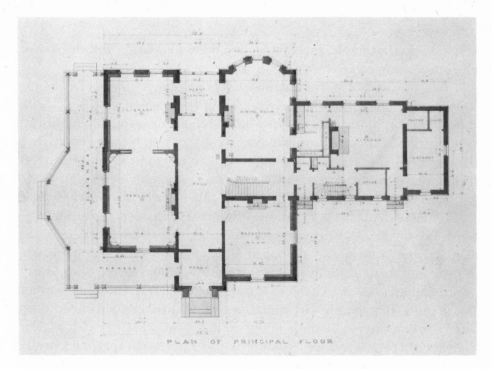

PLAN OF PRINCIPAL FLOOR

49. Gallaudet President's House, plan.

Colling's plates 29 and 36; the delicate rows of ferns and moldings on the pier capitals (Figure 46) combined details from two separate illustrations for stone capitals, plate 39 and plate 49 (Figure 42, E). Scaled down from the main portal of the Newburgh Savings Bank, this vaguely ecclesiastical frontispiece, unknown in houses by Downing and in Withers's 1850s designs, extends a liberal invitation to enter the comfortable interior.

Inside, Withers made use of a broad central hall extending from the vestibule to an enclosed plant cabinet (Figure 47) at the other end of the house. This cabinet, placed between the library and dining room, suggests that Withers knew Robert Kerr's recent book *The Gentleman's House*.[64] To facilitate circulation in dwellings where large groups of people would gather, Kerr had advised that an anteroom join two primary rooms. As an illustration, he offered a detail from his plan for Dunsdale in Kent[65] (Figure 48), which showed, at the end of a long hall, an anteroom and conservatory linking the dining room and drawing room. The southern end of the president's house approximates such an arrangement (Figure 49); the dining room and library, on opposite sides of the hall, are connected by the plant cabinet. Scaled down from Kerr's more spacious example, this cabinet embodies in a single unit the charm of a conservatory and the utility of a passageway.

The president's house was the *chef d'oeuvre* of Withers's Downing–Ruskinian domestic style. Displaying a full complement of High Victorian Gothic ornaments, as well as a commodious plan for the interior, it demonstrated the final possibilities of Withers's antebellum syntax. For the next several years he continued to build houses like it, but after 1868 he also began to explore different notions of domestic design.

The First Presbyterian Church in Highland Falls, New York (Figure 50), renewed Withers's association with literary ministers. Reverend Edward Payson Roe,[66] who was soon to gain renown as a novelist, had assumed the pastorate of the small Hudson River parish in 1868. He immediately made plans to erect a new church. Money raised by lecturing on his experiences as a chaplain during the Civil War and donations of "large sums from wealthy city churches and from friends" enabled Roe to build the church that Withers designed in 1868.[67]

The small picturesque building stands on a slope that rises in the west to the Hudson Highlands. The body of the church is a large rectangular room with a ceremonial end arranged like that of Withers's Yale Memorial Chapel project. The facade, which is preceded by a tower and vestibule and ornamented by a handsome rose window and sturdy kingpost brace, is simple and dignified.

Although the facade harks back to the Tioronda School of 1865 (Figure 28), the Highland Falls church appears also to have been influenced by an English building. *The Ecclesiologist* in 1859 had praised G. E. Street's new church at Howsham, Yorkshire,[68] for its unusual western elevation, which, by the arrangement of its elements, could easily have been the model for the First Presbyterian Church:

> The plan comprises . . . a nave with a narthex-like porch at the west end, and a tower engaged at the north side of the narthex. This is an admirable and novel plan, and admits of great internal comfort in the nave, and of much good architectural combination externally . . . [where] the narthex is roofed with a lean-to . . . [and] a circular window above the lean-to of the narthex is a good feature.

Not bound by the strict rules of Episcopal ecclesiology, Withers returned to the slightly earlier schoolhouse for the church tower (which also resembles that of Chapel Hall) and the fenestration pattern of the vestibule.

50. First Presbyterian Church, Highland Falls, N.Y., 1868.

Withers otherwise broke the flatness of the elevation exactly as Street had done, by bringing the tower and porch forward from the plane of the end wall to form an L-shaped mass before the facade.

Withers's First Presbyterian Church, like the country churches of Street, responds ardently to its natural surroundings. It strikes an expressive alliance with the native granite of which it is built and seems to embrace the essence of Roe's pronouncement that "we build from the rock with the rock, and trust that the great Spiritual Rock, will underlie it all."[69] By means of rough texture and broad mass, Withers integrated the building architectonically as well as pictorially into its hilly environment.

51. St. Luke's, Beacon, N.Y., 1869.

Equally scenic is Withers's most outstanding rural church, St. Luke's in Matteawan (modern Beacon), New York, which dates from 1869 (Figure 51).[70] A model of correct ecclesiology, St. Luke's like the Highland Falls chapel, is in perfect accord with its setting. Because two of Downing's friends, Henry Winthrop Sargent and John Monell,[71] were vestrymen of the parish and instrumental in the erection of the church,[72] the choice of Withers as the architect was inevitable. Of all who had been associated with Highland Garden, he alone had emerged as the standard bearer of Downing's ideas of church design. Built of hammer-dressed Schenectady stone now weathered to a soft grayish tone and standing within the churchyard and cemetery that Sargent planted with a wealth of botanical specimens,[73] St. Luke's conveys an impression of bucolic reverence that Downing would have admired.

Entered through the porch on the south side, St. Luke's consists

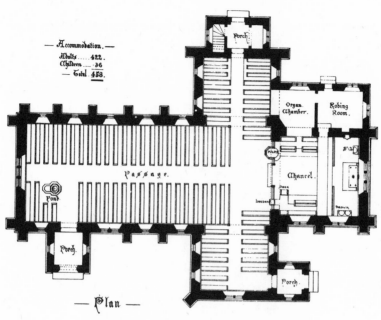

52. St. Luke's Beacon, N.Y., plan.

internally of a broad nave, full transepts, and a deep chancel (Figure 52).[74] A heavy collar-braced timber roof, the most impressive of Withers's career, hovers over the low walls of the nave and transepts (Figure 53). To solve the "crucial problem of a transeptual church with an open timber roof," which Schuyler defined as "the experience and appropriate framing of the crossing,"[75] Withers boldly elaborated the structure of the timber framework at that point and marked the crossing with a construction of braces, struts, and pendants.

Thoroughly Anglican in character and mood, St. Luke's resembles All Saints, Leyton, Essex, by William Wiggington (1829–90), which *The Building News* published in 1865.[76] Withers improved upon Wiggington's church by his substituting for Wiggington's tall, eccentric, stone belfry a timber belfry, a feature closely identified with the medieval parish churches of Essex.[77] Using All Saints as a model, Withers created one of the most refined examples of Gothic Revival architecture in America.

The vicarage Withers built at St. Luke's was an unusual house (Figure 54).[78] Constructed of roughly dressed squared stones with quoins

53. St. Luke's, Beacon, N.Y.,
interior.

and belt courses of red brick — a combination of masonry Withers had proposed for St. Michael's, Germantown, and had used in the Frost house of 1859[79] — it bears little resemblance to his earlier villas. The irregular facade, distinguished by a chunky entrance tower, which appeared in a more stout form on the Thurlow house (1874) in Wilkes-Barre, exhibits none of the Ruskinian decoration of the Gallaudet president's house.[80] Rather, the cottage stems from the romantic craftsmanship tradition of William Butterfield's parsonages of the 1840s (notably, that at St. Saviour's, Coalpit Heath) and a newer structure, Philip Webb's Red House in Kent, built in 1859 for William Morris. The informality of the St. Luke's parsonage may have been prompted by the desire to accommodate the dwelling to the churchyard, in which Sargent planned to recreate a medieval glebe. Withers, for his part, must have felt that something more vernacular than his customary scheme was demanded.

By the late 1860s, Withers had acquired an enviable reputation in his profession. It is a mystery, therefore, why, in 1869, he withdrew from the American Institute of Architects.[81] In 1857, he had been elected one of its first fellows[82] and he had served as the institute's national secretary

54. St. Luke's, Beacon, N.Y., Rectory, 1864.

between 1867 and 1869.[83] No statements appeared in the records of the institute or the contemporary press to explain Withers's action, but it is perhaps significant that Calvert Vaux and Leopold Eidlitz both quit the institute at the same time.[84] The reasons for their actions are equally obscure, although Eidlitz and Withers had recently worked together on a commission that may have caused tension between the two men. In any event, Withers's decision to disassociate himself from the organization did not adversely affect either his career or his standing in the professional community. It was after 1869 that he received some of his most important commissions.

The withdrawal of both Withers and Eidlitz from the institute may have been in some way related to their involvement in the project for a new church and rectory for the Church of the Holy Trinity (now destroyed) at 42nd Street and Madison Avenue in New York City. In 1869 a competition resulted in the acceptance of Withers's rectory design and the rejection of his scheme for the church in favor of one by Eidlitz.[85] Withers published the large Early English church as Design No. XVI in *Church Architecture* under the title "Church with semi-detached Tower."[86] That element along with the apsidal chancel, the only instance of the

55. Rectory of Holy Trinity Church, New York, N.Y. (demolished).
Architect's watercolor drawing.

form that appeared in Withers's designs before the 1880s, may reflect
influence from Street's famous St. James the Less in London (1858). The
only other innovation was the large porch on the front, which derived
from similar features on Chapel Hall and Reverend Roe's church. In
contrast to Withers's overall preference for quiet Early English, Eidlitz
employed colorfully patterned brick walls, variegated designs in the roof,
and an imposing belfry composed of stubby granite columns supporting
banded, pointed arches.[87]

The pastor of Holy Trinity was the controversial and volatile
Stephen Tyng,[88] who was reprimanded in 1868 by an ecclesiastical tri-
bunal for his ecumenical and evangelical views. He may have found
Withers's church too responsive to High Church ecclesiology for his
brand of religion. The rectory[89] (Figure 55), on the other hand, did not

56. Edom Bartlett Memorial Chapel, Annandale-on-Hudson, N.Y., 1869.

display these associations; its attractive High Victorian Gothic facade could well have appealed to an unconventional minister. Unlike Withers's church design, it was an example of progressive urban architecture.

The rejection the same year of another of Withers's competition designs, this one for St. James Episcopal Church in Brooklyn, New York, further suggests that his religious architecture was beginning to appear old-fashioned to some of his contemporaries. Like all of Withers's large churches, St. James had a symmetrical ground plan. In this case, however, the elevation grew into an irregular composition that a British critic praised in *The Building News*[90] for its "details." The successful integration of grand scale, ease of circulation, and picturesqueness made this design a particular favorite of Withers, who kept a framed copy of it over his desk.[91]

From the expansiveness of St. James, Withers turned his attention

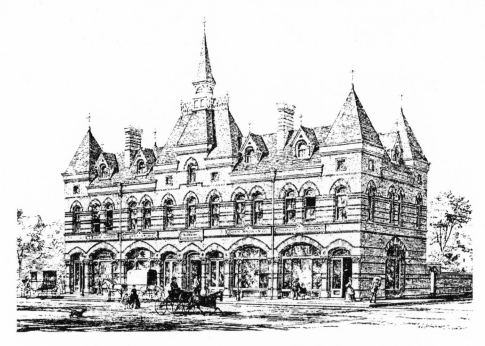

57. Block of Stores, Riverside, Illinois, 1870.

later in 1869 to the diminutive Edwin Bartlett Mortuary Chapel in Annandale-on-Hudson, New York[92] (Figure 56). Bartlett built the railway across the isthmus of Panama in 1848 and was the first merchant to import guano fertilizer into this country, a fact to which the three birds in the tympanum must delicately allude.[93] For the design of the stone tomb, Withers delved for inspiration into his repertory of ecclesiastical forms. He abstracted the entrance porch from the English parish church and gave it the autonomy of a self-contained structure. Texture and ornamentation accentuate the intimate scale and add virility to the compact fragment.[94]

Also in 1869, Withers became associated with one of the nation's early suburban development schemes, the village community of Riverside, Illinois. Three years before, the Riverside Improvement Company had engaged Olmsted and Vaux to lay out parklike grounds on a tract of land bordering the Des Plaines River near Chicago. Olmsted, who found Withers "a patient, amiable, accommodating young man" whose church architecture he especially admired, had Withers draw the plans for the community chapel in the center of the town.[95] In 1870, *The American*

58. Design for a Park Gateway, 1869 (project).
From Architect's perspective drawing.

Builder reported that the Improvement Company was erecting "a handsome block of stores and offices" near the chapel.[96] Designed by Withers, this High Victorian Gothic building (Figure 57) was one of the earliest commercial structures in the United States intended expressly for a planned suburban community.

The brick and stone building, which appeared as the frontispiece of A. J. Bicknell's *Detail, Cottage and Constructive Architecture* (1873),[97] had space for a market, hardware store, drug store, grocery store, and post office on its ground floor and offices for the Improvement Company on the second. Linking the building's three pavilions by arcades at the street level reiterated a fanciful design for an imposing park gateway that Withers exhibited at the National Academy of Design in 1869 (Figure 58)[98] and which may have been envisioned for Central Park. The relationship was more than coincidental, for the Riverside building was intended to have a ceremonial character; the Improvement Company brochure described it as occupying a landmark position in the landscape: "With the depot on the right, and the River with Picnic Island in the distance on the left . . . it is . . . centrally located to accommodate all Riverside residents."[99]

Withers's store block, represented by the Improvement Company as "harmonizing well with its surroundings,"[100] installed the High Victorian

Gothic style as a feature of American suburban life. Ironically, two decades later, Withers's renowned associate, Frederick Law Olmsted, laid
out the grounds for the World's Columbia Exposition in Chicago less
than twenty miles from Riverside and helped inaugurate the Neo-
Classical City Beautiful movement in America. But for the development of suburban communities in the later part of the nineteenth century, the quaint medieval character of the Riverside block was influential
in determining the artistic flavor of many suburban shopping centers.

While the work at Riverside progressed, Vaux, Withers and Company were engaged by the painter Frederick Church to help him realize
his vision of Olana, his imposing home and studio surveying the Hudson
from Church Hill, near Albany, New York.[101] The architects seem to
have acted chiefly as professional advisors; Olana's seductive potpourri of
Near Eastern and Gothic forms owed itself to Church's luxuriant fancy.
Withers, however, may have suggested to the artist that he employ rubble
with red brick dressings for the walls. A similar combination Withers had
used with good effect at St. Luke's parsonage. With the addition of delicate oriental details and colorful tiles around the entrance and windows
an unconventional amalgam was produced that neatly signified the ex-
oticism and naturalism of Church's artistic personality.

A TIME OF FULFILLMENT
(1871–1877)

BETWEEN 1871 and 1877, Frederick C. Withers produced the works that most entitle him to a place in the history of American art. He published *Church Architecture,* designed the Jefferson Market Courthouse in New York City, and created the William Backhouse Astor Memorial Reredos for Manhattan's Trinity Church. Working in an atmosphere of growing materialism and changing economic and social patterns, Withers asserted his full potential as the Gothic Revival was losing its grip on the imagination of America's architects. As new ideals, especially Richardson's Romanesque and Hunt's French Renaissance, appeared on the horizon, Withers continued to enunciate the principles of English Victorian medievalism.

Withers began the decade of the American centennial with his only known work in cast iron, a five-story store (Figure 59) that stands at 448 Broome Street in New York's SoHo district. Illustrated in A. J. Bicknell's *Wooden and Brick Buildings* (1875),[1] the warehouse was erected in 1871–72 for Mrs. A. G. Ullman. Montgomery Schuyler, writing from the perspective of the early skyscraper era, considered it one of the significant achievements of the High Victorian Gothic interlude. A firm rationalist, he appreciated the "characteristic treatment of metal, in which the application of Gothic principles resulted in a wide departure from Gothic forms."[2] Avoiding the temptation to apply pointed arches, Withers expressed on the exterior the horizontals and verticals of the internal rectilinear frame. He had practiced the fundamental truth of Gothic architecture — structural veracity — in spite of the insistent horizontality that resulted. As the men of the Chicago school would do in the 1890s, Withers had accepted the realities of metal construction as the basis for facade design.

In 1872, the year before he documented his attainments as an

59. Mrs. A. G. Ullman Cast
Iron Store, New York, N.Y.,
1872–72.

ecclesiastical architect in the pages of *Church Architecture,* Withers conceived what was perhaps his most perfect house of worship, St. Thomas Church in Hanover, New Hampshire (Figure 60). The faultlessly ecclesiological Early English church, recognized as one of the nation's "notable Episcopal churches,"[3] was the quintessence of romantic scholarly medievalism. Endowed with timeless dignity and beauty, St. Thomas, which was built of local granite laid in random courses of small rock-face stones, exemplifies the letter and spirit of the Gothic Revival in America and marks the zenith of Withers's career as a designer of churches.

Withers's book *Church Architecture* was itself an impressive Victorian object; a contemporary reviewer said the typography was "unexcelled, if not unequaled, by any similar work"[4] yet produced in America. In it the author illustrated his church designs from 1857 to 1873. Each carefully executed line drawing created a handsome graphic image on the folio-size bordered pages. The broadly conceived style recalled English architectural illustrations in *The Building News* and *The Architect.* The interior views with their exaggerated wide-angle perspective were indebted

60. St. Thomas' Church, Hanover, N.H., 1872.

for their treatment to the same source. Addressed to the serious layman as well as to the builder, *Church Architecture* demonstrated a degree of professionalism little known in American architectural publications until the appearance of *The American Architect and Building News* in 1876. Intended for the drawing room table as well as the library, *Church Architecture* was among the first American works on architecture to be considered elegant literature.

The subject of modern Gothic ecclesiastical architecture had been a popular one in America since the days of Downing, who had included church designs in *The Horticulturist*.[5] *Ancient English Ecclesiastical Architecture* (1850) by the English immigrant architect Frank Wills[6] was the first American book on church design that authoritatively discussed the principles of ecclesiology. Although physically it recalled Wills's volume, Withers's book lacked the missionary emotionalism of his predecessor's prose. Neither did Withers indicate, as Wills had done, that he anticipated the evolution of a new architecture from a careful consideration of medieval design; the day for such ideas was past. Richard Upjohn's *Rural Architecture*[7] (1852) had been frequently consulted because it provided examples of inexpensive wooden churches that parishes with limited means could build. *Parish Churches*[8] (1857), a lesser-known work by the New York architect John C. Hart (dates unknown), offered English Gothic masonry examples and was closer in spirit to Withers's book than Upjohn's, but Hart's emphasis on the differences and development of the historical Gothic styles reduced the appeal of his writing for the American reader. The closest publication in date to Withers's, and the best for comparison, is *Church Architecture* of 1871[9] by Henry Hudson Holly (1834–92). Like Withers, Holly presented designs for urban as well as country churches and ostensibly addressed his work to the same class of readers, educated Protestant laymen, churchmen, and architects. But Holly's pretentious air of authority and his large but coarse drawings underscore by contrast the uniqueness of Withers's volume. Holly, a well-known architect in New York City,[10] filled his treatise with all the information on the subject of churches he could command and then garnished it with lengthy chapters on subjects like the history of the conversion of England and the origin of the Book of Common Prayer. The architectural discussion offered little to compare with Withers's *Church Architecture,* for instead of a complete set of drawings for each building, such as Withers provided, Holly illustrated only perspective views of his churches, in which, as an irritated English critic pointed out, there was "not one feature that has not been drawn from modern English works."[11] Holly boasted that he had created a modern American ecclesiastical architecture. The designs themselves, though English inspired, were needlessly complicated and frequently ill proportioned; they showed none of the thoroughness and subtlety in detail and massing that characterize Withers's church designs.

Imitating the format of Downing's *The Architecture of Country Houses* (1850) and Vaux's *Villas and Cottages,* Withers began with an advisory introduction, followed by a portfolio of twenty-one of his churches, designated as "designs"[12] and arranged from the smallest to the largest. The crisp illustrations (many of which were not identified) showed ground plans, elevations, cross sections, and perspective views of each church. A descriptive essay accompanied each illustration. Two schoolhouses concluded the book, and drawings of two rectories, several church details, the Bartlett tomb, and Chapel Hall embellished the second part as "vignettes" beneath Withers's short commentaries.

The first part of *Church Architecture* dealt with the practical points of church building. Such matters as choosing a favorable site, the factors effecting the cost of construction, the arrangement and necessary parts of the plan, and the types of furnishings to be included were described succinctly. Despite the strong Ruskinian tinge of the prose, Withers's manner was direct and factual. His literary style was not that of a pedantic man.

Withers's philosophy of church design, however, had not evolved since 1858, when "A Few Hints" appeared in *The Horticulturist.* The statements in the introduction to *Church Architecture* merely elaborated the notions derived earlier from Pugin, Ruskin, and the literature of the English Gothic Revival. Worded like a quote from Ruskin's *Seven Lamps,* the text began by informing the reader that the work was offered "to demonstrate the great advantage of truthfulness and reality in building, as a matter of policy as well as of principles."[13] Under the heading "Style," Withers restated the arguments of appropriateness and practicality to justify the erection of Gothic churches. As he had in 1858, he said:

> The style of every building should be so characteristic that a simple glance may be able to decide the purpose to which it is devoted. The graceful spire or less pretentious bellcot, when rightly designed, will

be found to require no other interpreter. There is no style so admirably adapted to all wants and requirements as that of the medieval gothic, since it is one which can be made to accommodate itself to every necessity whether of site, or material.[14]

Furthermore, he wrote, "This style [Gothic] when rightly conceived, admits of no deceit or sham of any kind, and will not permit any attempt to disguise a necessary feature, or allow any false construction."[15] Thinking it necessary, even at this date, to reiterate Downing's and Pugin's condemnation of the Classical style as deceitful and impractical, Withers insisted that "the Grecian or Roman styles construct decoration by repeating features, not because they are required, but in order that the two sides of a building should be symmetrical."[16] Even the practical suggestions that Withers offered indicated that he had reread Pugin. The advice on the proper construction of stone walls — "a wall two feet thick, with good projecting buttresses at proper intervals, is stronger than a three foot wall without them"[17] — was a reflection of Pugin's observation in *True Principles:* "a wall of three feet in thickness, with buttresses projecting three feet or more at intervals is much stronger than a wall of six feet thickness without buttresses."[18]

Under "Materials," Withers dismissed wood as "impermanent" and, therefore, "not to be used extensively in the construction of churches,"[19] an English notion his years in America had not dispelled. By avowing the superiority of stone and brick and excluding timber churches from *Church Architecture,* Withers reduced the appeal of his book; many rural American parishes found wood not only an inexpensive and available building material, but one that had been hallowed by tradition dating back to the meeting houses of the seventeenth century.[20] Withers's unwillingness to recognize the beauty and validity of wood must be considered one of his serious shortcomings.

Withers did not subdivide his churches into groups, but as the designs in *Church Architecture* progress from smaller to larger, three categories of ground plans become evident: simple nave churches (Designs I–VII) for congregations with less than 450 people; aisled cruciform buildings (Designs VIII–XV) for parishes of more than 450 but less than 800 people; and aisled nave, and usually transeptual, churches (Designs XVI–XXI) for congregations with over 800 members. Almost without variation, Withers considered these fixed patterns the proper solutions to the spatial requirements and construction budget of any parish. Rather than add aisles to a small church to obtain the space of a medium-sized building, for example, he resorted to the simpler addition of transepts, thereby avoiding the introduction of costly arcades. Within the limits of Withers's fairly expensive architecture, each type of plan housed the intended number of worshipers with relative economy.

In addition to similar ground plans, many of the buildings in *Church Architecture* display similarities in their design elements. Withers's fondness for revision also induced him to construct elevations of different styles from the same ground plan. The "Curvilinear Gothic" church in Design II and its Early English vignette were both, Withers said, "taken from the same plan . . . and introduced for the purpose of showing that two churches can be erected on the same plan, one being very elaborate in detail, and the other plain, yet both equally correct in style."[21] The Early English vignette was copied from Robert Withers's St. Llandgwyd Church in Cardigan (Figure 24), which had inspired the design of St. Paul's. In *Church Architecture,* the Welsh church served as the less expensive optional plan for the costly American variation that was Design II.

Just as he conceived the ground plan of his secular buildings first and let the elevation follow from it, Withers also held historical style second to function. One of Withers's strengths as a Gothic Revival church designer was his ability to accept the limitations imposed upon him by a tight budget and not to sacrifice quality in construction or accuracy in detail to superficial elaboration. Many of his less scrupulous colleagues ignored his example; they preferred the opulence of Gothic architecture in wood and plaster. By providing a simpler interpretation of the intricate elevation of the church in Design II — an action that was analogous to Withers's 1858 development of the design of St. Michael's from the church in "A Few Hints" — Withers presented what, to his Ruskinian mind, must have seemed an honest alternative to imitation.

Despite its conservative character, *Church Architecture* was received enthusiastically by the architectural profession in the United States. *The American Builder* proclaimed it "altogether . . . the most admirable work on church architecture that has ever come under our supervision. It will be found most useful to the student as well as a valuable addition to the library of every architect, gentleman of taste, and lover of the beautiful."[22] The book continued to be respected even in the face of the changes in taste that occurred after its publication. As late as 1883 the editors of *The American Architect and Building News* recommended it as an authoritative text on ecclesiastical building.[23]

The cold reception that the British architectural press afforded *Church Architecture* contradicted the welcome the book received in America. An unsigned article in *The Building News* in 1873[24] entitled "Church Architecture in America" reviewed it in detail. While the writer found no fault with the ideas expressed in the introduction, he perceived that "the remarks and suggestions generally are such as might have been, and often were made, in this country in the very first years of the Gothic Revival; they remind us of Rickman and Pugin — of the *Glossary of Architecture,* and the early numbers of *The Ecclesiologist.*" The writer became more caustic when he discussed Withers's churches, which, like the commentaries, he judged antiquated.

> We may say at once that they [the designs] . . . are quiet in character, and very much on the level of our own 'regulation church' of twenty years ago. There is little conspicuously bad detail, and still less that is conspicuously good. There is no advance in planning beyond the outworn types. . . .
>
> Many of the designs, in fact, have so little individuality about them, that we seem to have seen them — and doubtless have seen something almost undistinguishable from them — over and over again. The chapels indeed, like most chapels in this country have a sort of irrepressible ugliness which is in itself a kind of distinction. . . . There is really, however, little of any kind to be said about the greater part of the designs illustrated.
>
> There is nothing so wearisome as dead level, and if an architect can not rise above it, one is sometimes perversely tempted to wish that he would fall below it, by the way of a change. Mr. F. C. Withers does neither, and his work is far from being amusing as it is from being suggestive; but it shows a knowledge of detail which might be turned to better use.

Withers's churches were indeed *retardataire* by British standards.[25] Although, as a writer in *The Building News* conceded, Withers was "sufficiently advanced to recommend brickwork," his designs, with the notable exceptions of the Dutch Reformed Church and St. Mark's, generally ignored the developments that had taken place in ecclesiastical architecture in Britain since the erection of Butterfield's All Saints. The shift within the Revival from a pure English Gothic to a mixed Gothic style had already reached maturity by 1866 when *The Building News,* in a review of the new Daylesford church in Worcester by J. L. Pearson (1817–97),[26] summarized the character of that stylistic transformation that Withers had elected to ignore:

> A few years since, it required no small amount of courage on the part of a church architect to deviate in any degree from our national variety of the Gothic style, so long as he closely adhered to that, tameness and formality were pardonable. If his work were but copied from orthodox models, antiquarian critics were ready to overlook the feebleness of the imitation. The duty to which they exhorted him, was to plod contentedly in the footsteps of those who had gone before, to resist the temptation to Continental studies, and above all to shrink with horror from inventing anything for which a precedent could not be found. Originality in design was thought little better than heresy in doctrine. . . . Too much propriety, however, is apt to become wearisome. A reaction has set in toward French and Italian detail, and the combination of these with our native forms, modified by present requirements, seems to likely result at last in something like a genuine practical style. . . . Breadth of treatment and largeness of parts are taking the place of minute and frittered decoration. Horizontal cornices, bands, strings are becoming prominent features; parapets and pinnacles are chiefly reserved for vaulted structures; sculpture is improving in character as well as increasing in quantity, while elaborate tracery abandoned by nearly all who can do without it, is "the last refuge of the destitute."

By 1873 even the supremacy of the Gothic style in English ecclesiastical architecture had ended, for Anglican architectural standards had been rejected by the non-Anglican denominations. Addressing the Architectural Association of London, the architect Edward C. Robins (1830–1913)[27] upbraided dissenting congregations for their unthinking emulation of the architecture of the National Church:

> Let the High Church party retain its recognized forms of expression, but let the Broad Church love its distinctiveness and with the Low Church, and those in sympathy with it, cease to imitate that which they have no sympathy. Rather let their buildings express themselves and be distinguished by their individuality, and let them be as vigorous in the expression of their church building views as hitherto they

have been weak and frail, timidly tempering and coqueting with symbolic forms to which they attach no meaning, and submitting to what is vaguely termed ecclesiastical propriety and precedent, which are not but convenient veils to disguise indolence and apathy, and hinder the progress of realistic art and original design.

Indignant at the fact that the energetic campaign of the Gothicists had cut the non-Anglican Protestants off from their rightful architectural heritage, Robins suggested that the temple churches of the eighteenth and early nineteenth centuries should be reconsidered.

The ecclesiastical buildings in the Classic style, so prevalent in the earlier part of this century, must not be altogether passed over in silence, although they are out of fashion now. The horizontality of their leading lines offers great facilities for covering large spaces with flat ceilings unsupported by internal arcades and they offer good opportunities for coloured decorations.

In America, too, disillusionment with Gothic prevailed. Boredom with and reaction against the Revival was expressed by Russell Sturgis, himself once a Revivalist, in 1871 in *The North American Review,* where he confessed to a loss of faith in ecclesiology.

The tacit understanding that churches are to be Gothic, and the codicil to that, that the best Gothic is the most like thirteenth-century Gothic, are hindrances to artistic progress. Let it be remembered how hard it is for anyone to do well in art, in these modern times, with little encouragement to strive, with little sympathy for his best efforts, with no ancestral designing to appeal to, with his pecuniary interest almost directly opposed to his sense of what is right and what is lovely. If achievement is made still harder and languid acquiescence easier by the exhortation to copy — to copy, moreover, admirable art confessedly beyond the power of living artists to equal, and capable of giving great delight to the student of its characteristics — modern art is deprived of its one remaining chance.[28]

Sturgis also attacked Gothic as an inflexible and impracticable style for American religious buildings:

If a modern designer can say of his work that it is in this style or in that, he is on the wrong path. Not that the adapting of details and forms is always wrong. . . . Any really able artist is allowed to plagiarize, for he knows how to use his thefts to the advantage of all. So that the vicious imitation is not the appropriating of details, a bit here and a bit there; it is the trying to build a chapel as a chapel would have been built in the thirteenth century — in form and in plan and in material, that is. What propriety is there in building a church for Protestant congregational worship with two rows of columns in it? Churches for this purpose are generally only just as large as they have to be, to seat the eight hundred or twelve hundred people expected every fine Sunday morning. These people sit in their places and listen to a service of which a very large part is a sermon. These churches should be made to see and hear in, and everything should be held subordinate to those primary requirements as thoroughly as in the case of a concert-hall.[29]

While Withers was contending that "there is no doubt but that Gothic architecture is the most suited for churches, for this style has the advantage over every other in its applicability to all sites and requirements,"[30] dissenting arguments had already appeared. In 1868, the editor of *Harper's Magazine* had questioned another fundamental aspect of the Revival, its associational appropriateness for Christianity. "There is an austerity in the Gothic style," wrote the editor, "which recalls rather the gloom of German forests and a crude, savage theory of Christianity, than the sweetness of Syrian sunshine, which is its natural atmosphere." Asserting that it was in the brightly lit old-fashioned meeting house where the true religious spirit could thrive, the writer added, "The smooth open Palladian arches seem a more truly Christian style. . . . It is a placid, smiling southern feeling which they convey, under them should be preached the truth that the kingdom of heaven is as a little child."[31] Such a statement in a popular and influential magazine was but another indication that American architectural taste was changing.

The American non-Episcopal community also was withdrawing its support from the Gothic Revival. Emulation of the architecture of the Episcopalians had prevailed since the 1850s. *The Churchman,* the magazine of the church, had viewed it as one of the "preparatory fruits" indicating an ecumenical "harvest" for Anglicanism.[32] By 1876, this amity was ended. In an article in *The American Architect and Building News,* an unidentified but perceptive writer foresaw the demise of the authority of Gothic and the ritualism that attended it in all but the Catholic community. Perceiving that American religion had moved away from ceremony toward evangelism, he criticized the plans and mystery of the Gothic church as encumbering:

> The only sect among us to which the Medieval form of church is really appropriate is the Roman Catholic. They alone have congregations large enough or a ceremonial inspiring enough to need it. It is not likely or desirable that they should depart from it; and since they build larger and more elaborate churches than the Protestants, they will have it in their power to produce the best architectural works. . . . The ritual and tradition of the Anglican church incline toward the Medieval forms of building; but its congregations are not large enough, and the sermon has become in a good part of the body in the United States too important in the service, to allow a complete and effective church on the Medieval model, in which in a modern parish either half of the space must be unoccupied, or half of the congregation be out of hearing of the sermon.[33]

The stylistic heterodoxy that religious building had assumed by the mid-1870s was illustrated by three churches that appeared in *The New York Sketch-book of Architecture* in 1875. None of them acknowledged the presence of Withers's book, published just two years earlier. Gambrill and Richardson submitted an unidentified competition design for a cruciform church with a central tower.[34] The building, of a freely interpreted Romanesque style, reflected their achievement in Trinity Church, Boston. The other two examples were not Romanesque but represented popular alternatives to Withers's ecclesiological Gothic. One was a design by Henry M. Congdon (1854–1922) for Calvary Episcopal Church, Utica, New York,[35] and the other was by A. J. Bloor (1828–1917) for an Episcopal church near Shrewsbury, New Jersey.[36] The former was clearly influenced by post-Pugin developments in church architecture in England. Still basically English Gothic, it nonetheless sported contrasting stone courses and arched portals on squat, polished granite columns — the polychromatic High Victorian style applied to church architecture. The church by Bloor, which was considerably more eccentric than the others, might be called Stick Style. It is an interesting building to contrast with the solid works of Withers, for Bloor had been close to Withers personally as well as professionally.[37] Bloor understood the current in American architecture of the 1870s that exploited the constructive properties and esthetic possibilities of wood as a native building material. The spindly thinness and exaggerated proportions, both characteristic of much church architecture in rural America during the 1870s, may have been inspired by an interest in Scandinavian stave churches. The New Jersey church bordered on pure fantasy. In comparison with Bloor's church, Withers's strong, scholarly designs must have seemed unexciting.

By 1873, virtually all of Withers's fellow Gothicists — William A. Potter, J. Cleveland Cady (1838–1919), and Russell Sturgis among them — had rejected the canons of the English parish church revival to which Withers adhered. Neither in its intent nor its examples did *Church Architecture* look forward. It added little to the ideas of Pugin, Wills, and the other British and American ecclesiologists. Instead, Withers had prepared a definitive summation of the principles of correct ecclesiology and confirmed the respectability of Gothic purism, a notion that was to endure a long time in American ecclesiastical architecture.

In contrast to *Church Architecture,* the history of the Jefferson Market Courthouse (Figure 61), Withers's best-known work, is as colorful as the building itself,[38] for it is immersed in the notorious politics of the Tweed Ring and Tamany Hall. The idea to erect a new municipal building on the site of the Jefferson Market was born in the Albany legislature; by 1870 it had become one of the many "pork-barrel" bills fostered by the Tweed political machine.[39] In the autumn of 1873, after $150,000 had been appropriated and spent, the city still had for its investment nothing but a pile of rotting building materials.[40] New commissioners were appointed at the beginning of 1874. The fact that the original scheme would have cost "several millions to complete"[41] caused the new commissioners to accept the suggestion of Andrew Green, the city comptroller, that it be discarded. Withers was hired to draw up a new plan.[42]

Withers's initial design for the courthouse was approved by July 1874[43] and appeared only slightly altered in *The New York Sketch-book of Architecture* in June 1875.[44] Construction began, and soon accusations,[45] contractors' disputes,[46] and citizens' investigations were renewed,[47] all of which continued even after the building was completed.

The courthouse, which eventually cost $550,000,[48] was located on the edge of one of the city's poorest neighborhoods. This fact, in part, accounted for the continual attacks upon it as a waste of public funds. At one point Withers and Vaux, who was nominally associated with the work,[49] were both accused of being incompetent and insane.[50] The Municipal Society self-righteously denounced the project and said it

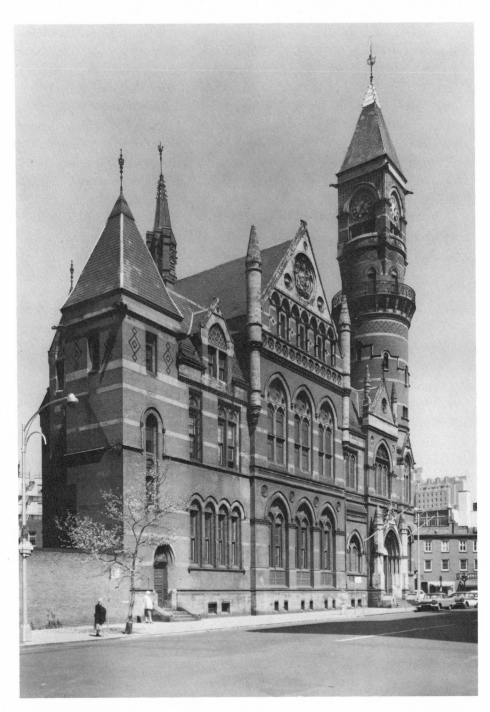

61. The Jefferson Market Courthouse, New York, N.Y., 1874. Sixth Avenue facade.

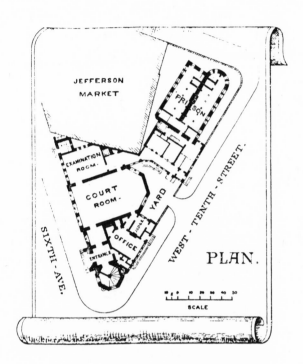

62. Jefferson Market Courthouse, plan.

would give "to the criminal brought to it a suggestion of the gaudy vul-
garity connected with gilded dens of infamy."[51] *The New York Times,*
which noted that the building was an "elegant architectural structure,"
irascibly dubbed it "a jewel in a swine's snout."[52] Contrary to citizens'
expectations, however, Withers emerged from the ordeal of public re-
criminations with his good name and professional reputation intact. An
expensive architect, he merely had spent the ample amounts placed at his
disposal by a less than scrupulous legislature bent on relieving the city's
depressed economy with an expensive building project.

The Jefferson Market Courthouse is a group of buildings that replaced the sprawling Jefferson Market and a dilapidated prison which
stood on a triangular plot defined by Sixth Avenue on the east, Greenwich Avenue on the west, and West Tenth Street on the north. Associated
in the minds of New Yorkers of Withers's class with "everything that is
bad, mean and unsavory,"[53] the old Jefferson Market, which had housed
a dingy police court over a saloon,[54] had been clustered without architectural pretense around a wooden fire tower. The architectural complex

Withers envisioned (Figure 62) on the cramped site consisted of four distinct units, which included the courthouse facing Sixth Avenue, a five-story prison enclosed by a high wall on Greenwich Avenue[55] and incorporating cells for sixty male and thirty female prisoners, as well as an exercise area beneath the roof, and a fire and bell tower attached to the courthouse at the corner of Sixth Avenue and West Tenth Street. The fourth unit on the site was a market,[56] which was projected by Withers but designed by Douglas Smyth in 1883, remarkably in harmony with the existing buildings by Withers. It stood in the southern wedge formed by Sixth and Greenwich Avenues.

In the courthouse building, which was separated from the prison by a small receiving yard, Withers incorporated the functions of police court, district court, and fire observatory in the structure that was his masterpiece.[57] Its plan (Figure 62) was his most ingenious organization of spaces, for the arrangement of rooms exhibited even greater inventiveness than that of Chapel Hall. Ease of communication between the various parts had been a major consideration in Chapel Hall; in the Jefferson Market Courthouse, Withers intentionally isolated the compartments from one another as he exploited the unusual site to obtain as much usable space as possible. Perhaps taking his cue from the three-cornered piece of ground, Withers mapped out his plan in two roughly triangular areas. The larger of these contained the police courtroom, which faced Sixth Avenue and which had its polygonal end in the apex of the larger triangular area. In the smaller triangle, the clerk's office facing West Tenth Street occupied a comparable space. These two large and small units were fitted into the acute angle formed by the junction of the narrow street and broad avenue. The corner staircase, which is in the base of the tower, led to the district courtroom on the second floor and, as it were, hinged together the two triangles of the courthouse plan.

The bell tower (Figure 63) shows how Withers reconciled the varied portions of the complex. The tower's function as a fire lookout was not related to the activity beneath it, yet it was incorporated structurally with the judicial building. Withers cleverly solved the difficult esthetic and practical problem of integrating the tower into the composition when he used its base to house the main staircase of the court building but isolated the upper stage to serve only the fire watchmen who gained access to it through an inconspicuous doorway and narrow stair turret on West Tenth Street. This clever compromise permitted him to exploit the dramatic visual potential of the corner by placing the tower there.

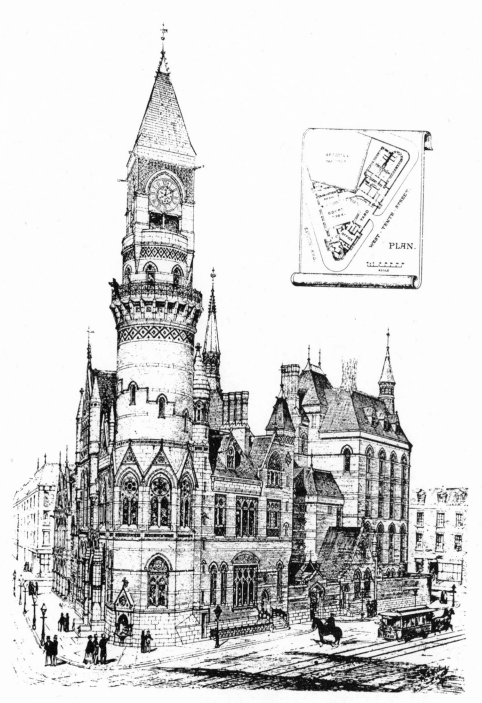

63. Jefferson Market Courthouse, tower.

64. Jefferson Market Courthouse, fountain at the base of the tower.

The red pressed brick and Ohio stone exterior reflects the arrangement of the multipurpose interior and draws together that intricacy into a coherent external composition. Projecting from the center of the Sixth Avenue side (Figure 61), the two-story stone courtroom unit, with its rows of Venetian windows and blind arcades, is the dominant element of the design. Its bulk and symmetry stabilize and coordinate the asymmetry of the elevation. The twin turrets flanking the gable augment the central section's verticality and punctuate the movement from the small stair tower on the left to the majestic fire tower on the right. Thus, the facade's syncopated rhythm of openings and masses is controlled by the regular and climatic progression from stair tower to central pavilion to bell tower.

An opulent but controlled profusion of ornament garnishes the facade. Carved details enhance the entrance portal and accumulate in the diapered panels under the windows, around the polygonal base of the tower, on the capitals of the numerous colonnettes, and in the pediments of the gables. A handsome canopied water fountain with reliefs depicting the weary traveler and the life-giving pelican (Figure 64), is at the bottom

65. Jefferson Market Prison, 1874.

of the bell tower. The most ambitious pieces of sculpture are the mighty
state seal in the main gable and the epigrammatic frieze representing the
trial from Shakespeare's "Merchant of Venice" in the tympanum over the
window above the entrance.[58]

In contrast to the judicial building and the tower, the prison on
Greenwich Street (Figure 65) was much less ornamental. Here Withers
most clearly expressed the High Victorian Gothic perception of the wall
as a surface wrapped around space and pierced by voids where necessary.
The curved bay, which terminated the male half of the prison, was fused
with the side and rear by means of unbroken horizontal bands of stone
and brick, which gave to the walls the character of a continuous taut
fabric from which the tall pointed windows lighting the cell corridors
seemed to have been carefully cut.

Though new for New York City, High Victorian Gothic had been employed for public buildings in Britain since the 1850s. Street's London Law Courts of 1866 and the Manchester Assize Court (1859) (Figure 66) by Alfred Waterhouse (1830–1905) are relevant predecessors of the Jefferson Market Courthouse. Withers's use of a gabled pavilion with triple-arched openings as the centerpiece of his courthouse facade suggests that there was more than a typological relationship between the Manchester and the New York buildings, for a similar arrangement distinguished the elevation by Waterhouse. Yet it is the fanciful quality of the Jefferson Market Courthouse that suggests another source for its design. The elaborate skyline and a number of details link it to the work of William Burges (1827–81), the English architect whose designs, in the words of Robert Jordon, "belong to the Medieval missal — such as that of Paul D. Limbourg — rather than to the real world."[59] In particular, Withers's fire tower[60] displays a debt to Burges's competition drawings for the London Law Courts published in *The Builder* in 1867[61] (Figure 67). Quite clearly, Withers adapted passages from Burges's scheme. Withers's tower, for example, is ringed near the base with pedimented windows similar to the ones that appeared on the twin entrance towers on the Strand side of Burges's design (left in Figure 67). The upper stages of Withers's tower, which he made circular to facilitate its use as a fire observatory, surely derived their inspiration from the square bell tower at the far end of the Strand elevation in Burges's drawing (right in Figure 67). Elements conspicuously shared by both structures include clock faces inscribed under pointed arches, ranges of pointed windows, projecting parapets, and Italianate arched belfries with pyramidal roofs. Burges's taste for continental Gothic may also have prompted Withers to introduce French elements, notably the impressive flèches over the court and prison.

The Jefferson Market Courthouse is the climax of a line of thought Withers had timidly begun in 1859. The sheer, continuous wall surface emphasizing and unifying the complex volumes, the rich and abundant naturalistic and ornamental carving, the syncopated yet architectonic rhythm of the fenestration, and the functional clarity of the ground plan combine ideas from the Dutch Reformed Church, the Newburgh Savings Bank, the Yale Chapel, and Chapel Hall. But the Jefferson Market Courthouse was not only larger and more complex than Withers's earlier works. It was also more challenging because of its exceptional location at

66. Alfred Waterhouse. Assize Courts, Manchester, 1859.

67. William Burges. Competition design for the Royal Courts of Justice.

68. College Hall, Gallaudet College, Washington, D.C., 1875.

the convergence of smaller streets with a major avenue. Withers's solution was to exploit the scenic potential of the acute angle at Sixth Avenue and West Tenth Street, the point at which the haphazard street patterns of Greenwich Village meet the gridiron of upper Manhattan. Placing the tower there, where it commanded a view uptown and downtown, and dramatizing the facade beneath it on Sixth Avenue, a sweeping north-south thoroughfare, Withers created a work that today, in greatly altered surroundings, remains a landmark.

A symbol of place to several generations of Greenwich Village residents, including John Sloan who depicted it in many of his paintings, "Old Jeff" in the early 1960s became the object of a vigorous preservation campaign. Its successful conversion in 1967 to a branch of the New York Public Library insured its continued existence while providing that it would play a new and vital role in the life of the community.

Throughout the 1870s Withers kept in touch with Edward Miner Gallaudet, and in April 1874, "studies for the plans of the college building"[62] were sent to Washington from the White Mountains, where the architect vacationed each year. These first sketches were the beginning of

69. College Hall and Chapel Hall, Gallaudet College.

Withers's last important High Victorian Gothic commission. The design of College Hall (Figure 68) was completed in April 1875. In February 1878, it was dedicated by President Rutherford B. Hayes.[63] The new brick and stone administration and dormitory building set the variegated exuberance of the Jefferson Market Courthouse down beside the sedate dignity of Chapel Hall. Yet for all its ostentation, College Hall, when seen from the grounds of the nineteenth-century campus (Figure 69), assumed an admirable relationship with its neighbor. Withers achieved this union of opposites by employing, in his College Hall design, bands that corresponded to the belt courses in Chapel Hall, a lowered roof line on the portion of College Hall nearest the older building, and a northwest corner *tourelle* of the same height as the spire on Chapel Hall.

Internally, College Hall was a typical institutional building in which the rooms on each floor lined both sides of a long corridor. Only the

70. Professor's House, Gallaudet College, Washington, D.C., 1874.

museum, which had a bay window in the base of the turret, and the vaulted lyceum room, which had a large stained-glass window on the north side of the third floor, were exceptional.

·Withers lavished his attention on the exterior of College Hall. In addition to carved floral ornament, sawtooth courses of black brick, herringbone brick gable fronts, corbeled brick bay windows, and muscular segmental arches on slender polished granite columns (in the arcade connecting the building to Chapel Hall) invigorate the fabric of the building.[64] It almost seems as if Withers sensed the end of Ruskinianism and deliberately gave free reign to his imagination, which had always run toward built-in ornamentation. The corbeled and buttressed belfry of St. Michael's, the decorative brickwork of the Newburgh Savings Bank, the forceful color contrasts and robustly three-dimensional belfry of the Jefferson Market Courthouse, as well as the stepped brick gable on an 1874 house for one of Gallaudet's professors[65] (Figure 70), were the spiritual antecedents of many of College Hall's details.

Yet the walls of College Hall owed their realization to Street's *Brick and Marble,* which Withers opened for the last time. Street's words on

71. College Hall, detail of arcade.

"Constructional Colour" read like a description of College Hall itself, for Withers transcribed Street's suggestions into a finale for his own High Victorian experience:

> There certainly appears to me to be a certain extent to which we may safely go in the way of inlaying or incrustation: we may, for instance, so construct our buildings as that there may be portions of the face of their walls in which no strain will be felt, and in which the absence of strain will be at once apparent; obviously, to instance a particular place, the spaces enclosed within circles constructed in the spandrels of a line of arches can have no strain of any kind. They are portions of the wall without active function, and may safely be filled in with materials the only object of which is to be ornamental. All kinds of sunken panels enclosed within arches or tracery would come under the same head, so also the spaces between stringcourses might vary frequently, if, as in old examples, the stringcourses were large slabs of stone bedded into the very midst of the wall.[66]

On College Hall the black sawtooth courses occur where, in the words of Street, "no strain will be felt," that is, in the spandrels of the arcade connecting the building with Chapel Hall (Figure 71) and along the top of the first floor between the windows. The remainder of unorthodox brickwork is likewise confined to nonessential structural areas, such as gable fronts. The building therefore retains the impression of strength and stability despite the great variety of its surface.

College Hall completed the ensemble of buildings Olmsted and Vaux had proposed in 1866 for the Washington campus. Today the college constitutes one of the country's notable examples of High Victorian Gothic architecture and romantic landscape planning.

The worldly Jefferson Market Courthouse was Withers's architectural masterpiece. *Church Architecture* was his literary achievement. The William Backhouse Astor Memorial Altar and Reredos in Trinity Church in New York (Figure 72) was his most prestigious commission.

Initially proposed at a vestry meeting on 10 April 1876[67] by Astor's son John Jacob Astor, Jr., the idea to replace the original wooden altar with a more grandiose one of stone was "cordially accepted" by the church. The Reverend Dr. Morgan Dix, rector, chose Withers as the architect and conducted the negotiations between the designer and the Astors.[68] The donors at first rejected as too expensive Withers's plan, which was ready on 10 June 1876.[69] Several days later, however, they reconsidered and adopted the $40,000 scheme.[70] The vestry then ordered the remodeling of the chancel to better accommodate the new altar and approved the erection of a one-story addition at the back of the church for a sacristy (Figure 73).[71] This important work was also entrusted to Withers, who supervised the entire project through completion in June 1877.[72]

The elaborate iconographic program of the altar and reredos[73] seemed to embody Mrs. Jameson's contention that the symbolism of religious art could give rise "to a thousand ennobling and inspiring thoughts."[74] Done in the Perpendicular style to harmonize with Upjohn's church, the program of the reredos followed the two main axes of the low screen.[75] The central vertical compartment over the altar contains reliefs of the Passion and Resurrection. In ascending order, they are: the Last Supper, reproduced in stone from Leonardo's fresco; the Crucifixion, inscribed within a cusped arch in the center of the reredos; the Resurrection and the Ascension in roundels to the left and right above the Crucifixion; and Christ in majesty in the tympanum. Three horizontal bands

72. William B. Astor Reredos, Trinity Church, New York, N.Y., 1876.

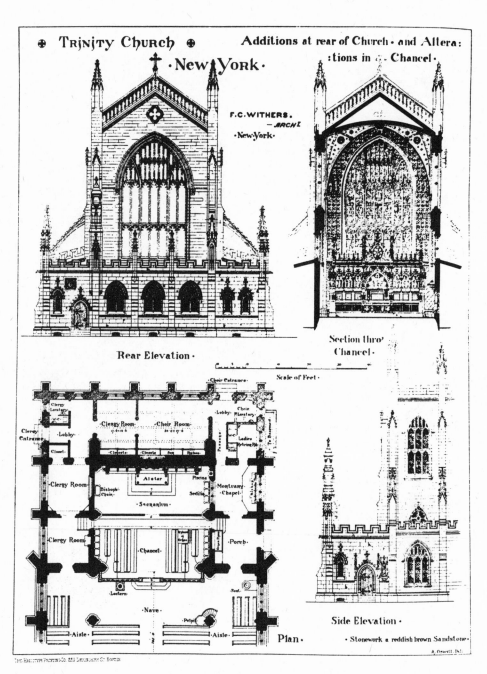

73. Alterations to chancel, Trinity Church.

flank this vertical section; at the base of the reredos on each side of the altar are decorative panels of diaper work; above them are six scenes in low relief from the life of Christ, and above these a row of statues of the Apostles and doctors of the church flanks the central Crucifixion scene. Musical angels, standing on the pinnacles of the four buttresses that subdivide the entire screen into three compartments, crown the ensemble. Throughout the reredos, the principle of division by three — an obvious symbolic reference — was maintained.

Withers's altar and reredos, like *Church Architecture*, looked backward rather than forward in its style, which recalled English works of the 1860s, and in its iconography, which followed the popular British practice of displaying Leonardo's *Last Supper* at the altar.[76] The combination of Gothic structure and Renaissance pictures in altarpieces had been discussed and justified in England as long ago as the 1850s, when the sculptor John Bell had called the combination irrational. A writer who signed himself "E. S." in *The Building News* of 1859[77] had staunchly defended the propriety of the mixture on the grounds that "there is no limit to the facilities, resources, and elasticity of Gothic architecture for the due exhibition of works of high art." By the middle of the 1860s the use of the *Last Supper* on altars had become so commonplace in England that *The Ecclesiologist* found it necessary to criticize the practice. In 1865, the British journal, irritated by the symbolic inappropriateness of Leonardo's painting for altars because it "cannot except prophetically fulfill the idea of Eucharist . . . the Sacrifice was not complete; the Blood was not shed; the Body was not broken," argued that at the altar the scene distracts the communicant, who "hardly wants at that time and place to strain his faculties by making out James from Peter, or Matthew."[78] The journal reserved special condemnation for the custom, repeated in Trinity Church, of translating the *Last Supper* into stone:

> If I remember rightly, it was at Durham that this fashion of putting an iconographical "Lord's Supper" over the altar began. . . . This was a mere copy, done in *alto relievo* of Leonardo's fresco, and is, of course, very ridiculous . . . it was a childish absurdity committed at Durham of doing Leonardo's "Cenacolo" in marble just reduced to one-tenth size of the original. The treatment necessary to a picture, that is to a coloured attempt on a flat surface to represent facts, is not the treatment required to represent facts in relief or pure sculpture. The whole method and idea is different.[79]

Notwithstanding this severe criticism, by 1876 an aura of doctrinal correctness, which had been reinforced by the decision in 1865 to erect a mosaic copy of Leonardo's work over the high altar of Westminster Abbey, overrode all objections.[80] Dr. Dix and Trinity Church were conservative; it was the Reverend Phillips Brooks and H. H. Richardson at Trinity Church in Boston who were setting new standards of ecclesiastical design in America in 1876.

While critics found little fault with the Astor reredos, they gave it little more than conventional acclaim. So prominent a work would have elicited more serious discussion had its date been 1846 or 1856, instead of 1876. The only important review of the reredos appeared in *The American Architect and Building News* shortly after the dedication in 1877.[81] The article reported the critical comments made by the guests who had been invited to view the work at a private showing prior to the consecration ceremony.[82] No questions were raised concerning either the appropriateness of the altar's iconographic program or of the mixture of Perpendicular Gothic and Italian Renaissance components. The most severe criticism was leveled, quite justly, at its truncated appearance. But even those who thought that "the skyline in this, a Gothic piece of work, was not sufficiently marked," were forced to modify their position when they reflected that "the work was done with a great colored chancel at the back, and without the opportunity of setting the work out some feet, and getting that relief which it now lacks." Despite this drawback, good things were said of the altar, although the general tone of the remarks was decidedly subcelestial: "the execution is magnificent as a specimen of workmanship" remarked the reporter, "almost too good, leading one to feel like tasting it, as a richly ornamented bit of confectionary."

The shortcomings of the Trinity high altar are obvious. Not only does its stout horizontality conflict with the slender height of the chancel and church, but the numerous scenes and figures are too small and too crowded to be clearly legible from beyond the altar rail. With the exception of the central Crucifixion group, the artistic character of the pictorial scenes is insipidly traditional and uninspired. Nonetheless, when seen from a distance, especially from the church vestibule, the altar's bright Caen stone surface, luminous from the remote chancel, provides a radiant focal point to the otherwise somber church interior.

"The scene was like a fairyland," wrote Dr. Dix of the ceremony of dedication,[83] at which he effusively praised the altar and its architect.

Extolling Withers as "one who fears God and loves the Church,"[84] the rector, who had been involved with the medieval movement from its earliest stages,[85] uttered one of the last testimonials to the Gothic Revival: "Men of the first ability have been at work with pencil and chisel, each band filled with an honorable ambition to make their part the best; so that really much of the spirit of the old craftsman has gone into this labor, and now lives under yon sculptures."[86] Dr. Dix's words and Withers's high altar were both monument and epitaph to the vital period of ecclesiology in the United States.

6

ARCHITECTURE
IN A GENTLER MOOD
(1878–1901)

MONTGOMERY SCHUYLER stated that the centennial year "brought with it our architectural Declaration of Independence"[1] from England. This new spirit of liberty, which infused both secular and religious architecture, took much of the luster from Withers's long-held reputation as an emissary of a respected foreign culture. Now Richardson's unpolished Romanesque became the first among a number of eclectic styles which owed their existence more to native impulses than to European example. Notable were the Colonial Revival, directly encouraged by the centennial celebration with its reminiscences of America's past; the Renaissance Revival, fostered by Richard Morris Hunt; and Neo-Classicism, identified with the stellar careers of Charles F. McKim (1847–1909), Larkin Mead (1846–1928), and Stanford White (1835–1906). Complicating matters further was the fact that even the authority of historicism was being challenged by the commercial architects of Chicago, who were growing impatient with all revival modes.

In this regard, the demise of High Victorian Gothic was seen to be the result, as Henry Van Brunt put it, of architects who had followed its cause but accepted modern conditions of structure, materials, and use, which "entirely smothered the letter and spirit of medievalism." Montgomery Schuyler echoed Van Brunt's point of view when he wrote:

> The Gothic revivalists wrought in a style that responds to our "ethnic" sentiments, but it was too remote, historically, for us to be in real sympathy with it. Its practitioners declared that the principles of Medieval architecture were capable of producing new and modern forms. That would have been a fair contention if they really modernized Gothic, but they never did.[2]

These characterizations were particularly appropriate to Withers's career. His two most important Victorian Gothic buildings, Chapel Hall and the Jefferson Market Courthouse, had provided no new structural or design ideas. In his cast iron store, which did offer a new approach to design in metal, as Van Brunt had said, Gothic forms were smothered under an honest expression of modern structure. Withers was thus beyond Gothic revivalism. But the new way lacked appeal for him. Instead of rising to the challenge of new circumstances, as he had done after the death of Downing and when the Civil War had dimmed the antebellum Downing tradition, Withers, in the last two decades of his career, retreated into complacency, rejecting, in the words of Van Brunt, "that more copious vocabulary which has grown out of our new life and our larger experience."[3]

Although conservative, Withers maintained a consistently high level of quality in his works. Continuing to display imaginative composition and direct expression of materials, his later buildings often possess a mellow, quiet beauty. It would be unjust to dismiss this architecture solely because it was not progressive; the last years of Withers's career are an honorable postscript to his two decades of leadership as a Gothic Revival church designer and his decade of adventurous creativity as a High Victorian Gothic secular architect.

With the rectory of Hartford's Christ Episcopal Church, designed in 1879[4] (Figure 74), Withers rejected High Victorian Gothic. The random ashlar brownstone residence was part of the comprehensive remodeling scheme for a prominent church[5] that had been constructed in the Perpendicular style in 1829 from the plans of Ithiel Town (1784–1844) and A. J. Davis. One of the early examples of the Gothic Revival in the United States, it had been built without a chancel. Withers corrected this embarrassing deficiency and added a new high altar and reredos. A low parish hall was also erected adjacent to the eastern end of the church with the new rectory on its north side.[6]

Located on a crowded street in the center of the city, the rectory, according to *The Churchman*, was architecturally "of a somewhat later" style of Gothic than Christ Church itself.[7] The mullioned and transomed windows and the engaged chimney with strapwork ornament were generally Tudor, a style that came under the broad heading of "Queen Anne," and represented Withers's desire to match the building to Town and Davis' church. The vivid contrast of materials, Italianate details, tall

74. Rectory of Christ Church, Hartford, Conn., 1874.

pointed arches, and the steep verticality of Withers's High Victorian Gothic urban houses, such as the Kimball house (Figure 33) and the rectory of the Church of the Holy Trinity (Figure 55), were missing. In addition, the emotional reserve of the Hartford building typified the mood of Withers's late architecture.

In the area of church architecture, Withers's vision remained unchanged. This was demonstrated in 1880 when he turned his attention to the commission for St. Luke's Episcopal Church, the only representative of that denomination in Altoona, Pennsylvania[8] (Figure 75). The parish, described as having "invariably consisted to some extent of the resident officials of the Pennsylvania Railroad Company,"[9] was typical of the well-to-do congregations that had hired Withers since the 1860s.

Old St. Luke's Church, erected in 1853 and used as a station on the Underground Railroad,[10] had been donated by a philanthropic New Yorker, General John Watts DePeyster, who was also consulted on the decision to build the new church.[11] DePeyster, or possibly the rector, the Reverend Alan Woodle, who had come to Altoona from Christ Episcopal Church in New York City,[12] must have asked Withers to design the new building. In any event, the erection of the church was more than a local endeavor. Thomas Scott, the president of the Pennsylvania Railroad, contributed $17,000 for construction, and George Whitney, "one of the most philanthropic, patriotic and estimable citizens of Philadelphia," gave more than $12,000.[13] The bells were donated by a New York family.[14] St. Luke's was clearly intended to be a faithful example of High Church Episcopal architecture in a city that had grown in less than thirty years from farmland into a major industrial center.

In various respects St. Luke's differed from the churches Withers had illustrated in *Church Architecture*, but essentially it followed ecclesiological dictates.[15] St. Luke's plan was nave with aisles, a type that he had prescribed for large parishes, although the actual seating capacity of 500 persons was only in the medium range according to his calculations. Because of the smallness of the site and the need to use all available space, the plan was rectangular rather than cruciform, even though Withers had generally used the latter for churches of this size. The dimensions of the plot prevented the full development of the chancel, which was simply marked at its junction with the nave by a turret on the roof and by buttresses on the sides. Instead of the stone tower typical of his urban churches, Withers adorned the western end of the nave with a

75. St. Luke's Church, Altoona, Pa., 1880.

wooden belfry that recalled the one at St. Luke's in Matteawan, New York. Built of roughly dressed sandstone, the Altoona church, because of its unbroken roofline and simple rectangular volume, shares a certain affinity with the contemporary churches of James Brooks (1852–1901) in England, particularly his Church of the Transfiguration (1880), Lewisham, and conveys an impression of elemental sturdiness.[16]

St. Luke's offered reassuring evidence of tradition in its raw surroundings, where it quickly gained a warm patina from the sooty air in the busy railroad town. (Recent cleaning has restored the original light buff color to the stone.) Solidly conservative, it was demonstrative of the

76. "Whitecaps," James Dunbar House, Monmouth Beach, N.J., 1880 (demolished).

character of the parish that it housed. Its simple lines and straightforward volumes, however, made it unusual in the street architecture of Victorian Altoona, a city distinguished for its wooden houses laden with "gingerbread" ornament.

St. Luke's was conventional. The Dunbar house, however, bore no relationship to Withers's earlier suburban residences. Whitecaps, as it was titled in *The American Architect and Building News* in 1881[17] (Figure 76), was situated on the ocean at Monmouth Beach, New Jersey. By virtue of its large leaded glass windows, wooden shingles, slender chimney stacks, and steeply pitched roofs, the house generally resembled Norman Shaw's Leyswood (1868) in Sussex, England, and Richardson's Watts-Sherman house (1874) in Newport. Withers certainly knew of the Watts-Sherman house, which had introduced the Queen Anne style to America, and may have even seen it, for he had family connections in Newport. But Whitecaps also reflected the influence of the British pavilion at the Centennial Exposition where architectural drawings displayed by the British government of similar domestic structures had impressed Americans. In a review of the drawings, several of which were by Roland Plumbe, Withers's assistant in Newburgh during the 1850s,[18] *The American Builder* recognized the special appropriateness of the style for seaside dwellings and extended the following invitation, which Withers accepted in the design of the Dunbar house:

> It is hoped that the next millionaire who puts up a cottage at Long Branch will adopt this style, and he will have a house ample enough to entertain a Prince, yet exceedingly cozy, cool in summer, and yet abundantly warm in winter, plain enough, and yet capable of the highest ornamental development.[19]

Withers chose the style, which *The American Builder* called "Elizabethan," as expressive of spacious, informal comfort. But the clapboard sheathing of the Dunbar house, although it had enjoyed popularity among American Stick Style architects of the 1870s, was without precedent in contemporary English architecture. Recognizing that Elizabethan was a timber style and also, as *The American Builder* had pointed out, well suited for America, Withers combined the English elements of design with the traditional American exterior finish. However, the use of clapboard to enclose the internal timber framework that supported the house ignored the ingenuity that Withers had displayed in his honest articulation of the exterior of the Broome Street store. There he had called to mind the iron frame in the facade design. On the Dunbar house, he concealed construction. Even the handsome rafters in the head of the central gable and on the *porte cochere* — devices that, along with the tall second-story window, he may have derived from a house built in 1879 on Mount Desert Island, Maine,[20] by the Boston architect William R. Emerson (1856–1936) — were decorative extravagances rather than structural embellishments.

In his design for Whitecaps, Withers attempted, as others, particularly Dudley Newton (1845–1907), had, to develop an Anglo-American style of domestic architecture. Availing himself of the freedom that the English Queen Anne style offered, he created a bold composition of inflated volumes, varying roof lines, and arbitrary fenestration. With these characteristics he combined the traditional American porch and substituted clapboard for the plaster of English half-timber construction. Yet the Dunbar house was the only one of its kind by Withers.

More squarely in the cozy "olde English" style of the Watts-Sherman

77. J. Pierrepont Davis House, Hartford, Conn., 1881.

house was Withers's residence for Dr. J. Pierrepont Davis in Hartford
(Figure 77). The red brick house, which appeared in *L'Architecture Amé-*
ricaine (1886),[21] comprised half-timbered and shingled gables, decorative
terra-cotta panels and gargoyles, steep chimney stacks, and a two-story
bay of mullioned and transomed windows. The porch at the entrance
and the verandas on one side of the front imparted a characteristically
American expression of domestic comfort and may have accounted for
the French interest in the building.

Withers's unsuccessful entry in the competition for the New York
City Produce Exchange building[22] in 1881 marked the end of his career
as a commercial architect. The competition, which one contemporary
critic called "an architectural opportunity that in some respects was the
best that ever has been offered in New York,"[23] stipulated that the building, which was to stand at Broadway and Beaver Streets, should contain
an exchange hall several stories high and ample office space for the
Exchange members. In addition, the street-level rooms would be rented
to other businesses. By the middle of January, 1881, seventeen prominent architects had submitted designs to the building committee.[24] Early

78. Competition design for the New York Produce Exchange, 1881.

in March the Exchange membership approved the plan presented by George B. Post.[25] Constructed in a modified form, Post's scheme helped to establish as an integral part of American urban architecture Renaissance-inspired imagery and metal frame construction, of which it was an advanced example.[26]

The Produce Exchange competition signaled the end of Gothic in commercial architecture in the United States, as Trinity Church in Boston had challenged its authority in ecclesiastical architecture and the Philadelphia Exposition had diminished its standing in domestic architecture. Three of the best-known medievalists, Withers, R. M. Upjohn, and Leopold Eidlitz, had competed in the Exchange competition and lost. They were defeated because ostensibly their schemes were impractical. One would suppose, however, that the Exchange membership preferred to have their building usher in a new era rather than monumentalize an old one. Clarence Cook reported that Withers's drawings "were not even taken out of their portfolio."[27] At the opening of a new decade, the competition for the largest commercial building ever proposed for New

York City was animated by a desire for change. The simple unity of the arcaded facade of Post's design made a direct appeal to the judges of the competition, as did the ingenuity of its supporting structure. The Renaissance style of Post's building may also have pleased the exchange members, who, in the new age of corporate wealth, may have wished to fancy themselves not as the descendants of medieval burghers but rather as latter-day merchant princes.

Although purged of Italian Gothic allusions, Withers's design[28] (Figure 78) was consistent with his earlier standards. Distinguishing the prominent Broadway and Beaver Street corner, a majestic tower, recalling St. Stephen's tower on the Houses of Parliament (and containing the main staircases and service rooms), closed the symmetrical Broadway elevation on the south and a lower staircase tower framed it on the north. Both of these service towers asserted their independence from the core of the building by their higher window levels and by their slight projection from the facade. Above the arcaded ground floor of the central section, the three-story exchange hall was defined by a molded stringcourse beneath and by a wide band of patterned brick above. The horizontal roof was enlivened by a series of identical turreted gables, and throughout the elevation Withers standardized and repeated a limited number of later English and continental Gothic forms. Taking the medieval guild hall as his point of departure, and also undoubtedly thinking of Barry's Parliament building, Withers attempted to express the repetitious nature of the office and commercial spaces, the breadth and importance of the hall, and the functional isolation of the stair and service units.

The modest Van Schaick Free Reading Room (Figure 79) that Withers designed for the community of Westchester, New York, in 1882[29] recalled his picturesque earlier buildings. A snug little structure of reddish brown brick, it partook of the predilection for substantial comfort that pervaded middle class American taste in the 1880s. Returning to his earlier architecture for inspiration, Withers revised the towered facade and the ground plan of the Tioronda School of 1865 (Figure 28). The form of the library tower was more massive than its predecessor, and it appeared again in Withers's Vassar Brothers Hospital (1885) at Poughkeepsie.[30]

Although Withers used the Tioronda School as the basis for the Van Schaick library, he ignored the polychromatic wall fabric of the earlier

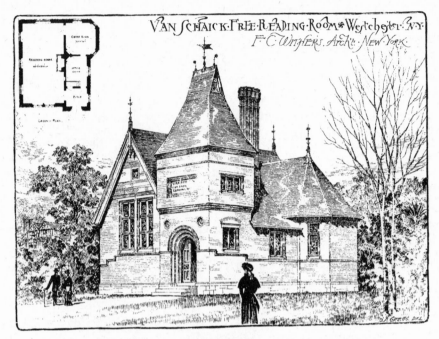

79. Van Schaick Free Reading Room, Bronx, N.Y., 1882.

brick building in his new design. Forgetting High Victorian dark and light ornamental patterns, Withers revived the monochromatic sobriety that had characterized his pre-Civil War brick houses. Here was a purified conception of brick architecture as a planometric, monochromatic expression of simple volumes. This was the most significant development in Withers's later career. When he chose to employ it, he created buildings that were impressively architectonic even though they were remote from the most vital artistic traditions of his day.

The competition for the Soldiers and Sailors Monument in Hartford of 1882 brought Withers more recognition than had the Produce Exchange contest, but it did not result in the construction of his entry.[31] After awarding Withers third prize, the selection committee, which paid the competitors but declined to accept any of their plans, asked Withers to prepare an alternate scheme. The committee also rejected this proposal (Figure 80) and eventually went to George Keller (1842–1935), who designed the present memorial, which was erected in 1886.

Withers's monument, which recalled his 1869 scheme for a park gateway (Figure 58), took the form of a marble and limestone Gothic

80. Soldiers and Sailors Monument, Hartford, Conn., 1882.
Architect's watercolor drawing.

triumphal arch with a tall mansard roof emphasizing the broad middle opening. The arch was to have been centered on a bridge over the Park River, at the entrance from the city to Bushnell Park. The pretty scenery in the presentation drawing demonstrated that the design was conceived in the spirit of the picturesque gardening tradition that Downing had loved and to which Withers had remained sympathetic through his relations with Calvert Vaux and Frederick Law Olmsted. A Gothic fantasy showing the way to an idyllic landscape, the monument vividly embodied allusion to the heavenly gateway that awaited those who had "crossed over" in the service of their country. Suggestive of the Gothic entrances to many American rural cemeteries, the memorial would have conveyed its message to all but the most irreverent citizens. In light of the many ponderous monuments the Civil War brought forth, it is regrettable that Withers's charming conception was never carried out.

Also projected as an ornament within a landscaped setting was the 175-foot-high brick water tower that Withers designed in 1883 for the

81. Water tower for Hackensack Water Co., Weehawken, New Jersey, 1883.

Hackensack Water Company in Weehawken, New Jersey (Figure 81). Built to maintain even pressure throughout the water system, the tower held a 165,000 gallon tank at the height of 300 feet above sea level. The superhuman scale and stark forms that less artistic utilitarian structures of this kind generally possessed had no fascination for Withers or his patrons. Instead, Withers imparted an "architectural" character to the tower by introducing picturesque variety and embellishment and by relating the design to the secular towers of the Middle Ages. At the top, the presence of the water tank is indicated by the expanse of solid masonry supported by corbels and by the pyramidal roof that rises above the parapet. Enriching this upper area with a net pattern of black brick and creating an irregular skyline with the turret (which caps a stairway that runs from the base of the tower to the roof), crenelations, and flagpole, Withers effectively mitigated a top-heavy appearance.

Together with its romantic look, the Weehawken tower incorporated

innovative principles of construction. Described by *Engineering News* as
"the most important structure of its kind in the country,"[32] the tower
made use internally of pointed arches to support the tank, which weighed
over 620 tons when full. This arrangement, which was regarded as "bold
at the time when built," proved superior to iron trussing because it reduced to a minimum the "springing of the bottom of the tank when filled
or emptied." Boilers housed in the basement level provided the power
needed to pump the water up to the tank. Undoubtedly, much of the
credit for the tower's structural system must go to John F. Ward, the civil
engineer who worked with Withers on the project (and for whom Withers designed a handsome dwelling in Jersey City in 1884).

Demonstrating the nineteenth-century dichotomy between "architecture" and "building," Withers translated utility into the language of
Victorian associationism. By giving the structure the aspect of a medieval
guard tower, he expressed its function as a sentinel maintaining the
efficiency of the water system. Nor was this exercise in "speaking architecture" lacking in more literal meaning; beneath the tank, the shaft of
the giant watchtower housed the administrative office of the water company, as well as quarters for employees.

The scheme that Withers prepared in 1885 for the remodeling of St.
George Episcopal Church (erected in 1819) in Newburgh, New York,[33]
was one of only two Romanesque ecclesiastical designs of Withers's career
(Figure 82). The proposal, which fortunately was never carried out,
would have removed the renowned Greek Revival steeple of the Newburgh church and decorated the simple gabled western end with heavy
Romanesque ornament. Standing south of the church, a tall square cam-
panile threatened to dwarf unceremoniously the low nave and facade,
the proportions of which were fixed by the original structure.

Although Romanesque, Withers's design showed no influence of
Richardson, whose personal adaptations of Angevin Romanesque domi-
nated American architecture in the 1880s. Like T. H. Wyatt and David
Brandon in their 1847 plan for St. Mary's Wilton, Wiltshire,[34] Withers
took his inspiration from northern Italian Romanesque, rather than
from French medieval architecture, which had fascinated Richardson,
and treated the style with the same exactitude as he had the Gothic. All of
the requisite elements of paneling, corbel tables, and round arches were
incorporated into a design that literally reproduced the historical style.
He did not find in Romanesque a vehicle for imaginative self-expression,

82. St. George Church,
Newburgh, N.Y., 1885
(project).

as Richardson had. The exaggerated proportions and the accentuated textures, as well as the disregard for accurate ornamentation, that characterize the Richardsonian Romanesque, eluded him. St. George Church made only a slight departure from Withers's conservative ecclesiological Gothic style.

Withers's career as a domestic architect all but ended in 1885 with his design for the Frank Hasbrouck house in Poughkeepsie, New York (Figure 83). The large red brick dwelling that Withers, in *The American Architect and Building News,* claimed was Queen Anne style,[35] is graced with terra-cotta ornament, inset floral panels, and molded stringcourses. Displaying a picturesque asymmetry, the main elements of the house are enhanced by a variety of bays, dormers, and gables, which lend considerable liveliness and interest to the overall composition. Built of brick, the house is appropriately endowed with a strong sense of planarity.

83. Frank Hasbrouck House, Poughkeepsie, N.Y., 1885.

The same quality characterizes the masterpiece of Withers's later years, the Chapel of the Good Shepherd built in 1888 on Roosevelt Island (formerly Blackwell's and Welfare Island) in New York City (Figure 84). The church, a gift of the banker George Bliss[36] to the Episcopal City Mission Society, until recently served the inmates of the island's municipal hospital, prison, and insane asylum. Originally to have cost $5000, the brick chapel eventually exceeded $75,000, due to the ever-increasing demands and generosity of its donor.[37] The investment has had lasting value, for the handsome structure, which has been skillfully restored, has merited the status of architectural landmark and continues to play an integral role in the life of the island, now transformed into a residential community (Figure 85).[38]

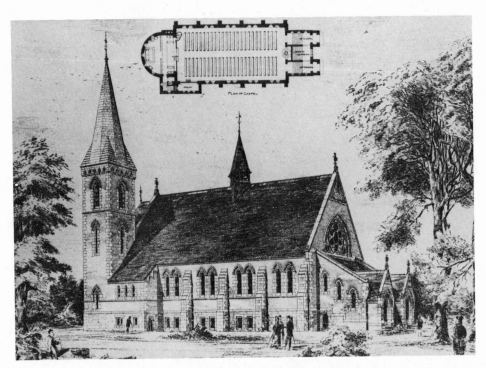

84. Chapel of the Good Shepherd, Roosevelt Island, New York City, 1888.

The nature of the Welfare Island parish compelled Withers to devise an unusual church for the society. To maintain the segregation of the male and female inmates, Withers introduced twin entrance porches, one for each sex, on the western elevation. The portals lead into a deep vestibule, which contains two stairways in line with the entrances. These flights of steps ascend to doors in the north (male) and south (female) sides of the wide nave. Between the stairways, a central flight of steps descends to a reading room and other facilities in the basement. This triple division is developed on the entrance wall of the nave, where the baptismal font sits in a large niche between the two portals.

The present interior preserves the warmth and simple dignity of Withers's original scheme. "The brick walls are . . . faced on the inside with brown enamelled brick as high as the stone string-course under the windows," records a contemporary description, "and above it the whole of the interior walls are of buff-colored pressed-brick laid in red mortar. . . . The roofs (of the nave and apse) are open timbered, constructed of Georgia pine and finished in panels with moulded ribs, etc."[39]

85. Chapel of the Good Shepherd, Roosevelt Island, New York City, 1888.

In the northeast corner of the nave, Withers located the organ chamber, which projects on the exterior to form an L-shaped mass with the tower. By placing the tower at the juncture of the nave and apse, Withers avoided the jumble of forms that would have resulted had the tower been positioned near the western facade. The location of the tower on the north side also insured a satisfactory composition for the elevation that faced the primary approach road (Figure 84). The Chapel of the Good Shepherd illustrates that Withers still possessed the ability to seek imaginative solutions for out-of-the-ordinary commissions. He expressed obvious pride in the work by conspicuously placing his monogram in the apex of the facade gable.

86. George Truefitt.
St. George's Church,
Worthing, Sussex,
1867.

Within the limits of the lingering tradition of the Gothic Revival, Withers achieved the finest expression of the plain manner he introduced with the design of the Van Schaick library. Fabricated of red Croton face brick with a foundation of granite and dressings of freestone, the strong unadorned volumes of the broad nave, bulky apse, and sturdy tower stand forth without ornamental elaboration and build into a powerful aggregate of masses (Figure 85). Withers undoubtedly was indebted to James Brooks for much of the character of expression of the Chapel of the Good Shepherd. Brooks built many brick mission churches in poor parts of London in the 1860s. These buildings, in Eastlake's words, depended "for their effect entirely on their plans and proportions."[40] St. Chad's, Haggerston, like Withers's building, was faced internally with brick and employed an apse rather than the English Gothic chancel, as had Street's St. James the Less, another brick church for an indigent parish. The eastern end of the Chapel of the Good Shepherd also bears a close resemblance to St. George's Church at Worthing, Sussex, of 1867, by George Truefitt (Figure 86). Truefitt had accompanied Vaux on a tour of the Continent before Vaux met Downing. The bold apse and general "muscular" character of Truefitt's church undoubtedly originated in his experience with French Gothic. Distilling his plan from these

87. Competition design for the Cathedral of
St. John the Divine, New York, N.Y., 1889.

sources, Withers created a compact design that, in its quiet monumentality, shares the spirit, if not the form, of the architecture of Richardson.

Yet none of this feeling was present in the scheme Withers unsuccessfully submitted in 1889 in the competition for the Episcopal Cathedral of St. John the Divine in New York City (Figure 87). His proposal was one of sixty sets of drawings received by the cathedral building committee, which awarded the commission to George L. Heins (1860–1907) and C. Grant LaFarge (1862–1938) who had based their design on Richardson's Trinity Church.[41] Predictably, Withers had not looked to an American model but to recent English example for guidance; the western elevation and crossing of Withers's cathedral clearly emulated J. L. Pearson's Early English and French style Truro Cathedral of 1880.[42]

Although it was published in *The American Architect and Building News* in November 1889,[43] before the building committee had made its choice,

88. Trinity Church, Hartford, Conn., nave.

Withers's scheme was never seriously considered. Even though there was conservative opposition to the Heins and LaFarge plan,[44] the prosaic accuracy and tight linearism of Withers's design conflicted with the dominant taste of the day, which gravitated toward the weighty Richardsonian style. Coming too late in his career, the opportunity for Withers's greatest ecclesiastical achievement found him too far removed from the mainstream of American church architecture to meet the challenge.

Despite this fact, in 1891 Withers drew the plans for the largest church ever erected from his designs, Trinity Episcopal Church in Hartford, Connecticut.[45] Withers's friend and Trinity's former pastor, the Reverend Francis Goodwin, personally supervised the new church construction.[46] Described as an "expert on Gothic architecture,"[47] Goodwin may even have influenced the design. The connected group of dark red brick buildings consisting of a tall freestanding tower (derived from the tower of Magdalen College, Oxford), an aisled church, a parish hall, and a rectory, was unique in Withers's architecture. The broad nave of the church (Figure 88), which featured a splendid hammer beam roof, proved that Withers could still create inspired architecture. But the lofty interior was a personal achievement for the man, not significant for his art.

After he designed Trinity Church, Withers was called upon less and less to design ecclesiastical buildings. In 1893, he donated his services as architect of the diminutive St. Matthew's Chapel in Sugar Hill, New Hampshire.[48] Withers's only wooden church, St. Matthew's served as the summer chapel for the Episcopalians who vacationed, as he did, at the Sunset House and the other hotels in the vicinity of the White Mountains resort. The Episcopal Church of St. John the Evangelist overlooking the bay in Newport, Rhode Island, was Withers's last church.[49] Designed in 1893, the scholarly Decorated style building concluded the architect's career as a church designer on a resonant cord of High Church traditionalism.

Despite the absence of ecclesiastical building commissions, throughout the 1890s Withers continued to design church furnishings. Association of his name with the Astor Reredos brought him the patronage of some of New York City's most important Episcopal parishes. The Swope Memorial Reredos (1892) (Figure 89),[50] composed of Siena marble and Caen stone and decorated with the Crucifixion scene, and the oak Cotheal Memorial Pulpit (1897)[51] for Trinity Chapel, ornamented with Ghibertian reliefs illuminating the theme of preaching, were impressive commissions. Another was the lych gate that a member of the Astor family gave to the Church of the Transfiguration in 1896 (then already known as "The Little Church Around the Corner") (Figure 90). Built of wood on a stone foundation and painted dark brown to harmonize with the earlier church, the lych-gate was described as "the one touch necessary to make the surroundings of the Church of the Transfiguration the most picturesque and charming of any in New York."[52] Together with the Zabriske Memorial Altar and Reredos (1895)[53] in the chancel of the same church, these works demonstrated that Withers still commanded the respect of the city's conservative churchmen.

The final commission of Withers's long career, the New York City Prison at Leonard and Center Streets (Figure 91), involved the architect

89. The Swope Memorial Reredos, Trinity Chapel, New York, N.Y., 1892.

90. Lych Gate, Church of the Transfiguration, New York, N.Y., 1896.

in another municipal scandal. In 1896 Withers and his partner of later years, Walter Dickson (1835–1903),[54] who together did a large amount of institutional planning for the city of New York, presented their scheme for the city's biggest jail to the mayor and his architectural adviser, George B. Post.[55] Early the following year the plans were approved and construction was begun.[56] One year later, however, the new commissioner of correction, Francis Lantry, announced "that the plans were defective and the structure insecure."[57] The controversy arose over the installation of the steel cell blocks, which were designed by another pair of architects, Horgan and Slattery. The city administrator contended that the original granite structure that Withers had designed was too weak to sustain the weight of the cells. Since Post, as well as Withers and Dickson, had approved the original plans, it was inconceivable that so gross a miscalculation would have been overlooked. The responsibility rested with the less renowned, less respectable Horgan and Slattery, who had made the cells too heavy. In a sharp editorial, *The New York Times* said

91. New York City Prison, 1896.

what many citizens had voiced in private about the affair: that the accusations against Withers were inspired by politicians seeking to turn the commission over to favorites.

> The firm of architects appointed to displace a well-known and respected architect is entirely unknown to New Yorkers interested in architecture. The suspicion that they are only architects "ad hoc" may be unjust, but it is entirely natural. It is hoped that the courts may be successfully invoked to prevent the consummation of this threatened outrage not only upon the architects but upon the public.[58]

The struggle to discharge Withers was unresolved at the time of his death on 1 January, 1901. The building was eventually completed according to his plans, but it was demolished in 1948 to make way for the present municipal jail.

Withers's prison design developed the château-fortress form of the Jefferson Market Prison of 1874. The facade of the new building was divided horizontally into two large stories, which, in turn, were each subdivided into four tiers of cells. Contained between two semicircular towers, the elevation was distinguished by a central turreted pavilion and a massive entrance portal. Beneath the high roof, attic windows opened onto an "airing court" that provided space for the prisoners to exercise but barred "the possibility of either escape, or of communication with the outside world."[59] Other features showed that penitentiary architecture had become considerably humanized since 1836 when John Haviland (1792–1852) had designed the original "Tombs" prison, the building that Withers's structure replaced. In addition to the airing court, the new building contained a restaurant where prisoners could buy their own meals, water closets in every cell, and special rooms "for prisoners of the better class, who are sometimes thrust into prison on mere suspicion."[60]

The exterior of the prison was more unified than the elevation of Withers's earlier Produce Exchange. The château-fortress format, however, did not offer any fundamentally new suggestions for the design of large buildings. The New York City Prison, which Schuyler called "by no means a bad building, but by no means its architect's best work or most characteristic,"[61] was unallied to the growth of a new American architecture at the turn of the century.

↝7↜

EPILOGUE

To APPRECIATE the true and enduring merit of Withers's architecture, one must turn to his most significant achievement, the Jefferson Market Courthouse, and to the comments of the man who in Withers's lifetime was most sympathetic to his work, Montgomery Schuyler. *The American Architect and Building News* in April 1877 printed his evaluation of the building, which was the best to appear.[1] Opening his discussion with high praise for New York City's only High Victorian Gothic municipal building, Schuyler commended the courthouse elevations for their honest derivation from the interior plan:

> The distinction of the buildings now opened in Sixth Avenue is that the design is distinctly an expression of the purposes of the building, that it varies as they vary, and that the ground plan being established by the exigencies of the building alone, the architecture is rigidly developed from the ground plan.

Elaborating on this statement, the writer set down the most perceptive criticism of Withers's architectural talent ever recorded:

> Whatever style it is attempted in, it is evident that what is attempted in the Third District Courthouse is a much harder thing to do than to set up in front of a New York court-house and jail the front of a medieval town hall or a Palladian palace. The difference is essentially that in the former case architecture is treated as a living art and in the latter as dead. The architect of the Sixth Avenue buildings, by committing himself to a sound basis of design, was forced really to "design" a new building. With so intricate and so peculiar a programme he could not compile it. Details, of course, he could find in abundance, but details would not serve him, nor even pieces of elevations, which perhaps he might have found. The whole resulting from the combination of these multivarious parts must be original. In such an attempt even a moderate success is a creditable feat while to say of such a work it is better in perspective than in elevation, and

better in mass than in detail, is to assign its author a very high rank as
an architect. This may truly be said of the architect of the new buildings. He has made a whole which is better and greater than any of its
parts.

The preceding remarks defined Withers's greatest strength as an
architect: his ability to make clear the universal fundamentals of plan and
space through the poetry of historicism. This gift enabled him to be
original in his work, as each commission was unique in the challenge it
posed. Thus, the Jefferson Market Courthouse is Withers's most complicated and eloquent design because its requirements were the most complex he confronted in his career. Withers did not attempt to needlessly
disinvolve the plan by balancing its elements or equalizing the size and
shape of its units, for that would have been antithetical to the nature of
the design problem to incorporate several functions within an irregular
area. In other cases, such as Chapel Hall, where an uncomplicated spatial
arrangement—the alignment of rooms along a single axis—resulted nat-
urally from the physical conditions governing the commission, Withers
exploited simplicity in the ground plan and harmony in the elevation to
create a design of equal originality, but one whose esthetic character was
different. Conditioned by his appreciation of Ruskin's rationalism, Withers's talent for developing his designs from a thoughtful understanding
of what was demanded of the building and the finesse with which his
works proclaimed that perception, as well as his ripe scholarship, sustained the reputation of his best buildings even when his stylistic idiom
was beginning to look outdated. As late as 1885, the Jefferson Market
Courthouse was voted one of the "ten best buildings" in America.[2] In a
later period, when the Gothic Revival was all but forgotten, Withers
continued to be recognized as one of the important American architects
of his time.[3]

Withers shared with many of his colleagues ideals that flourished
during the first three-quarters of the nineteenth century. Devotion to
reform and search for a means of embodying cherished sentiments, notions born during the Greek Revival, were essential to the Gothic Revival.
Jefferson and the Greek Revivalists, who piloted American building from
the late eighteenth century until shortly before Withers's arrival, saw
their style as redeeming architecture from superficial Georgian elegance.[4] They also believed, as the Gothic Revivalists did, in the associational values that architecture might possess. The ennoblement of the

free citizen by means of monumentally dignified buildings and the calling to mind of the ancient and honorable roots of republicanism inspired, in part, the resurrection of the antique style.

The Classical attitude prevailed well into the Jacksonian era. Then pragmatism, extolled as the civic virtue of the common man, laid the social foundation for the acceptance of the more relaxed patterns of Gothic Revival design. The Gothicists of the 1830s and 1840s saw the conventionalism of the Greek style as physically and mentally stifling. Put forth in the name of progress, their ideas were defended as improvements in the well-being of the nation. Men like Downing and his follower Withers sought, through convenience and informality, to accommodate a new world view.

Enlightenment associational values were also revised by the romantic Gothicists who reaffirmed the role of faith in modern life. They no longer extolled the strictly public virtues. Pugin, Ruskin, Street, and Withers intended rather to remind nineteenth-century man of his Christian heritage and his obligations to God as well as to his society.

As the Gothic Revival evolved into the High Victorian Gothic style, Withers and his colleagues, such as J. C. Cady, W. A. Potter, and Leopold Eidlitz, sustained by the philosophy of Ruskin, retained the attitude of moral rightness toward the system that was their inheritance from the earlier phase of the Gothic Revival. During the rampant eclecticism of the Grant era, this moral tone distinguished High Victorian Gothic from its numerous rivals. The Second Empire, Egyptian, Moorish, and Renaissance styles were fundamentally decorative in their approach to architectural design. Their practitioners did not defend their use on moralistic grounds. None of these idioms inspired the quantity or quality of scholarly and speculative writing that had attended the Greek and Gothic revivals. While their existence diluted and retarded the effectiveness of the High Victorian Gothic crusade, they offered no threat to Withers's principles. He and his fellow Gothicists plodded along in the hope that the world would see the correctness of their way; they regarded their competitors more with indifference than with passionate fear.

It was the Richardsonian Romanesque that ultimately dimmed whatever hope the American followers of Ruskin may have had of obtaining dominion over public taste. The Richardsonian Romanesque presented a serious alternative to the reformist and associational ideals of the Gothic Revival. The Richardsonians did not employ the Romanesque with the intention of turning the thoughts of Americans back to the Dark Ages. Instead, Richardson sought a more fundamental expressiveness for modern architecture, one that was esthetic rather than philosophical. The "symbolic expression"[5] of Richardson's designs conveyed their essential architectural character, such as airiness in a resort house or containment in a prison, and showed other architects that they too could commit themselves to genuine artistic ideals without becoming preoccupied with encumbering metaphysical content.

Led by one towering individual, the Richardsonian Romanesque conquered not by rational philosophical arguments, but by sheer creative energy. By reexamining space, texture, and design, Richardson repeated the process the Gothic Revival had initiated fifty years earlier by revolting against the Greek style. As Montgomery Schuyler recognized,[6] Richardson's answers were too decisive and too harmonious with the age to be resisted by the weary heirs of Pugin.

On another, more prosaic level, Withers's Gothic Revival idealism, which saw beauty only in the medieval past and primarily in terms of traditional materials, suffered defeat at the end of the nineteenth century by the technology that produced the skyscraper. Although Withers had not been adverse to introducing modern products such as iron structural beams, elevators, and metal staircases into his buildings, he sought to amalgamate them into his High Victorian Gothic ideology. They did not profoundly affect his mental outlook as they did Louis Sullivan's. But Withers's values could not serve the America of the 1890s, when emphasis came more and more to be placed on large size and fast, cheap construction. These pragmatic imperatives were at odds with his Ruskinian philosophy.

By 1901, the America Withers had found upon his arrival had disappeared. His career had mirrored the change. Starting as a domestic architect and growing into a major ecclesiastical designer, he partook of the metamorphosis of America from a rural to an urban culture. Withers's architecture, which exemplified sound building allied with earnest purpose, contributed in a small but important way to the evolution of the new civilization that mounting wealth and a growing population produced in later Victorian America.

NEC HABEO NEC CAREO NEC CURO

Frederick Clarke Withers.

Withers's bookplate.

❧NOTES❧

CHAPTER 1

1. For a history of the English parish church revival in America see Phoebe Stanton, *The Gothic Revival and American Church Architecture: An Episode in Taste, 1840–1856* (Baltimore: Johns Hopkins University Press, 1968). Stanton's *Pugin* (New York: Viking Press, 1971) is the definitive study of the ideas and works of that influential Gothicist.

2. For the literary background of Ruskin's influence in America see Henry-Russell Hitchcock, "Ruskin and American Architecture or Regeneration Long Delayed," *Concerning Architecture,* ed. John Summerson (London: The Penguin Press, 1968). A more thorough account of the entire Ruskinian phenomenon in American culture is Roger Stein, *John Ruskin and Aesthetic Thought in America, 1840–1900* (Cambridge, Mass.: Harvard University Press, 1967). Also helpful are David W. Dickason, *The Daring Young Men: The Story of the American Pre-Raphaelites* (Bloomington, Ind.: Indiana University Press, 1953), Kristine Garrigan, *Ruskin on Architecture* (Madison, Wisc.: University of Wisconsin Press, 1973), and John Unrau, *Looking at Architecture with Ruskin* (Toronto: University of Toronto Press, 1978).

3. George Edmund Street, *Brick and Marble in the Middle Ages, Notes of a Tour in the North of Italy* (London: John Murray, 1855), p. 279.

4. For a discussion of the relation between Butterfield's architecture and Ruskin's writings, see Henry-Russell Hitchcock, *Early Victorian Architecture in Britain* (New Haven, Conn.: Yale University Press, 1954), vol. 1, chap. 17, "Ruskin or Butterfield? Victorian Gothic at the Mid-Century." Also see Paul Thompson, *William Butterfield: Victorian Architect* (Cambridge, Mass.: M.I.T. Press, 1972).

5. For a discussion of Ruprich-Robert's designs, see Theodore Turak, "French and English Sources of Sullivan's Ornament and Doctrine," *The Prairie School Review* 11(Fourth Quarter, 1974): 5–28.

6. Charles Eastlake, *A History of the Gothic Revival* (London: John Murray, 1872), p. 319.

7. [Russell Sturgis], "Viollet-le-Duc's French Medieval Architecture," *The Nation* 9(1869): 134.

8. Huss's work was a translation of the articles under "Construction" in Viollet-le-Duc's *Dictionaire raisonné.*

9. James F. O'Gorman, *The Architecture of Frank Furness* (Philadelphia: Philadelphia Museum of Art, 1973). O'Gorman's excellent essay on Furness is a valuable contribution to the study of the origins of the American High Victorian Gothic movement.

10. For a discussion of Downing's association with Davis, see Edna Donnell, "A. J. Davis and the Gothic Revival," *Metropolitan Museum Studies* 5(1934–36): 183–233.

11. The most complete study to date of

Downing's career is George B. Tatum, "Andrew Jackson Downing, Arbiter of American Taste" (Ph.D. diss., Princeton University, 1950). William H. Pierson, Jr., carefully treats the importance of Downing's career for American architecture in *American Buildings and Their Architects,* (Garden City, N.Y.: Doubleday, 1978), vol. 2, pt. 1, *Technology and the Picturesque, The Corporate and Early Gothic Styles,* chap. 7, "Andrew Jackson Downing: Villa, Cottage, and Landscape."

12. For an analysis of this aspect of Downing's work, as well as the structuralism implicit in the Stick Style, see Vincent Scully, "Romantic Rationalism and the Expression of Structure in Wood: Downing, Wheeler, Gardner, and the 'Stick Style,' 1840–1876," *Art Bulletin* 24 (June 1953): 121–42.

13. For the history of this house and illustrations see Tatum, op. cit., pp. 169ff. For a thorough study of Downing's house, which he may not have habitually called Highland Garden, see Arthur C. Downs, Jr., "Downing's Newburgh Villa," *Bulletin of the Association for Preservation Technology* 4(1972): 1–113.

14. Tatum, using Downing's terms, succinctly characterized his architectural principles as: "(a) Fitness or Unity, (b) Expression of Purpose, (c) Expression of Style." Tatum, op. cit., p. 149. Ruskin's words first appeared in 1838 in Loudon's *Architectural Magazine* and later in *The Poetry of Architecture, Cottage, Villa, etc.* (New York: John Wiley and Sons, 1886), pt. 4, p. 140.

15. Dennis Francis is currently doing research on the life and work of Vaux preliminary to writing a book.

16. Quoted in Stein, op cit., pp. 201–2.

17. See *The Church Journal* 3(14 June 1855): 154.

18. "Frederick C. Withers," *Harper's Weekly,* 19 January 1901, p. 9. The obituary was probably written by Withers's friend Frederick Bangs. (Withers is buried in Trinity Cemetery in New York.)

19. For the best general study of the style see George L. Hersey, *High Victorian Gothic, a Study in Associationism* (Baltimore: Johns Hopkins University Press, 1972).

20. John Ruskin, *The Seven Lamps of Architecture* (New York: John Wiley and Sons, 1886), p. 71.

21. Withers's first wife was Emily De-Wint. His second was Beulah Alice Higbee.

22. *Reports, Constitutions, and By-laws of the Century Association for the Year 1900* (New York: Century Association, 1901), p. 50. This is an obituary of Withers. His name appeared in the association's membership register as early as 1875. Withers's enrollment was proposed by Frederick Law Olmsted and seconded by the journalist John H. Platt.

23. Withers's name appeared on the membership roll in *The Church Club Yearbook* from 1889 through 1894.

CHAPTER 2

1. Talbot Hamlin, "Frederick C. Withers," *The Dictionary of American Biography* 10(1936): 435.

2. Letter from Margaret Withers, the architect's daughter, to Alan Burnham dated 2 February 1958. In the files of the American Architectural Archive, Greenwich, Conn. (The Archive also possesses an undated typescript recording the history of the Withers family.)

3. Ibid.

4. Robert Jewell Withers (1824–94)

studied architecture with Thomas Hellyer. An ecclesiastical architect, he married Catherine Vaux, a sister of Frederick Withers's partner, and enjoyed a moderately successful practice in London, where Frederick visited him in 1876 and 1878 and perhaps at other times as well. His outstanding work was considered to be St. James, Great Grimsby, of 1875. He also designed the English churches in Brussels and Wildbad. The library of the Royal Institute of British Architects has a card index compiled by Goodhart-Rendel of Withers's church work. Listed are approximately one hundred commissions, many of which were to restore churches in Wales, where in 1859 Withers also built the municipal buildings at Cardigan (illustrated in Roger Dixon and Stefan Muthesius, *Victorian Architecture* [London: Oxford University Press, 1978], p. 169). Eastlake, in his *History of the Gothic Revival* (1872), referred to Robert Withers as one of the architects who was influenced by William Burges and his attachment to French medieval work. An obituary appeared in *The Building News,* 12 October 1894, p. 518.

5. H. H. House, *The Sherborne Register* (London: William Clawes and Sons, 1893), p. 34. The school is presently known as the Sherborne School.

6. "Indentureship of Apprenticeship for Five Years from Sixteenth April, 1844, F. C. Withers to Mr. Edward Mondey." New York Historical Society.

7. I am indebted to R. Peers, curator of the Dorset County Museum in Dorchester, for his attempt to locate information on Mondey.

8. Letter from Withers to Edward Miner Gallaudet, president of the Columbia Institution for the Deaf and Dumb, dated 21 June 1875. In the collection of the Gallaudet Memorial Library, Gallaudet College, Washington, D.C.

9. Paul Waterhouse, "Thomas Henry Wyatt," *Dictionary of National Biography* 21(1922): 1104–5.

10. A. C. Pugin and A. W. N. Pugin, *Examples of Gothic Architecture* (London: Thomas Walker, 1836), vol. 3, title page.

11. A photograph of this church is reproduced in Hitchcock, *Early Victorian Architecture,* vol. 2, plate IV, no. 6.

12. In a long letter, dated 18 July 1852, to Marshall P. Wilder, Vaux related how he came to know Downing. This letter, which is in the Historical Society of Pennsylvania, apparently furnished information Wilder included in "Andrew Jackson Downing" *The Horticulturist* 7(November 1852): 493. Frederick Law Olmsted recalled that Vaux, after "returning from a professional tour on the Continent, contributed drawings for an exhibition in London, the subjects of which and their treatment led to his being sought by Mr. A. J. Downing. . . ." (letter to the editor of *The American Architect and Building News* 2[2 June 1877]: 175.) A sidelight to Vaux's arrival in Newburgh was related in "Our New York Letter," *The American Builder* 1(December 1868): 14. The writer, probably Clarence Cook (the initials C. C. appeared at the end of the article), wrote: "I well remember what a quiet but effective revolution Mr. Vaux worked years ago in the town of N——, where he lived when he first came from England. How he astonished masons and appalled the carpenters, and disgusted them both by exposing their ignorance and attempting to set them in the right way. Some found his doctrine

too austere, and some, with true American spunk, bolted outright, but Vaux, with an imperturbable good nature veiling an inflexible will, kept the track, and when the old ones refused to learn, set to train the young ones. His effort was not long in making itself felt, and many well-built houses in that town bear witness to the thoroughness which characterized his own work, and which he insisted on in the work of those he employed."

13. Letter from Downing to Smith dated 29 March 1853. Printed in *The Horticulturist* 6(April 1856): 162.

14. Interview with Margaret Withers by Alan Burnham, 19 May 1958. Notes from this interview in the American Architectural Archive. *The Builder* regularly printed employment notices and it may have been with that journal that Downing placed an advertisement.

15. For a discussion of Downing's plan for Washington and an illustration of the arch that may have been designed by Vaux, see Wilcomb Washburn, "Vision of Life for the Mall," *Journal of the American Institute of Architects* (March 1967). Vaux had been in Washington to deliver the sketch for the arch when he met Withers at the Astor House on his return to Newburgh. See also Daniel Reiff, *Washington Architecture, 1791–1861* (Washington: U.S. Commission of Fine Arts, 1971), chap. 4, "James Renwick and A. J. Downing in Washington."

16. Letter from Withers to Maria Jewell Withers, his mother, dated 21 February 1852. A copy of this document is in the Avery Library of Columbia University in the Withers file box. The original is apparently lost. Withers is listed as one of thirty-five passengers on the *Atlantic* from Liverpool to New York, 26 February 1852, on U.S. Department of State Passenger Lists of Vessels Arriving at New York, #150.

17. Letter from Withers to his mother, loc. cit.

18. Withers indicated that he had letters of introduction from an "uncle Jewell" (his mother's maiden name) to "W. Pittis who is one of the 'upper tens' as the moneyed people are termed, and W. Hearn, his brother-in-law. . . ." He also was introduced to a "Mr. Maitland . . . one of the first people in New York." W. Pittis must have been a member of the prosperous English family that had immigrated to New York City and become successful real estate brokers. See the biography of Albert Pittis in *Cyclopedia of American Biography* 20(1929): 459. In the 1855 edition of *The Wealth and Biography of the Wealthy Citizens of the City of New York* (New York: The Sun, 1855), p. 51, R. L. Maitland, a director of the Bank of New York, was listed as having a fortune valued at $150,000. In the 1845 edition of the same pamphlet, Maitland had been described as "Scotch, and some of his wealth comes through his wife, daughter of Robert Lennos."

19. Letter from Withers to his mother, loc. cit.

20. John Peter DeWint (1787–1870) was the son of the Dutch immigrant of the same name whose home is now a state museum at Tappan, New York. The younger DeWint was a principal landholder in the area of the modern town of Beacon, New York, and at one time was involved with the development of the railroad system in the Hudson Valley. In addition, he owned the ferry that serviced the eastern and western banks of the river at Newburgh. This was a major link in the chain

that joined the western part of New York with New England. DeWint's wife, Caroline, was the grand-daughter of John Adams, the second president. For further bio-graphical information on the fam-ily, see Frank Hasbrouck, *The His-tory of Dutchess County, New York* (Poughkeepsie, N.Y.: S. A. Ma-thieu, 1909), vol. 2, pp. 705ff.

21. In the Newburgh city directory for 1860–61, Withers was listed as living at 199 Montgomery Street. In the census record of 1860, a number of unrelated persons were also listed at that address, indicating that it was a boarding house (Eighth Census of the United States: 1860).

22. "Sale of Mr. Downing's Residence," *The Horticulturist* 7(October 1852): 482.

23. Letter from Downing to Smith, loc. cit.

24. *The Horticulturist* 7(October 1852): 483.

25. Frederika Bremer, *The Homes of the New World* (New York: Harper and Brothers, 1854), vol. 2, p. 628.

26. The editorial appeared in *The Hor-ticulturist* 6(August 1851): 345–49. See Tatum, op. cit., pp. 135ff. for a discussion of Downing's role in stimulating interest in the Central Park project.

27. Calvert Vaux, "Should a Republic Encourage the Arts," *The Horticul-turist* 7(February 1852): 74–78.

28. Clarence Cook "A Visit to the Home of the Late A. J. Downing," *The Hor-ticulturist* 8(January 1853): 21–27. Cook, who signed himself "C. C.," wrote in *The Horticulturist* 8(Feb-ruary 1853): 103, that: "It was the winter of 1851–52 that the writer first saw Downing." Jo Ann Weis has written a doctoral dissertation (Johns Hopkins University, 1977) on Cook. Along with Vaux and Cook, Frank Jessup Scott (1826–

1919), another assistant, who later enjoyed a successful career as a landscape architect, would have been on hand when Frederika Bremer visited Downing in Sep-tember 1851. After Downing's death, Scott became an architect in Toledo, Ohio, but withdrew from practice in 1859 to follow a number of diverse pursuits. One of them was the publication in 1872 of a book on landscape gardening enti-tled *The Art of Beautifying Suburban House Grounds of Small Extent* (New York: D. Appleton and Co., 1872), which reflected the influence of his association with Downing, to whom the book was dedicated "with affec-tionate remembrance." Biographi-cal data on Scott comes primarily from an article in *The Toledo Daily Blade,* 13 February 1881 (with a portrait), an obituary in *Eclaireur de Nice,* 12 June 1919, and miscellane-ous manuscript material in the files of the Maumee Valley Historical Society, Toledo, Ohio. See also Ar-thur Channing Downs, Jr., "Victo-rian Premonitions of Wright's Prairie House in Downing and Scott," *Nineteenth Century* 2(Summer 1976): 35–39. Scott's book was re-printed by the American Life Foundation in 1978. It is also likely that Charles W. Elliott (1817–83), who served as a commissioner of Central Park in New York, was present during Bremer's visit. At the time, Elliott was also working under Downing.

29. Cook, op. cit., pp. 21–22.

30. Vaux provides information on the projects with which he and Down-ing were engaged in the letter to Marshall Wilder dated 18 July 1852 and referred to in n. 12.

31. Tatum, op. cit., pp. 311–13. Vaux wrote to Marshall P. Wilder (see n. 12) in July 1852 that at the time

of Downing's death the office "had commissions in Newburgh, along the Banks of the Hudson, Boston, Newport, Georgetown, Albany, etc."

32. "Design for a Marine Villa," *The Horticulturist* 8(April 1853): frontispiece and p. 190.

33. See n. 14.

34. "Church in the Lombard Style," *The Horticulturist* 7(August 1852): frontispiece and p. 94.

35. Ibid. Downing had earlier aired his views on ecclesiastical architecture in an article titled "A Short Chapter on Country Churches," *The Horticulturist* 6(January 1851): 9–12. Other notices of churches appeared in *The Horticulturist* in 1851 in the May and December issues. On at least one occasion, Downing (undoubtedly with Vaux's assistance) furnished a correspondent with a sketch for a rural church. It was "a simple Gothic church to be built of stone" and to cost about $6,500. See "Answers to Correspondents: Village Church," *The Horticulturist* 6(January 1851): 56.

36. Clarence Cook, "The Immortal," in Louise Cook, comp., *The Poems of Clarence Cook* (New York: privately printed, 1902), p. 41.

37. "Sale of Mr. Downing's Residence," loc. cit.

38. Letter to the editor of *The Horticulturist* 8(October 1852): 482.

39. For a discussion of Alger's connection with the Downing house, see Tatum, op. cit., pp. 199–200 and Downs, "Downing's Newburgh Villa."

40. "Downing and Vaux, Architects, Newburgh-On-Hudson," *The Horticulturist* 8(March 1853): back cover. Clarence Cook apparently remained in Newburgh at least until March 1853. A letter he wrote on 14 March 1853, headed "Mr. Downing's, Newburgh," can be found in the manuscript division of the New York Public Library.

41. "Downing and Vaux, Architects, Newburgh-On-Hudson," *The Horticulturist* 8(June 1853): inside front cover. For more on this subject see letter by Arthur C. Downs, Jr., and my reply in the *Journal of the Society of Architectural Historians* 36(March 1977): 61–62.

CHAPTER 3

1. Calvert Vaux, *Villas and Cottages* (New York: Harpers and Brothers, 1857), pp. vi–vii.

2. When the first Newburgh city directory was published in 1856, Vaux's residence was listed as 225 West 31st Street, New York City, rather than in Newburgh. Nor did he maintain his name under the "Architects" classification in association with Withers. This indicates that by 1856 no formal professional arrangement existed between the two men. Therefore, the partnership referred to by Vaux must have lasted from 1853 to 1856. It is also interesting to note that in 1867 William R. Ware remarked that Vaux had nearly given up the practice of architecture for landscape design. See Ware, "On the Condition of Architecture and Architectural Education in the United States," *Sessional Papers of the Royal Institute of British Architects, 1866–1867* (London: By the Institute, 1867), p. 83. The Bank of New York was designed under the Vaux and Withers firm name in 1856, but on stylistic grounds, as well as for other reasons, I consider it to be a

work entirely by Vaux. See my letter in "Correspondence," *Journal of the Society of Architectural Historians* 36(March 1977): 61–62.

3. A.K.H.B., "Concerning Villas and Cottages," *Frazer's Magazine* 58(December 1858): 701.

4. The A. C. Gray House in New York City (Design No. 34) and Design No. 23 for an unnamed patron in Worcester, Mass., had this type of roof.

5. Calvert Vaux, "Hints for Country House Builders," *Harper's New Monthly Magazine* 11(November 1855): 763–78.

6. Pugin and Pugin, op. cit., vol. 2.

7. A.K.H.B., op. cit., p. 704.

8. The position of Withers's initials in the drawing, on the bottom of the stone rather than at the edge of the sketch, the normal position for the signature of the artist who had merely delineated the object, also suggests his authorship. A headstone of this exact design stands in the cemetery of St. George Protestant Episcopal Church in Newburgh, not, as Vaux had indicated, in the Newburgh City Cemetery, further suggesting his unfamiliarity with the work. It marks the grave of Jasper Cropsey and is inscribed in Gothic letters: "Died March 19, 1854. Blessed are the dead which are in the Lord." The probable source of the design was a grave by Scott illustrated in W. H. Kelke, *The Churchyard Manual: Intended Chiefly for Rural Districts* (London: C. Cox, 1851), p. 39, which was published a year after Vaux had left England. It is very probable that Withers brought the little book with him to America.

9. Parish records of St. George P. E. Church, Newburgh, New York, p. 243. The notation indicates that Withers became a member of the parish in 1855.

10. Edward M. Ruttenber, *History of the County of Orange* (Newburgh, N.Y: E. M. Ruttenber and Son, 1875), pp. 241–42. Ruttenber discusses the founding of St. Paul's and gives a copy of the letter petitioning the rector of St. George Church for the establishment of the new parish. Withers signed this letter.

11. Vaux and Caroline Downing became the godparents to Withers's daughter Alice Maria in 1859. Parish records of St. George Church, Newburgh, New York, p. 76 (23 October 1859). See Hamlin, loc. cit., which states that drawings owned by New York City indicate that Withers was associated with the work at Central Park as early as 1860. In the 1864 edition of *Villas and Cottages,* Vaux illustrated, on page 178, a park boat ramp that was labeled "V&W."

12. Newburgh city directory for 1856–57, p. 76. The following year he moved to Washington Hall (now destroyed) on Water Street, but maintained his residence at 286 Grand Street, where John J. Monell also lived (city directory for 1858–59, p. 85).

13. In the Newburgh city directory for 1858–59, Roland Plumbe was listed at Withers's office. In the 1870s, he became a successful architect in London and eventually became a fellow of the RIBA. In the 1860–61 directory, the names of Frederick H. Knevitt (p. 60) and Edward D. Edwards (p. 38) were listed.

14. There were two other architects living in Newburgh at this time in addition to Withers. They were Rembrandt Lockwood and John Weller Priest. The latter was the more important of the two. He

maintained his office in New York City and used his home in Balmville as a second office. Elkanah K. Shaw, a pupil of Priest, managed business for his employer in the smaller city and lived in Priest's home. Priest had been associated with the New York Ecclesiological Society and had gained renown as a church architect through the society's good graces. The little wooden church of St. Michael's Reisterstown, Md. (1854), on the grounds of the former Hannah Moore Academy was his most prestigious commission before tuberculosis cut short his promising career. (For a discussion of St. Michael's, see *The Church Journal* 2[3 August 1854]: 211–12.) He and Withers must have found a common bond of friendship in their devotion to Gothic architecture, although no documents have come to light substantiating a relationship between the two men. Priest's views on the nature and value of the Gothic Revival were different from those of Withers, who seems to have conceived of the Gothic style as an end in itself, especially in church architecture. Priest viewed it as a means of leading modern architects to the discovery of a new, contemporary style. The fullest account of Priest's career currently available is in Stanton, op. cit., pp. 193–207. See also Hitchcock, "Ruskin and American Architecture," which discusses Priest's writings, but only his initials, J. W. P., are furnished. John J. Nutt in *Newburgh: Institutions, Industries and Leading Citizens* (Newburgh, N.Y.: Ritchie and Hull, 1891), p. 256, explains the relationship between Shaw and Priest.

15. Stanton, *The Gothic Revival and American Church Architecture*, p. 160, n. 30.

16. Review of *Dr. Oldham at Greystones and His Talk There* in *The Architects' and Mechanics' Journal* 2(14 April 1860): 12.

17. Ibid.

18. For more on this topic, see Arthur Channing Downs, Jr., "Victorian Premonitions."

19. Review of *Dr. Oldham*, loc. cit.

20. "Description of a Country House," *The Horticulturist* 12 N.S. (May 1857): 230–32. The exterior has been painted white and extensive alterations, in the Adamesque style of the early twentieth century, have been made to the interior.

21. *The Horticulturist* called attention to this with the remark that: "The outside angles of the library are cut off, and the windows and chimney are placed in such a way, that a person sitting by the fire may, at the same time, enjoy the lovely prospect which this room commands." Ibid., p. 232.

22. Nutt, op. cit., stated that the estate originally consisted of a "handsome dwelling and commodious outbuildings and beautiful . . . grounds with ornamental trees, winding walks, and lawns" (p. 99). St. John resided here until his death in 1890.

23. Extensive alterations were made to the house around 1900. Oak paneling, opalescent stained glass, and high mantelpieces — all of which blend well with the original structure — were installed at that time.

24. Vaux, *Villas and Cottages*, p. 259.

25. Ibid.

26. For a discussion of the importance of Robert Kerr, *The Gentleman's House* (London: John Murray, 1864), see Vincent Scully and Antoinette Downing, *The Architectural Heritage of Newport* (New York: Clarkson and Potter, 1967), pp. 153–54. Part of the Goodwin house

is preserved in the Connecticut Historical Society. Henry-Russell Hitchcock, *The Architecture of H. H. Richardson and His Times* (Cambridge, Mass.: M. I. T. Press, 1961), p. 31, n. VI-4 discusses the plan of the Goodwin House and refers to the Reeve House.

27. The house, which stands on Downing Avenue adjacent to the former home of Charles Downing, is owned by Peter Cantline, who also possesses the original plans, prepared by Withers for Walter Vail and dated 1859. The format of these plans reflects the arrangement used in *Villas and Cottages,* which invariably included a roof plan in addition to floor plans. Their layout stemmed from the graphic style of the Downing office. (I am indebted to Professor Tatum for this observation.) The house was built by William Hilton, a prominent builder who, according to Nutt, op. cit., p. 201, erected "scores, almost hundreds" of houses in Newburgh and its suburbs.

28. *Wealth and Biography of the Wealthy Citizens of New York City* (New York: The Sun, 1845), p. 9.

29. The house, which was estimated to cost $16,000, was mentioned as from designs by Withers in "Building Progress," loc. cit. I am indebted to Nancy Ferguson, research assistant at the Metropolitan Museum, for sharing with me the information she unearthed that led to the identification of the house as the one Withers planned for Deming. Her master's essay (Columbia University) studies the building.

30. "Architectural Drawings in the National Academy of Design," *Architects' and Mechanics' Journal* 2(2 June 1860): 81.

31. The house is presently owned by Craig House. The dwelling was listed in "Building Progress" in *The Architects' and Mechanics' Journal* 1(17 March 1860): 192, where the cost was given as $26,000.

32. "Architectural Drawings at the National Academy of Design," *The Architects' and Mechanics' Journal* 2(16 June 1860): 101. The drawing was number 12 in the 1860 exhibition. The house was actually built of yellow brick, not red brick, which the critic's remarks imply appeared in the watercolor drawing.

33. For more on Downing's legacy in this regard see Scully, loc. cit. In addition to the houses discussed here, *The Architects' and Mechanics' Journal* 2(17 March 1860): 191, mentions as "in hand" by Withers "five cottage residences at Newburgh, on a lot of 28 acres, commanding one of the finest views of the Hudson River, for Dr. Heard, Professors Greene, Hackley, and Henry, Captain Strong, U.S.N., etc." This area is on Carpenter Avenue between Gidney and Cottage Avenues. The Newburgh city directory for 1864–65 lists Dr. John Heard and the Reverend Caleb S. Henry as living on the west side of Carpenter Avenue (no street numbers indicated). Captain James H. Strong was listed at that address only in the 1862–63 directory. Nutt, op. cit., p. 201, states that William Hilton (see n. 27 of this chapter) built a house for Professor George Washington Greene, as well as the Reverend Mr. Henry's residence. Hackley may never have erected a home in Newburgh, for his name is absent from the city directories. The two dwellings presently on this stretch of Carpenter Avenue nearest Cottage resemble those Withers designed in the 1850s, and

I assume that he was responsible for them. Three others are in the Second Empire style, a mode Withers never employed in documented commissions and, hence, I am reluctant to attribute them to him.

34. [Montgomery, Schuyler], "Frederick C. Withers," *Record and Guide*, 12 January 1901, p. 17.

35. Frederick C. Withers, "A Few Hints on Church Building," *The Horticulturist* 13(July 1858): 348–52.

36. Ibid., p. 348.

37. Ibid., p. 349.

38. Pugin had stated the same objection in *True Principles of Pointed or Christian Architecture* (London: H. G. Bohn, 1853), p. 41.

39. Withers, loc. cit. Pugin had said much the same thing when he wrote: "Practical men know that flat-pitched roofs, which are exceedingly ugly in appearance, are also but ill calculated to resist the action of weather" (*True Principles*, p. 11).

40. Withers, loc. cit. See also Pugin, *True Principles*, p. 2.

41. Withers, op. cit., p. 3.

42. Pugin had stated "Nothing can be more execrable than making a church appear rich and beautiful in the eyes of men, but full of tricks and falsehood . . . " (*True Principles*, p. 3).

43. See Stanton, *The Gothic Revival*, pp. 108–11 for a discussion of the seminal importance of St. James the Less. William Pierson's chapter "Richard Upjohn, Trinity Church, and the Ecclesiological Gothic Revival," op. cit., also sheds light on the beginnings of the scholarly phase of the Gothic Revival in America as well as its English background.

44. Raphael Brandon and J. Arthur Brandon, *Parish Churches: Being Perspective Views of English Ecclesiastical Structures* (London: Bogue, 1848).

45. Stanton, *The Gothic Revival*, p. 300.

46. The church is now known as Calvary Presbyterian Church. Indicative of the progressiveness of the congregation was the controversy that erupted in 1856 over the choice of the dynamic Dr. Sprole, the former chaplain at West Point, as the new minister. A small group of parishioners bolted the church over the issue and established Calvary Presbyterian Church. The split had the appearance of an old school–new school antagonism. The First Presbyterian Church chose to rival its economic counterpart, the St. George Protestant Episcopal Church, in an effort to revitalize the parish. The effort proved successful and the congregation grew to considerable stature in New York State. In 1870 the union of the state's old and new school factions took place here. The best history of the church is found in James Hall, *Centennial Celebration of the First Presbyterian Church* (Newburgh: By the church, 1884).

47. On the history of ceremonial reform within the Presbyterian Church see Julia Melton, *Presbyterian Worship in America* (Richmond: John Knox Press, 1967). Withers's Newburgh church was overlooked by Andrew Drummond in *Church Architecture of Protestantism* (Edinburgh: Clark, 1934). He stated that "the first Gothic church in America of which the Non-Liturgical denomination may be proud, was the Central Congregational Church, Boston, designed by R. M. Upjohn [1867]" (p. 92).

48. Ruttenber, op. cit., p. 300, for the trustee's resolution adopting With-

ers's plan. The presence of John J. Monell on the board of trustees may have accounted for Withers's success, for in addition to being a friend of the architect, Monell was sympathetic to the architecture and ritual of the Protestant Episcopal Church. After the Civil War he rejected Presbyterianism and became a prominent member of St. Luke's Protestant Episcopal Church in Matteawan (modern Beacon), New York. The contract for the construction of the Newburgh church was let to a local builder, George Veitch, for the sum of $27,500. The work began in August 1857, and the church was dedicated prior to the completion of the stone spire in November 1858.

49. Brandon and Brandon, op. cit., vol. 1, p. 45.

50. Edmund Sharpe, *A Series of Illustrations of the Decorated Style of Ecclesiastical Architecture* (London: John Van Voorst, 1849), plate 5.

51. Ibid., p. 10. The glass in this window was donated by Withers and bears his monogram in the top roundel.

52. Ibid., p. 9. Withers presented his Presbyterian neighbors with a tour de force of ecclesiology, one in which the aficionado of Gothic architecture might even discern a sort of internal development from earlier to later construction, for the windows in the eastern end were considerably simpler and more "transitional" in character than those of the western elevation. Those in the tower are the most complicated and "advanced" of the entire church. Thus the usual medieval pattern of building from the ceremonial end toward the entrance was signified by the character of the details.

53. Vaux, *Villas and Cottages* (1864) p. 117. The church is illustrated on p. xxiv.

54. "First Presbyterian Church, Newburgh, New York," *The Crayon* 6(February 1859): 49. From the description one can appreciate that the original appearance of the interior (illustrated in Plate 39 of Withers's *Church Architecture*) is largely intact. The area that has undergone the most drastic change is the pulpit wall, which is now filled with a memorial to Eliza Bush, installed in 1884 and possibly designed by Withers. Originally the arched recess behind the elevated oak pulpit was to have been "decorated with a row of beautiful encaustic tile; the space above filled with fresco drapery, and below a hanging of pink and gold will reach to the top of the ornamental oak framing at the back of the pulpit. Above the arch will be written in illuminated letters on a scroll 'Give unto the Lord the glory due unto His name. Worship the Lord in the beauty of holiness.' " *The Architects' and Mechanics' Journal* 2(17 March 1860): 194, stated that the stained glass windows were made by Henry Sharp of New York, except for two that were done by Lavers of London. The church was lighted by gas standards, one beneath each arch in the nave, which were manufactured according to Withers's designs by the well-known firm of Cornelius and Baker. The church was built by George Veitch of Rhinebeck, New York.

55. "Dr. Spring's Church," *The Crayon* 5(January 1858): 22.

56. "Notes and Answers to Correspondence," *The Ecclesiologist* 20 (April 1859): 142.

57. The church, which is located on High Street and known now as the

Church of God, was severely damaged by fire in 1912. After that it was rebuilt and enlarged, preserving very little of Withers's original design.

58. "Architectural Drawings at the National Academy of Design," *Architects' and Mechanics' Journal* 2(16 June 1860): 101.

59. "St. Michael's Germantown, Pennsylvania, U.S.A.," *The Ecclesiologist* 21(August 1860): 215.

60. The facade of St. Michael's presents an intriguing comparison with two designs that the New York architect John Coleman Hart published in *Designs for Parish Churches in the Three Styles of English Church Architecture* (New York: Dana, 1857). The church, in the Early English style, had a facade composed of two lancet windows flanking a tall central buttress that reached to the bellcot — an arrangement very similar to that of St. Michael's, except that St. Michael's had the unique projecting turret. It is possible that Withers had been impressed by the design from Hart's book, which, of all the American publications on ecclesiastical architecture, would have attracted him because of Hart's historical accuracy, high-quality designs, and frequent references to the major English sources of the Gothic Revival.

61. "St. Michael's Church and Parsonage, Germantown, Pennsylvania, U.S.A.," *The Building News* 5 (November 1859): 1000.

62. The Reverend Dr. Suydam was newly ordained when he received the pastorship of the Dutch Reformed Church in 1857. As early as 1864, he began his career as a novelist (*The Crugar Family* and *Cruel Jim* were popular). For a biographical sketch of Suydam, see *Appleton's Cyclopedia*, vol. 6., p. 3.

63. Minutes of the vestry of the Dutch Reformed Church, Beacon, New York, 19 May 1858.

64. Ibid., 24 October 1859. Concerning John DeWint's relation to the Church, Frank Hasbrouck, the historian of the county and a patron of Withers, reported that "among the principal donors of land and money to the church was John Peter DeWint" *The History of Dutchess County New York* [Poughkeepsie, N.Y.: S. A. Mathieu, 1909], vol. 2, p. 330.

65. The process of gathering funds and pledges took more than one year. It was reported on 24 October 1859 in the minutes of the vestry that: "Whereas the Building Committee appointed by this church to erect a new church edifice have requested this consistory to advise them in relation to proceeding to build an edifice which they have in contemplation at the estimated cost which may reach nearly or quite the sum of $15,000 and possibly subject the church to a debt of between $4000 and $5000. Therefore Resolved. That we do advise said committee to proceed to make the contracts and secure the said proposals immediately and commence said building early this coming spring." Construction was begun as scheduled, at the start of the building season of 1860. Dedication ceremonies, in which an ecumenical representation of local clergymen participated, took place on 9 January 1861. Further historical data are contained in Mrs. Samuel Verplank, "Historical Notes of the Reformed Dutch Church of Fishkill Landing," *Centennial of the Reformed Dutch Church of Beacon, New York, 1813–1913* (Beacon, N.Y.: Printed for the church, 1913).

66. Withers, *Church Architecture*, Design XIII.

67. Although the interior bears no re-

semblance to an English parish church, Withers quoted from the Gothic past of his homeland in at least one detail. The curious bulbous stone brackets supporting the wall pieces and collar braces of the roof were modeled from a block from St. Mary's Church, Scarborough, which had been illustrated in James Colling, *Details of Gothic Architecture* (London: Bogue, 1856), vol. 2, plate 35.

68. "Architectural Drawings at the National Academy of Design," *Architects' and Mechanics' Journal* 2(2 June 1860): 81.

69. The large stone belfry was taken down in 1887. For details of other alterations, see Verplank, op. cit., pp. 34–42.

70. George E. Street, "On Italian Pointed Architecture," *The Ecclesiologist* 23(December 1861): p. 361.

71. For a discussion of Mould's church, see David Van Zanten, "Jacob Wrey Mould: Echoes of Owen Jones and the High Victorian Style in New York, 1853–1865." *Journal of the Society of Architectural Historians* 28(March 1969): pp. 41ff.

72. Withers, *Church Architecture*, Design III. A British writer commented as late as 1870 that in America "black bricks . . . are unknown, a want much felt by anyone attempting to design in brick" (L. F., "Notes from New York," *The Architect* 3[26 February 1870]: 99).

73. "Dutch Reformed Church, Fishkill Landing," *The Christian Intelligencer,* 10 January 1861. Quoted in Verplank, op cit., p. 35.

74. In "All Saints, Margaret Street," *The Ecclesiologist* 20(June 1859): 184, it was stated that Butterfield "was the first to show that red brick . . . was compatible with the highest flights of architecture." In the journal's review of Street's *Brick and Marble,* the same writer stated: "The present volume may be useful in more ways than one: in suggesting new thoughts to many of our architects and in persuading many of its readers of the beauties and merits of constructional polychrome in our buildings, as well secular as religious" (*The Ecclesiologist* 16[July 1855]: 305).

75. Street, *Brick and Marble,* p. 277.

76. George E. Scott, "On the Uses to be Made of Medieval Architecture of Italy." Paper read before the Ecclesiological Society in 1855 and printed in the appendix of his *Remarks.*

77. Withers, *"A Few Hints,"* pp. 348–49.

78. "St. Helen, Little Cawthorpe, Lincolnshire," *The Ecclesiologist* 20 (April 1859): p. 287.

79. St. Mark's was dedicated on 10 April 1861. For a photograph of the original building and a history of the parish, see Mrs. Thisbe Morgan, *St. Mark's Protestant Episcopal Church, Shreveport, Louisiana* (Shreveport: Castle Printing Co., 1957), p. 17.

80. Morgan, op. cit., p. 16.

81. Letter from Margaret Withers to Alan Burnham dated 2 February 1958. In the American Architectural Archive.

82. Johns D. Sigle, "Calvert Vaux, An American Architect" (Master's thesis, School of Architecture, University of Virginia, 1967), p. 24.

83. Dr. Sprole had been dismissed from West Point for his abolitionist views by Secretary of War Jefferson Davis. See Judge Fancher's address in *The Centennial Celebration of the First Presbyterian Church,* p. 21. The Reverend Dr. Suydam was described as "very active during the Civil War in arousing the patriotism of the people of his neighborhood" (Hasbrouck op. cit., p. 330).

84. Letter dated 20 April 1861 from

Cook to T. C. Farrar in the manuscript collection of the New York Public Library.

85. Miscellaneous records related to Withers's service in the Union Army are in the National Archives. The facts relating to this service are drawn from those records, unless otherwise noted. Other miscellaneous material on Withers's activities in the Civil War is in the New York Historical Society's manuscript collection.

86. *The War of the Rebellion: A Compilation of the Official Records of the Union and Confederate Armies* (Washington, D.C.: U.S. Government Printing Office, 1885), series 1, vol. 6, p. 186.

87. Gillmore summarized the meaning of the victory as having demonstrated "the power and effectiveness of rifled canon for breaching at long distances—at distances hitherto untried, and considered altogether impracticable, thus opening a new era in the use of this most valuable, and comparatively unknown, arm of service" (ibid., p. 148).

88. Letter from W. G. Stickney, attending surgeon, Volunteer Regiment Engineers, dated 13 April 1862. Stickney wrote, "I have carefully examined this officer and find that he is afflicted with neuralgia of the head and neck."

89. Letter from A. B. Snow, surgeon, Volunteer Engineers, dated 9 August 1862.

90. Emily DeWint Withers died on 1 July 1863 and was buried in St. George Cemetery, Newburgh.

91. The partnership was operating prior to 1 December 1863, for on that day Vaux wrote to Frederick Law Olmsted, "My business is in good shape and I have formed a partnership with Mr. Withers" (letter in the Olmsted Papers, Library

of Congress, manuscript division). The partnership ended in 1872.

CHAPTER 4

1. Withers's second wife, Beulah Alice Higbee, died in 1888.

2. It was stated in "Our New York Letter," *The American Builder* 1(October 1868): 16, that "George Fletcher, N. Babb, Mr. Cleveland, Mr. Cady, Mr. Eastburn Hastings, Mr. Frederick Withers, Mr. John Miller, and Mr. Russell Sturgis, Jr., with Mr. Littell, make up the list of those young men who are sure to place the architecture of our future on a better basis than it has hitherto occupied."

3. Schuyler, "Russell Sturgis' Architecture," p. 405.

4. "Correspondence," *The American Architect and Building News* 2(7 July 1877): 218.

5. Nutt, op. cit., p. 144. In 1869 Withers had designed a small Sunday School building for St. Paul's parish. Until the larger edifice was built, the one room building was used as the church. It still stands beside the incomplete building.

6. See chap. 3, n. 10.

7. The building is presently owned by the Seventh Day Adventist Tabernacle of Newburgh.

8. Withers, "A Few Hints," p. 349.

9. "Llandgwyd Church, Cardigan," *The Building News* 7(1 August 1862): 90. The church was designed in 1856–57.

10. A copy of Withers's watercolor elevation drawing for the bank is in the Avery Library at Columbia University.

11. Hitchcock, "Ruskin and American Architecture," p. 189.

12. The photolithographic copy of Withers's drawing is now in the

prints and drawings collection of the Royal Institute of British Architects. Ware's address to the Institute was reprinted in his "On the Conditions of Architecture and Architectural Education in the United States," loc. cit.

13. The house is located at 264 Grand Street. Original plans are in the possession of Oliver Shipp of Balmville, New York. The house makes an interesting comparison with Richard Upjohn's Douglas House in Geneva, New York.

14. After the death of his first wife, Monell married Downing's widow Caroline in 1865. Monell had maintained an elegant house and garden in Newburgh before he and Caroline moved into the new house that Withers designed for them across the Hudson. The area where the house stands was known as Fishkill Landing in the nineteenth century. For a description of Monell's Newburgh house see T. A. Richards, "Idlewild," *Harper's New Monthly Magazine* 16(January 1858): 157–58. For a biography of Monell see Nutt, op. cit., p. 165. The name Eustasia undoubtedly commemorates the island in the West Indies from which Caroline's father, John DeWint, had immigrated. Unfortunately, Eustasia, which has been nominated to the National Register of Historic Places, was seriously damaged by fire in 1979.

15. Andrew Jackson Downing, *Cottage Residences*, ed. George Harney and Henry Winthrop Sargent (New York: John Wiley and Son, 1873), p. 210. I attribute this house to Withers primarily on stylistic grounds and because it was crossed off the list of buildings by Vaux now in the manuscript division of the New York Public Library.

16. Howland, a religious man, stipulated in his donation that one of the upper rooms of the Tioronda School be used as a Sunday School. He personally conducted religious classes there, and according to his friend the Reverend George Prentiss, Howland made the building "his little domain," where he was "a sort of lay prophet, priest and king." See George L. Prentiss, *In Memorium, Joseph Howland 1834–1886*, p. 7. For a description of Howland's estate, which was landscaped by Henry Winthrop Sargent, see J. E. Spingarn, "Henry Winthrop Sargent and the Early History of Landscape Gardening and Ornamental Horticulture in Dutchess County, New York," *The Yearbook of the Dutchess County Historical Society, 1937*, p. 199.

17. Withers, *Church Architecture*, Design XXII.

18. See Stein, op. cit., for comments on the importance of *The New Path*.

19. Clarence Cook was the art critic of *The New Path* and probably wrote the review of the Tioronda School, since the writer's remarks appeared in a discussion of the painting exhibition at the National Academy of Design. Russell Sturgis was the journal's regular architectural critic.

20. "Architectural Designs in the Academy," *The New Path*, 2(July 1865): 114–15.

21. The building bore the date "AD 1866" in two roundels above the main entrance. According to Ruttenber, op. cit., p. 236, and Nutt, op. cit., p. 173, the construction of the building was begun in the summer of 1866. It was ready for occupancy in October 1868. The building, according to Nutt, cost $115,527, but according to Ruttenber, cost $130,000. In any case, the sum was considerable, especially for a brick building. The cost of the

architect's proposed design for a large stone memorial chapel at Yale University of approximately the same date was estimated at $125,000. The high cost of the Newburgh Savings Bank may have been due, in part, to the uniqueness of the design, which was the first in Newburgh to use so much carved work and molded brick (see Nutt, loc. cit., and Ruttenber, loc. cit.). Daniel B. St. John had become the president in 1858. Monell was one of the founders of the bank in 1852 (see Ruttenber, op. cit., pp. 35–36).

22. Ruskin's choice of humble water lilies as models for the capitals of the Oxford Museum undoubtedly inspired Withers to use distinctly aquatic plants on the entrance capitals. Even more fulsome leaves appeared on the capitals of the columns that separated the triple windows on the second floor above the entrance.

23. For a history and description of Vaux's Bank of New York, see Henry Domett, *A History of the Bank of New York, 1784–1884* (New York: G. P. Putnam's Sons, 1884), pp. 93–95. See also correspondence between me and Arthur Channing Downs, loc. cit.

24. Scott, *Remarks,* p. 201.

25. Ibid., pp. 193 and 194.

26. Ibid., p. 203.

27. The Newburgh Savings Bank also reflected the latest English advances in brick construction. In 1864, the July through December issues of *The Building News* ran a series of articles entitled "Examples of Brick Architecture," which illustrated many details from recent English brick buildings. The numerous chamfered brick voussoirs, terracotta cornices, and ornamental details shown there found generic counterparts on Withers's building.

28. For the attitude of New England intellectuals toward the Civil War, see George Frederickson, *The Inner Civil War, Northern Intellectuals and the Crisis of the Union* (New York: Harper and Row, 1965).

29. The earliest record of the Yale proposal is an entry in the *Minutes* of the Prudential Committee for 27 March 1866 stating that it had been "Voted in accordance with the request of a committee of graduates that a subscription may be circulated for the purpose of completing the fund for a new chapel and for the erection of a memorial building in connection therewith, in honor of the Yale soldiers, who have fallen in the war to sustain the Union." A number of architects, including Leopold Eidlitz and Emlen Littell, submitted competition drawings to the committee prior to the fall of 1866, but Withers wrote in *Church Architecture* (Design XX) that "preference" was given to his. Olmsted and Vaux prepared a plan for landscaping around the proposed building that was also accepted. The *Minutes* of the Prudential Committee for 7 December 1866 record the appropriation of $1000 for the preparation of preliminary drawings for Withers's scheme, but the project was never carried to completion.

30. Charles Eliot Norton, "The Harvard and Yale Memorial Buildings," *The Nation* 5(11 July 1867), p. 34.

31. Wayne Andrews, *American Gothic, Its Origins, Its Trials, Its Triumphs* (New York: Vintage Books, 1975), p. 112. Norton and Ruskin maintained close ties through correspondence, much of which appears in John Ruskin, *Letters of John Ruskin to Charles Eliot Norton,* 2 vols. (Boston: Houghton, Mifflin, 1904).

32. Norton, op. cit., p. 35.

33. For a full description of Withers's proposed design, see "Yale Memorial Chapel," *The American Builder* 2(April 1870): 85. Two slightly different plans also exist in the form of photolithographed drawings in the Withers file box at the Avery Library of Columbia University. The building also appeared in the English journal *The Builder* 25(12 October 1867): 747–48.

34. John Burchard and Albert Bush-Brown, *The Architecture of America* (Boston: Little, Brown and Co., 1961), p. 122.

35. *National Academy of Design, Winter Exhibition Catalogue, 1866,* No. 27. The drawing was exhibited under the Vaux and Withers firm name; however, the house appeared in Bicknell's *Wooden and Brick Buildings* and Withers's *Buildings* as the work solely of Withers. I assume that the drawing that is now in the Karolik Collection was the one shown at the National Academy of Design. According to A. J. Bloor, who worked for Vaux and Withers, the Kimball plans were finished 11 July 1865. Bloor's diary is in the New York Historical Society.

36. David Arnot, *Gothic Architecture Applied to Modern Residences* (New York: D. Appleton and Co., 1849).

37. "Our New York Letter," *The American Builder* 1(December 1868): 14.

38. The history of the formation of the hospital was recounted in "Hudson River Hospital for the Insane," *The New York Times,* 15 February 1867, p. 8. See also Alexander B. Callow, Jr., *The Tweed Ring* (New York: Oxford University Press, 1966), p. 156, for mention of the hospital as one of the numerous charitable projects that the Tweed Ring aided to win public support.

39. "Hudson River Insane Hospital," *The New York Times,* 25 December 1868, p. 8.

40. *First Annual Report of the Board of Managers of the Hudson River Hospital for the Insane* (Albany: State of New York, 1868), p. 7. This source also contains a detailed description of the hospital.

41. It was stated in the First Annual Report, loc. cit., that: "The interior plan of arrangements had been most carefully prepared by the medical superintendent, acting on his own knowledge of the necessities of such an institution, with the counsel and approval of eminent men employed in the care of hospitals for the insane."

42. See Thomas Hurd, *Institutional Care of the Insane* (Baltimore: Johns Hopkins University Press, 1919), vol. 1, pp. 207ff. for a summary of Kirkbride's "propositions."

43. "Building News," *The American Builder* 1(April 1869): 91–92.

44. The history of the construction of the hospital is outlined in Hurd, op. cit., pp. 165ff.

45. "Hudson River State Hospital, Poughkeepsie, New York," *The American Architect and Building News* 3(30 March 1878): 110 and (24 August 1878): 65. Considering that this was a public institution, the accommodations compared favorably with what was provided at the Hartford Retreat around this same time. With the opening of a state asylum at Hartford in 1868, the Retreat, whose indigent patients were transferred there, was remodeled by Vaux, Withers and Company. "These plans," according to Hurd, op. cit., vol. 2, p. 88, "involved a radical and thorough reconstruction of the buildings, and embraced improvements in heating, ventilation, the enlargement of the halls and arrangement of a series of

spacious single and also suites of rooms, consisting of parlor, bed and bath rooms, all arranged and adapted for occupancy by patients whose habits and mode of life render these extra accommodations a sort of necessity."

46. Along with the impending Romanesque Revival, the growing regard among doctors in the 1870s for decentralized or cottage-plan asylums foretold the end of Ruskinian Gothic buildings like the Hudson River Hospital. The economy and success of the contemporary Willard Asylum (1865; designed by Joseph Chapin), Ovid, New York, which was built on the cottage system, prompted many responsible people to question the soundness of such megalithic complexes as the Poughkeepsie hospital. In a paper read before the Conference of Boards of Public Charities in 1875, by which time the Hudson River Hospital, with over $2,000,000 spent on its construction, had become the second most costly asylum in the country, a New York City doctor named H. B. Wilbur decried the waste of public money that asylum construction had occasioned since the close of the Civil War. He especially attacked the eastern states for having spent over $2600 to accommodate each mental patient, while "the cost of the ten most expensive hotels in America would probably not exceed $1500 a guest" (Dr. H. B. Wilbur in *Report to the Conference of the Boards of Public Charities, 1875* [New York: The Conference, 1875], p. 147). But over and above the question of expense, Wilbur contended that huge asylums were ineffectual, for they substituted class treatment for individual attention. He noted that under the current system, "the ratio

of recoveries in our asylums seems to be a diminishing one." But Wilbur's conclusion was optimistic, for with the erection of the decentralized Willard Asylum — as well as the Moses Shepherd Asylum in Towson, Maryland, designed in 1862 by Vaux while Withers served in the Union army — Wilbur was able to say that "better views are beginning to prevail." The ascendancy of these "better views" made the cumbersome plan of the Hudson River Hospital nearly obsolete by 1878. For a discussion of the controversy between the opponents of the centralized asylum plan and its supporters see Hurd, op. cit., vol. 1, chap. 3. For a discussion of the Willard Asylum as "the first notable departure from the original propositions," see Hurd, op. cit., vol. 1, p. 208f. The drawings and plans for the present Shepherd-Pratt Hospital, which are dated 1863, are in the possession of the hospital. They document Vaux's role as architectural assistant to Dr. D. Tilden Brown. According to Hurd, Brown visited Europe at the request of the trustees of the hospital before preparing the plan that they approved (see Hurd, op. cit., vol. 4, p. 364). Withers continued to design buildings for Poughkeepsie into the 1880s (see "Building News Supplement," *Building* 5[24 July 1886], p. 4).

47. "New Churches: Holy Innocents, Hartford, Connecticut, U.S.," *The Ecclesiologist* 23(April 1867): 185.

48. I am indebted to Kenneth Cameron for information and suggestions concerning the identity of the Church of the Holy Innocents. Forty-nine sheets of drawings dated 20 March and 1 June 1866, are in the Stowe-Day Foundation, Hartford. See also Sarah B. Landau,

"The Colt Industrial Empire in Hartford," *Antiques* 109 (March 1976): 568–79.

49. A simpler version of the church than the one that Withers illustrated in *Church Architecture* is preserved in the Withers file box at the Avery Library of Columbia University.

50. Withers, *Church Architecture,* Design XII.

51. For a history of the institution see Albert W. Atwood, *Gallaudet College, Its First One Hundred Years* (Washington, D.C.: Gallaudet College, 1964).

52. Letter from Vaux to Gallaudet dated 20 December 1865. All correspondence relevant to the history of the Gallaudet College buildings is in the Edward Miner Gallaudet Memorial Library at the college, unless otherwise indicated. For the history of the college's Victorian buildings, see my article "Gallaudet College: A High Victorian Campus," *Records of the Columbia Historical Society of Washington, D.C., 1971–1972* (Washington: By the society, 1973), pp. 439–67.

53. The original plans and a large amount of correspondence from Withers are in the Edward Miner Gallaudet Memorial Library at Gallaudet College.

54. Although construction began at that time, the plans were not completed until April 1868. Writing to Gallaudet on 1 May 1868, Withers said, "the elevation, as completed, is liked by everyone who has seen it, and many say it is the best thing I have ever done." Chapel Hall makes an instructive comparison with H. H. Richardson's libraries of the 1880s and may have influenced them. The Crane Library (1880) in Quincy, Massachusetts, and the Billings Library (1883) in Burlington, Ver-

mont, bear a certain resemblance to Chapel Hall.

55. Prior to Withers's association with the institution, Gallaudet had employed a local architect named Emil S. Friedrich to design several buildings on the campus. These included the primary school (1859), the first college building (1865), and a shop building (1865). Virtually nothing is known about Friedrich except that he was employed as an engineer at the Washington Navy Yard and had worked with Thomas U. Walter at the Capitol.

56. Chapel Hall possessed the following in common with the New England buildings: commemorative purpose, Ruskinian Gothic style, congregational function, and wall space for memorial plaques.

57. The building, which Gallaudet called "this beautiful gift of the Government," was dedicated by President Grant on 29 January 1871. The general contractor was James Naylor of Washington. W. Vaughn provided the stained glass for the ten large windows that light the main hall.

58. Originally built of wood, this porch was transformed into a bricked-in corridor when College Hall was constructed in the 1870s.

59. The work first appeared in installments, beginning in 1864, in *The Building News.* The book, and others by the same author, was well known and respected in this country, and by the time the second edition was issued, in 1878, Colling had been made an honorary member of the American Institute of Architects (James K. Colling, *Art Foliage* [London: By the author, 1865]).

60. Ibid., pp. 39 and 42 for text to accompany plates mentioned in this discussion.

61. Norton, op. cit., p. 34.

62. The plans for the Gallaudet president's house were drawn in March 1867, and the building was ready for occupation by the end of 1868. A professor's house was erected at the same time to the north of the president's house.

63. The exterior, as constructed, is slightly less elaborate than the architect's drawing. The most notable deficiency in the actual building is the absence of quoins.

64. Kerr, op. cit., p. 114.

65. Ibid., plate 45.

66. For a biography of Roe see Mary Roe, *Edward Payson Roe, Reminiscences of His Life* (New York: Dodd, Mead and Co., 1899). The church records indicate an intention on the part of the parish to erect a new building as early as 25 March 1867. At that time a building committee was empowered to receive plans, and on 13 April 1867 the obscure firm of Wycliff and Baldwin was paid $385.00 for their services. These plans were never carried out (see *First Presbyterian Church of the Highlands: The One Hundreth Anniversary of the Church Building* [Highland Falls, N.Y.: By the church, 1968], p. 2). Further historical material is available in *A Century of Worship, 1850–1950* (Highland Falls, N.Y.: By the church, 1950).

67. Roe, op. cit., p. 97.

68. For a photograph and discussion of this church, see Basil Clark and John Piper, "Street's Yorkshire Churches and Contemporary Criticism," *Concerning Architecture*, pp. 209ff.; on p. 214 there is a description of the front of the church from *The Ecclesiologist*. The building was illustrated in *Examples of Modern Architecture, Ecclesiastical and Domestic* (London: Batsford, 1870).

69. Roe, op. cit., p. 100.

70. For a history of the parish, which was known as St. Anna's prior to 1869, see Hasbrouck, op. cit., vol. 1, pp. 333–35.

71. A brass plaque in the west wall of the church lists them as vestrymen at the time of construction.

72. The church was very costly and proved to be a financial burden on the parish. Withers estimated the cost at $45,000 (*Church Architecture*, Design XI). The building was not completely paid for until 1879, at which time it was consecrated (Hasbrouck, loc. cit.).

73. Hasbrouck, op. cit., vol. 1, p. 333–35 and Spingarn, op. cit., p. 200.

74. The following items illustrated in the introductory section of *Church Architecture* were from St. Luke's: the font on p. xv (for which there is a drawing by Withers in the Upjohn Collection at the Avery Library of Columbia University); the bishop's chair on p. xix; two sedilia on p. xix; and two stained glass windows on p. xix (the window labeled "Figure 35" was a memorial to Withers's first wife, Emily).

75. Montgomery Schuyler, "Trinity's Architecture," *Architectural Review* 25(June 1904): 423–24.

76. "All Saints Church, Leyton, Essex," *The Building News* 12(27 January 1865): 60–61.

77. "Medieval Timber Churches," *The Building News* 11(19 February 1864): 130–32. Concerning belfries it was stated, " . . . we find a good deal of timber work of a very interesting character in the churches of Essex. The timber belfries are so common as to form quite a characteristic feature of Essex churches and Essex landscapes." The article included several illustrations.

78. A fire completely gutted the interior

of St. Luke's parsonage in 1887. The fire also destroyed the architect's drawings and many parish records.

79. Scott had recommended this combination of materials for its "excellent effect" in rural districts (*Remarks*, p. 105). Withers designed the Frost house using these materials in 1859. The format of that building, which was illustrated in the 1864 edition of *Villas and Cottages* (Design 28), was in the tradition of Withers's other villas. The house was built at Clinton Point, New York, and was used by the Gallaudet Home for the Deaf before being destroyed.

80. The S. L. Thurlow house appeared in *The American Architect and Building News* 1(9 December 1876): 397. The imposing stone structure recalls, on a more modest scale, the country houses of Withers's master T. H. Wyatt, for example, Wyatt's Orchardleigh Park in Somersetshire of 1855.

81. *Proceedings of the Third Annual Convention of the American Institute of Architects, November 16 and 17, 1869.* (New York: By the Institute, 1870), p. 14.

82. Everard M. Upjohn, *Richard Upjohn, Architect and Churchman* (New York: Columbia University Press, 1939), p. 160. A. J. Bloor frequently recorded in his diary that the offices of Vaux and Withers were the scene of AIA meetings in the 1860s.

83. "Frederick C. Withers," *Quarterly Bulletin of the American Institute of Architects*, April 1901, p. 2.

84. *Proceedings of the Third Annual Convention of the American Institute of Architects*, loc. cit.

85. Eidlitz's church is now demolished.

86. Withers did not indicate the location or the name of the church, but his description of its site ("on a corner lot in the upper part of this city with frontage on the south and west") accurately corresponds to the situation of Holy Trinity. In addition, he explained that he placed the tower at the west end of the south aisle "on account of the principal approach to the church being from the south," that is, along Madison Avenue, which would have been the street running in front of the church. The architect inadvertently alluded to this fact when he wrote that the "narthex, facing on the avenue, is large. . . ." It is recorded in *A History of Real Estate, Building, and Architecture in New York City* (New York: Record and Guide, 1898) that the firm of Vaux, Withers and Co. submitted a plan for the Church of the Holy Trinity in 1869 (see listing of new and proposed buildings for that year).

87. The church was included by Rev. George W. Shinn in his book *Kings Handbook of Notable Episcopal Churches in the United States* (New York: Moses King, 1889), p. 106.

88. "Stephen Higginson Tying, 2nd," *National Cyclopedia of American Biography* 20(1909): 188.

89. Withers's original watercolor perspective drawing for the rectory is in the Avery Library of Columbia University.

90. "Church Architecture in America," *The Building News* 25(5 September 1873): 245.

91. I am indebted to Alan Burnham for a photograph, taken in the 1880s, of Withers in his office at 54 Bible House in New York City. St. James also appeared as Design XXI in *Church Architecture*.

92. Drawings of the mortuary chapel were published in Withers's *Church Architecture* as vignettes to Designs VI and X. See also *National Academy*

of Design, Winter Exhibition Catalogue, 1869, drawing number 79.

93. W. S. W. Ruschenberger, *A Memory* (Philadelphia: Privately printed, 1868), pp. 90ff. This is the only biography of Bartlett, whose estate — Rockwood — north of Tarrytown, New York, was illustrated in the 1865 edition of Downing's *Landscape Gardening.*

94. The chapel stands in an overgrown field beside the Bard College chapel. The land once belonged to Bartlett, who had moved there three years prior to his death in 1868 (Ruschenberger, op. cit., p. 90).

95. The first mention of the church appeared in "Riverside," *The American Builder* 1(December 1869): 229. The church, which was nearing completion, was described as "one of those few structures which derive their beauty from the element of pure simplicity, unsacrificed to mere ornamentation. . . . The interior is no less beautiful than the exterior. The ceiling, curved by massive trusses, rises with a Gothic arch to a height of forty-five feet above the floor; while the light, softened by the stained windows, fills the interior with that soft glow so seldom found in modern churches. . . ." The structure was seriously damaged by fire in 1879. It was rebuilt along its original lines, with the addition of a tower over the south porch. The church was enlarged in 1889, 1897, and 1928 (see *Riverside Then and Now* [Chicago: Riverside Historical Society, 1936], pp. 128–29). Olmsted's remarks were made to his father in a letter dated 17 August 1864 and now in the Library of Congress. In the letter Olmsted expressed a low opinion of Richard Upjohn as a church architect — "I don't think his work

is well-studied. It has a commonplace, stencilled look" — but praised Leopold Eidlitz and Edward C. Cabot.

96. "Riverside," loc. cit.

97. *Detail, Cottage and Constructive Architecture* (New York: A. J. Bicknell, 1873).

98. *National Academy of Design, Winter Exhibition Catalogue, 1869,* No. 79. The gateway was praised as "A handsome structure" appropriate for one of the entrances to Central Park in "Our New York Letter," *The American Builder* 2(July 1869): 138. Alan Burnham has suggested that the gate might have been intended not for Central Park, but for Washington Square, for he noticed the name "University Pl" on the side of one of the street cars in the foreground.

99. *Riverside* (Riverside, Ill.: Riverside Improvement Company, 1871), p. 40. I am indebted to Robert H. Heidrich of Riverside for information and photographs of the building.

100. Ibid.

101. I am indebted to Peter Stevenson and to Peter Goss, who has written a dissertation on Olana, for information concerning the role of Vaux and Withers in the project. Only a small number of the architectural drawings for the house have survived; however, there are several that are lettered in Withers's hand and bear the date May–June, 1870. A voucher for $300 (dated 21 September 1871) has also survived and it confirms at least one payment by Church to Vaux and Withers. The Olana commission was one of the last on which Vaux and Withers collaborated as partners. The firm of Vaux, Withers and Co. appeared in the New York City directory for the last time in 1871–72. Hamlin states

that the partnership ended in 1871 (Hamlin, loc. cit.).

CHAPTER 5

1. *Wooden and Brick Buildings,* vol. 2, Design 67, plate 87.
2. Schuyler, "Frederick C. Withers," loc. cit.
3. George W. Shinn, op. cit., pp. 168–70. See also "St. Thomas' Church, Hanover, New Hampshire," *The Churchman* 59(7 January 1888): 22–23. Withers also published the church as Design V in *Church Architecture*. The impressive entrance tower was never completed.
4. Review of *Church Architecture* by Frederick Withers in *The American Builder* 9(November 1873): 284.
5. See page 25 for a discussion of one of these. See also "A Short Chapter on Country Churches," loc. cit. and "A Church in the Romanesque Style," *The Horticulturist* 6(December 1851): 574.
6. Frank Wills, *Ancient English Ecclesiastical Architecture and Its Principles Applied to the Wants of the Church at the Present Day* (New York: Stanford and Swords, 1850).
7. Richard Upjohn, *Rural Architecture* (New York: George P. Putnam, 1852).
8. John C. Hart, *Designs for Parish Churches in the Three Styles of English Church Architecture* (New York: Dana and Co., 1857).
9. Henry Hudson Holly, *Church Architecture* (Hartford: M. H. Mallory and Co., 1871).
10. Holly, born in New York City, studied architecture under Gervase Wheeler from 1854 to 1856. After that he spent some time in England before establishing himself in New York. He was also the author of *Country Seats* (1863) and *Modern Dwellings* (1878). His most important achievement was designing the buildings at Nashville for the University of the South in the 1880s (see "A Group of American Architects," *The American Architect and Building News* 15[16 February 1884]: 76).
11. Review of *Church Architecture* by Henry H. Holly in *The Architect,* 5(18 May 1872): 261.
12. The churches, Withers stated, "were designed by the author during his late partnership with Calvert Vaux and Frederick Law Olmsted, several of them have been carried out under his direct supervision and nearly all were prepared for definitive localities" (Withers, *Church Architecture,* p. iv).
13. Ibid.
14. Ibid., p. vii.
15. Ibid.
16. Ibid.
17. Ibid., p. ix.
18. Pugin, *True Principles,* p. 3.
19. Withers, *Church Architecture,* p. viii.
20. For more on this point see Donald D. Egbert, "Religious Expression in America," *A Critical Biography of Religion in America,* ed. Nelson R. Burr (Princeton, N.J.: Princeton University Press, 1961), vol. 4, pt. 4.
21. Withers, *Church Architecture,* Design II.
22. Review of *Church Architecture* by Frederick Withers in *The American Builder* 9(November 1873): 284.
23. "Church Architecture," *The American Architect and Building News* 13(14 April 1883): 179.
24. "Church Architecture in America," *The Building News* 25(5 September 1873): 245.
25. In addition to the fact that the writer in *The Building News* was fundamentally discontent with Withers's churches because of their old-fashioned character, he also

criticized their relative plainness and smallness. The reasons for these qualities went beyond Withers's personal style. They were rooted in the economic realities of building in America. It is not by coincidence that none of Withers's designs in the "Curvilinear Gothic" style were constructed, for, as he indirectly admitted by offering the two methods of exterior finish for the same ground plan in Design II, Withers realized that the cost of such churches was prohibitive in the United States. This fact had been recognized earlier by the British architectural press. In an article entitled "American Architecture" in *The Architect* of 6 August 1870, an English writer stated that religious edifices in America "are all what our churchman would call chapels." He attributed the smallness of American churches to the absence of an established church and to the "numerous religious communions which divide the patronage of the public." But more important than the religious factor was the difference between the cost of labor and materials in America and England. Shortly before the publication of *Church Architecture*, Russell Sturgis had indicated that this fact was significant in determining the character of all American architecture. He considered it to be one of the five major "obstacles" that impeded American architects "in whatever attempts they may take to give the world better art." At the heart of the problem was the high cost of labor in America during the prosperous years after the Civil War. Sturgis attributed this situation to "all the philanthropic and reformatory movements which tend to the improvement of the lot of the less prosperous members of the community." He objected, however, to the high cost of well-made goods and the inflationary impact that higher wages had on construction. The effect was most serious in ecclesiastical architecture, for Sturgis wrote, "The difference in the cost of building a church with a good deal of decorative work about it, painted glass in the windows, ornamental tiles on the floors, carved oak in the pulpit and reading-desk and organ-case, wrought-iron leaf-work in the finials and gas-brackets and chancel-rail — the difference in the cost of such a church here and in England, is very great, perhaps as five here to two in England" (see Russell Sturgis, "Modern American Architecture, I," *The North American Review* 112[January 1871] and "Modern American Architecture, II," *The North American Review* 112 [April 1871]).

26. "Daylesford Church, Worcestershire," *The Building News* 18(27 April 1866): 270.
27. E. C. Robins, FRIBA, "On Congregational Church Building," a paper read before the Architectural Association of London, 14 November 1873, and printed in *The Architect* 10(22 November 1873): 271.
28. Sturgis, "Modern American Architecture, I," op. cit., p. 177.
29. Sturgis, "Modern American Architecture II," op. cit., pp. 388–89.
30. Withers, *Church Architecture*, p. vii.
31. "Editor's Easy Chair," *Harper's New Monthly Magazine* 38(October 1868): 847.
32. "The Teaching of Church Architecture," *The Churchman* 5(9 December 1871): 393.
33. "Some Practical Conditions of American Architecture," *The American Architect and Building News* 1(19 August 1876): 266.
34. "Competitive Design for a Village

Church, Gambrill and Richardson, Architects," *The New York Sketch-book of Architecture* 2(October 1875): plate XL.

35. "Calvary Church, Utica, New York, Henry M. Congdon, Architect," *The New York Sketch-book of Architecture* 2(March 1875): plate XV.

36. "Two Designs for an Episcopal Church near Shrewsbury, New Jersey, A. J. Bloor, Architect," *The New York Sketch-book of Architecture* 2(May 1875): plate XX.

37. See chap. 4, n. 35.

38. Officially known as the "Third Judicial District Courthouse," the structure is presently the Jefferson Market Branch of the New York City Public Library.

39. See Callow, op. cit., p. 217, for mention of the courthouse as a Tweed Ring project. For a concise history of its construction see *New York City Architecture: Selections from the Historic American Buildings Survey,* No. 7 (Washington, D.C.: U.S. Department of Interior, 1969), pp. 17–29.

40. Minutes of the Board of Aldermen of the City of New York, 28 October 1873. Printed in *New York City Architecture,* p. 18. The original architect is unknown.

41. "Jefferson Market and the New Court-House," *The New York Times,* 3 February 1874, p. 2.

42. "The Board of Aldermen," *The New York Times,* 9 December 1876, p. 2.

43. Withers's original design, details of which were later modified, first appeared in "Design for Court House, Third Judicial District, New York," *The New York Sketch-book of Architecture* 1(July 1874).

44. "Court House, Bell Tower and Prison, Third Judicial District, New York," *The New York Sketch-book of Architecture* 2(15 June 1875).

45. One of the first public accusations made against the project was a letter from "A Ninth Ward Resident and Taxpayer" in *The New York Times,* 9 July 1876, p. 2. He asked, "It was started by the Tweed Ring as a job; is it still one?"

46. In December of that year, Robert Cushing, a stone carver, submitted a letter to the Board of Aldermen that accused the president of the building commission "with wastefulness and extravagance in disbursing the funds." He also vitriolically referred to Withers and Vaux as incompetent and insane. At the hearing that was held later in the month to investigate the charges, Cushing accused Withers of having tried to persuade him to falsify his bill in order to take advantage of funds that would otherwise have not been needed. In public testimony, Cushing alleged that "In November, 1875, Mr. Withers and I stood in front of the court-house on Sixth Avenue. Mr. Withers said to me, 'I want to ask a favor of you. There is a special appropriation of $50,000 for building the tower. It will not cost so much, but I want to make it appear that it will. I will ask you to give me a receipt for $4000 worth of work on the tower, and I can also get a receipt for $4000 worth of other on it.' I told him I could not do that; the work for which the receipts were asked by Mr. Withers was not done" ("Local Miscellany" *The New York Times,* 28 December 1876, p. 2). The controversy carried into February 1877, when an investigation exonerated Withers of any serious misconduct. *The American Architect and Building News* revealed the damaging fact Cushing had initially "brought a bill of seventeen thousand dollars for extras, which the architects . . . refused to allow, and the Commissioners therefore re-

fused to pay. He then sued the City and lost his suit. Thereupon he brought a long list of charges against the architects accusing them of incompetency and misconduct in a variety of ways" ("The Third District Court-House," *The American Architect and Building News* 2[10 February 1877]: p. 41). For Cushing's charges in full, see *Proceedings of the New York City Board of Aldermen* 144(18 December 1876): 556–61. Two years after the completion of the courthouse, P. K. and J. A. Horgan, brick masons, submitted a bill in the amount of $44,000 for extra work occasioned, they insisted, by the long delays during construction. Withers, cast in the role of protector of the public treasury, exposed the claim as blatantly dishonest, since the Horgans claimed compensation for 47,000 square feet of brick surface on the Sixth Avenue elevation although there were only 37,000 square feet on the entire building. For details of the controversy, see "An Audacious Claim for Extras," *The American Architect and Building News* 3(1 February 1879): 37.

47. For the proceedings of the Municipal Society's investigation see "Municipal Extravagance," *The New York Times,* 8 May 1877, p. 2. A special committee was also formed by the Board of Aldermen to investigate the courthouse project (see n. 46).

48. "Municipal Extravagance," loc. cit.

49. Although published drawings of the courthouse generally include the name of Vaux along with that of Withers, the role of Vaux in the work seems to have been a minor one. Whenever the building was discussed in contemporary literature, it was clear that Withers was responsible for the design.

50. "Municipal Extravagance," loc. cit.

51. Ibid.

52. "The Jefferson Market Monument," *The New York Times,* 9 May 1877, p. 4.

53. "The Jefferson Market Monument," loc. cit.

54. "Jefferson Market Police 'Rum-House,' " letter signed "Justice to the editor of *The New York Times,*" 8 January 1874, p. 3.

55. The prison at the back of the courthouse had no formal facade, for it faced the small courtyard between the buildings and was seen by the public only from the rear. From the courtyard one entered a narrow corridor which led to the guard room from which access to the cell blocks on the first level was possible. The upper decks could be reached only by a steam-operated elevator at the end of a long passage leading from the south side of the guard room. Further details of the prison (now destroyed) are available in "Notes on Current Topics," *The American Builder* 11(October 1875): 223, which states, "The prison for the females will be on the second floor, arranged in two tiers, and that for the males on the floor above, arranged in four tiers. The cells will be placed back to back, the dividing wall being used for ventilation purposes with separate flues carried from every cell to the central shaft, in which is placed the iron smoke flue from the furnace. . . . The cells will be lighted by large windows in the outer walls, which will be set back ten feet from the street line, with a fence wall 18 feet high, surrounding the building." The prison wing was finished in 1877 but was not occupied by prisoners until the following year (see "Building Intelligence," *The American Architect and Building News*

2[23 June 1877]: v, and "The New Jefferson Market Prison," *The New York Times,* 14 April 1878, p. 2).

56. Withers's 1876 design for the market is now in the possession of the buildings department of New York City, which also has the drawings for the courthouse complex. It is not known why Withers's plan for the market was rejected, but Schuyler suggested that there were political reasons (see Schuyler, "Frederick C. Withers," loc. cit.). For a discussion of Smyth's market versus Withers's proposal, see "Jefferson Market," *Record and Guide* 7(15 September 1883): 683–84.

57. Plans, cross sections, and details of the courthouse complex, exclusive of the market, were made known to the English architectural profession by *The Building News* 29(9 July 1875): 36.

58. "Notes on Current Topics," *The American Builder* 11(October 1875): 223.

59. Robert F. Jordan, *Victorian Architecture* (London: Penguin Press, 1968), p. 156. The *Très Riches Heures* quality of the Jefferson Market Courthouse found expression also in Vaux and Withers's study for the New York City central court and prison published in *The New York Sketch-book of Architecture* in April 1874. Ennobled by a majestic tower, the design included a stately chamber recessed behind the low facade, a plan undoubtedly inspired by Street's Great Hall in the London Law Courts. Impressed by the design, Schuyler, in his obituary of Withers, said that it "would have been, if it had been executed, one of the most important monuments of the Gothic Revival in this country."

60. Withers's tower was emulated at least once by another architect (see "New Theological Hall, Hamilton, New York, T. I. Lacey, Architect," *The American Architect and Building News* 8[3 July 1886]). Sketches of the tower appeared in "Secular Towers, Modern," *The American Architect and Building News* 18(17 October 1885) and in *Building* 3(June 1885).

61. "The New Law Courts," *The Builder* 25(4 May 1867): 309–11.

62. Letter from Withers to Gallaudet dated 16 April 1874, in the collection of the Gallaudet Library, Gallaudet College. Withers generally stayed at the Sunset House in Sugar Hill, New Hampshire.

63. College Hall also served as an illustration of the fact that in English eyes, the American architectural profession had not improved since Withers's arrival in 1852. During 1876 William Fogerty (1829–99), a fellow of the Royal Institute of British Architects, who had spent several months in the United States, aired his unfavorable views on American architecture in *The Building News,* 11 March 1876, p. 45. Fogerty represented the building situation in the United States as dismal and the country as a ripe place for any bright young English architect who would immigrate as Withers had done. Later the same year, *The Building News* (28 July 1876, p. 93) published College Hall as one of its infrequent American entries, obviously using it as testimony to the truth of Fogerty's contention that America needed and appreciated English architects.

64. When the board of directors of the institution approved Withers's design, they had expressed reservations about the expensive ornamentation. Withers wrote to Gallaudet that by making certain unspecified omissions the cost could be reduced by as much as $12,000, but he

warned that "the building would then be bald and ugly, and I therefore trust your board will not consider it essential to cut down the design in detail" (Letter from Withers to Gallaudet dated 2 February 1875, in the collection of the Gallaudet Library, Gallaudet College).

65. For a full set of drawings and specifications for the house, which was known as "House A," see A. J. Bicknell's *Wooden and Brick Buildings with Details*, vol. 1, Design 31, plates 53–56. A house with an identical ground plan and only a slightly different elevation was constructed at the same time next to House A.

66. Street, *Brick and Marble*, p. 279.

67. Minutes of the Vestry, Trinity Church, New York City, 10 April 1876, p. 497.

68. Diary of the Reverend Dr. Morgan Dix, manuscript collection of Trinity Church, entries for 10, 15, and 23 June 1876 make it clear that Dr. Dix acted as an intermediary between Withers and the donors.

69. Ibid., 10 June 1876.

70. Ibid., 23 June 1876.

71. Minutes of the vestry, 27 June 1876, p. 505. Drawings of the chancel — which no longer retains Withers's decorations — and the sacristy were published in "The Illustrations," *The American Architect and Building News* 3(2 February 1878): 42.

72. During the summer of 1876 it was reported in *The American Architect and Building News* ("Correspondence," 26 August 1876, p. 279) that the preliminary arrangements for the work in Trinity Church were underway and that Withers was about to "leave for England in a few days, where the figures and bas-relief work will be executed by an artist employed on many of the Medieval restorations there." The English sculptor was Robert Smith and the mosaicist was Daniel Bell of London. The entire ensemble was assembled by the well-known New York firm of Ellin and Kitson. On 3 April 1877, the church was closed while work on the altar and chancel progressed. During this period a writer from *The American Builder* ("The Astor Memorial," July 1877, p. 150) visited the scene and was moved by the sight of "a carver who was moulding a bracket over the Piscina to the similitude of an angel with outspread wings. Absorbed in his task he was an embodied revival of that passionate devotion to the religious art which we are told by the Pessimistics of to-day died with the middle ages." The entire project was completed by 27 June 1877. Concerning the color scheme of the chancel, *The New York Times*, 17 June 1877, p. 2, noted: "The ground-work of the coloring is Venetian red, and the general tone of the ceiling vellum. . . . The stone shafts of all the arches in the chancel . . . are decorated in gold and colors, while the bosses, caps, and corbels are picked out in gold. The spandrils of the ceiling are adorned with shields bearing the sacred emblems of the Church richly illuminated."

73. A full description of the altar and reredos by the architect appeared in *The Year Book and Register of Trinity Church, 1878* (New York: By the church, 1878): 52–55. An illustration also appeared in *The Building News* 22(22 September 1876). See also "New York — The Altar and Reredos in Trinity Church," *The Churchman* 35(30 June 1877): 726–27.

74. Anna Jameson, *Sacred and Legendary Art*, quoted in Elizabeth Holt, *From*

the Classicists to the Impressionists (Garden City, N.Y: Doubleday Anchor Books, 1966): 144.

75. In its fundamental lines, the Astor reredos recalls the Civil War monument in St. James Episcopal Church in Chicago, which Withers designed in 1870. It appeared as the vignette to Design XX in *Church Architecture*.

76. For generic English predecessors, see Peter Anson, *Fashions in Church Furnishings, 1840–1940* (London: B. T. Batsford, 1960). Withers's Trinity altar, which Anson compares to similar works by G. G. Scott, is discussed on pp. 276–77. See also the Reverend John Wright, *Some Notable Altars in the Church of England and the American Episcopal Church* (New York: Macmillan Co. 1908).

77. E. S., "The Harmony of Gothic Architecture with High Art," *The Building News* 5(14 October 1859): 918.

78. "The Proposed Mosaic Reredos for Westminster Abbey," *The Ecclesiologist* 26(December 1865): 341. The altar was by G. G. Scott (see "New Reredos and Altar Table, Westminster Abbey," *The Builder* 25[9 November 1867]: 822–23, ill.).

79. "Proposed Reredos for Westminster Abbey," op. cit.

80. Ibid., p. 340.

81. "Correspondence," *The American Architect and Building News* 2(7 July 1877), p. 218. See also *The Churchman* 36(30 June 1877): 39; (14 July 1877): 37; and (28 July 1877): 32, ill.

82. The writer described the event, which took place on 27 June 1877, as an "occasion of which any architect might feel proud. Divines and literary men, journalists, critics, and fellow-architects, with a liberal sprinkling of the best class of general society, thronged the church for several hours, dividing their time between feasting their eyes upon the beautiful work and heaping congratulations upon Mr. Withers."

83. Diary of Dr. Dix, op. cit., 27 June 1877.

84. "Correspondence," loc. cit.

85. In 1852, Dix, while still a student at the General Theological Seminary, was a member of the executive committee of the New York Ecclesiological Society (see *Third Annual Report of the New York Ecclesiological Society,* 12 May 1851, p. 33).

86. "Correspondence," loc. cit.

CHAPTER 6

1. Schuyler, "Russell Sturgis' Architecture," p. 406.

2. Henry Van Brunt, "The Historic Styles and Modern Architecture," *The Architectural Review* 1(1 August 1892): 59–61; 2(2 January 1893): 1–4. Printed in William A. Coles (ed.), *Architecture and Society: Selected Essays of Henry Van Brunt* (Cambridge: Belknap Press of Harvard University, 1969), p. 297; and Montgomery Schuyler in Jordy and Coe, op. cit., vol. 2, p. 578.

3. Van Brunt in Coles, op. cit., p. 294.

4. "Chetwood," "Correspondence," *The American Architect and Building News* 5(8 March 1879): 78.

5. The project was originally proposed in November 1878 by the widow of Major James Goodwin as a memorial to her husband (see *Contributions to the History of Christ Church, Hartford* [Hartford: Belknap and Wakefield, 1895], p. 102).

6. The entire project was completed 27 December 1879, when the altar was consecrated. See "Chetwood,"

"Correspondence," *The American Architect and Building News* 7(10 January 1880): 13.

7. "Connecticut," *The Churchman* 41(3 January 1880): 9.

8. Minutes of the vestry of St. Luke's Episcopal Church, Altoona, Pennsylvania, 25 May 1880. See the passage of the resolution adopting Withers's plan.

9. Jesse C. Sell, *The Twentieth Century History of Altoona and Blair County, Pennsylvania* (Chicago: Richmond-Arnold Publishing Co., 1911), p. 369.

10. "The Heart of the Alleghenies," *Harper's New Monthly Magazine* 62(August 1883): 331.

11. Sell, op. cit., p. 368.

12. The Reverend Allan Woodle was once an assistant minister at Christ Church in New York City. He had also been a manager of *The Church Journal,* an important Episcopal periodical (information from an uncited obituary of Woodle in the possession of Sydney Billin).

13. S. H. S. Gallaudet, *St. Luke's Episcopal Church Centennial Yearbook: 1856–1956* (Altoona: By the church, 1956), p. 16.

14. The bells were donated by William G. Hamilton of New York (*The Altoona Morning Telegraph,* 5 September 1881).

15. The church was published in "St. Luke's Church, Altoona, Pennsylvania," *Building* 2(January 1884): 94, ill.

16. A photograph of Brook's church appears in Dixon and Muthesius, op. cit., p. 216.

17. "Whitecaps," *The American Architect and Building News* 10(29 October 1881). The house was built in 1880 at a cost of $15,000 (see "Building Intelligence," *The American Architect and Building News* 7(19 June 1880): 278.

18. "Miscellaneous Notes," *The American Builder* 13(August 1877): 191–92.

19. "English Architecture at the Exhibition," *The American Builder* 12(April 1876): 82.

20. "House on Mt. Desert Island, Maine, William R. Emerson, Architect," *The American Architect and Building News* 5(27 March 1879): 169.

21. This book is discussed in detail by Arnold Lewis in his introduction to *American Victorian Architecture: A Survey of the 70s and 80s in Contemporary Photographs* (New York: Dover, 1975). The Davis House is illustrated in Plate III, 13.

22. The project was first contemplated in 1877 (see "Building Intelligence," *The American Architect and Building News* 2(31 March 1877): v.

23. "Whitehall," "The Produce Exchange," *The New York Times,* 3 March 1881, p. 8.

24. "Produce Exchange's New Building," *The New York Times,* 19 January 1881, p. 5.

25. "The Produce Exchange Building," *The New York Times,* 6 March 1881, p. 7. For a critical appraisal of the competition, see "Whitehall," "The New York Produce Exchange Competition," *The American Architect and Building News* 9(12 March 1881): 128–29.

26. Carl Condit, *American Building* (Chicago History of American Civilization, Chicago: University of Chicago Press, 1968), pp. 116–17, discusses the importance of Post's produce exchange building in the evolution of metal skeletal construction.

27. Clarence Cook, "Architecture in America," *The North American Review* 35(November 1882): 252.

28. "Competitive Design for the New York Produce Exchange, Mr. F. C. Withers, Architect," *The American*

Architect and Building News 9(9 April 1881): 174.

29. The library, located at 9 Westchester Square in Bronx, New York, is presently called the Huntington Library. For a full discussion of the history of this building, see Francis Kowsky, "The Huntington Free Library and the Van Schaick Free Reading Room," *Journal of the Bronx County Historical Society* 7(January 1970): 1–8.

30. The tower motif was also present on Withers's Thurlow House (1874) in Wilkes-Barre, Pennsylvania. For more on the Vassar Brothers Hospital, see *Building* 3(August 1885): 126 and plate II.

31. The history of the competition is related in Melancthon W. Jacobus, "The Soldiers Memorial in Hartford," *Bulletin of the Connecticut Historical Society* 34(April 1969): 33–42.

32. "The Weehawken Water Tower," *Engineering News and American Contract Journal,* 16(6 November 1886): 292. The tower was also published in *The American Architect and Building News,* 14(8 September 1883): 114. The tower, which is no longer used, has been nominated to the National Register of Historic Places as part of the Hackensack Water Company at Weehawken complex.

33. "St. George Church, Newburgh, New York," *The American Architect and Building News* 18(2 January 1886).

34. See Hitchcock, *Early Victorian Architecture,* vol. 2, plate IV. 6, for an illustration of St. Mary's.

35. "House for Mr. Frank Hasbrouck, Market Street, Poughkeepsie, New York," *The American Architect and Building News* 22(2 July 1887). I am indebted to Elsa Hasbrouck for information and documents related to the house that Withers built for her father.

36. "The late George Bliss and the Church on Blackwell's Island," *The Churchman* 73(4 April 1896): 440–41.

37. Ibid.

38. The building, which is used as a community center and interdenominational church, was restored by Giorgio Cavaglieri, who also remodeled the Jefferson Market Courthouse for use as a public library.

39. "Chapel of the Good Shepherd, Blackwell's Island, New York, Mr. F. C. Withers, Architect," *The American Architect and Building News* 26(20 July 1889): 27.

40. Eastlake, op. cit., p. 364.

41. For a history of the competition, see Canon Edward N. West, "Rethinking Need Means Rethought Plan and Design," *Cathedral News,* May 1967, pp. 1–4.

42. Illustrations of Pearson's church were published in "Truro Cathedral," *The Churchman* 66(26 November 1887): 300.

43. "Competitive Design for the Cathedral of St. John the Divine," *The American Architect and Building News* 26(2 November 1889): 206.

44. West, op. cit., p. 1.

45. For an illustration of this church, see "Trinity Church Chapel and Parish House, Hartford, Connecticut," *The American Architect and Building News* 33(4 July 1891): 14.

46. Sherrod Soule, *Francis Goodwin, A Biography* (Hartford: Privately printed, 1939), p. 25. Goodwin personally supported the cost of the church, which was estimated at $175,000. In 1871, Withers had designed the Hartford home of Goodwin's brother James, and in 1885 he had been engaged by both brothers to plan model laborers' cottages. These were illustrated in *Building* 3(April 1885), plate 7.

47. Soule, op. cit. p. 24.

48. Information on the church was obtained from a letter dated 24 May 1958, by Margaret Withers to Alan Burnham (in the American Architectural Archive).

49. For photographs and a history of the church, see "Zabriske Memorial Church of St. John the Evangelist, Newport, Rhode Island," *The Churchman* 72(13 July 1895): 48–49.

50. "Reredos in Trinity Chapel," *The Churchman* 66(31 December 1892): 900–901. The altar was included, along with that of Trinity Church, in John Wright, *Some Notable Altars* (New York: Macmillan Co., 1908), p. 253.

51. "The New Pulpit in Trinity Chapel, New York," *The Churchman* 77(26 February 1898): 317.

52. "Church of the Transfiguration, New York City," *The Churchman* 64(10 October 1896): 441–42.

53. "New York City," *The Churchman* 71(8 June 1895): 808. See also Wright, op. cit., p. 254.

54. Walter Dickson was an architect from Albany, New York, who became associated with Withers in 1887. The only significant biography available is an obituary in *The American Art Annual 1903–1904*. It states that he designed the Albany post office building and that he had been "instrumental in the placing of bronze tablets throughout the city, commemorating Albany" (p. 139). Withers and Dickson's original partnership agreement is in the American Architectural Archive.

55. "Plans to change the Tombs," *The New York Times,* 5 June 1896, p. 12.

56. "New York City Prison," *The American Architect and Building News* 56(3 April 1897): 6.

57. "Work on the New Tombs," *The New York Times,* 30 November 1898, p. 2.

58. "The New Tombs Prison," *The New York Times,* 1 December 1898, p. 6.

59. "New York City Prison," loc. cit.

60. Ibid.

61. Schuyler, "Frederick C. Withers."

CHAPTER 7

1. [Montgomery Schuyler], "The Third District Court House of New York," *The American Architect and Building News* 2(12 April 1877): 127. (Reprinted from *The New York World.*)

2. The results of the poll, which was first proposed in the 21 February 1885 issue, were published in "The Best Ten Buildings," *The American Architect and Building News* 17(13 June 1885): 282–83.

3. Especially by Talbot Hamlin's biography in *The Dictionary of American Biography* 10(1936): 405.

4. For Jefferson's remarks on the Georgian see "Notes on the State of Virginia," *The Writings of Thomas Jefferson* (New York: Scribner's, 1884), vol. 3, pp. 257ff.

5. Samuel Green, *American Art: A Historical Survey* (New York: Ronald Press, 1966), p. 339.

6. Schuyler, "Russell Sturgis' Architecture," p. 406.

APPENDIX

A List of Works by Frederick Clarke Withers

THE FOLLOWING LIST records all of Withers's known works and projects, including those done in collaboration with Calvert Vaux and Walter Dickson. References to important notices have been appended to many entries, but for more comprehensive documentation the reader is referred to the bibliography. When original drawings or plans are extant, their location is indicated together with the work. Concluding the list is a catalog of the buildings for which documentation is incomplete or tentative. This group encompasses those churches in Withers's *Church Architecture* that cannot be identified. For each location, works are inventoried chronologically; firm names are used when it is not certain that the project was solely or chiefly designed by Withers.

LIST OF ABBREVIATIONS

AABN   *The American Architect and Building News*

AMJ   *The Architects' and Mechanics' Journal*

BLDGS   Frederick C. Withers, *Buildings Erected from the Designs of F. C. Withers* (New York: George P. Putnam Sons, 1877)

CA   Frederick C. Withers, *Church Architecture* (New York: A. J. Bicknell, 1873)

DNB   Docket of New Buildings, New York City Department of Buildings

Harper's   Calvert Vaux, "Hints for Country House Builders," *Harper's New Monthly Magazine* 11(November 1855): 764

NAD   National Academy of Design Exhibition Catalogues (each entry will be followed by the year and drawing number)

RG   *Record and Guide*

VC   Calvert Vaux, *Villas and Cottages* (New York: Harper and Brothers, 1857)

ALBANY, N.Y.

Cathedral of the Immaculate Conception, alterations (Withers and Dickson, 1891. *RG,* 17 March 1891, p. 436.

ALTOONA, PA.

St. Luke's P.E. Church (1880). *Building* 2(January 1884).
Fourth Ward School (1881). *AABN* 9(24 December 1881): xii.

ANNANDALE-ON-HUDSON, N.Y.

Edwin Bartlett Mortuary Chapel (1869). *CA,* vignettes to Designs VI and X; drawing in the Avery Library, Columbia University.

BALMVILLE, N.Y.

David M. Clarkson House, Grand Ave. (1856). *The Horticulturist* 12(May 1857); drawing in the Avery Library, Columbia University.
Daniel B. St. John House, Grand Ave. (1857). Drawing in the Avery Library, Columbia University.
Frederick Deming House (1859; later known as the Forsyth-Wickes House). *AMJ* 2(17 March 1860): 191; *AMJ* 2(2 June 1860): 81; *NAD,* 1860, No. 13. The library from this now-abandoned structure has been preserved in the American wing of the Metropolitan Museum of Art.
Walter Vail House, Downing Ave. (1859). Plans in the possession of Peter Cantline, the present owner.

BEACON, N.Y. (includes the nineteenth-century communities of Fishkill Landing and Matteawan)

Dutch Reformed Church (1859). *CA,* Design XIII; *BLDGS,* Design 19.
"Tioronda," Gen. Joseph Howland House (1859; presently owned by Craig House). *AMJ* 2(17 March 1860): 191.
Tioronda School (1865; presently owned by Craig House). *CA,* Design XXII; *BLDGS,* Design 3; *NAD,* 1865, No. 150.
"Eustasia," Judge John J. Monell House, Monell Pl. (1867). Downing's *Cottage Residences,* 1873 edition, pp. 209–12.
St. Luke's P.E. Church (1869). *CA,* Design XI; *BLDGS,* Design 13; *NAD,* 1869, No. 67. Drawing for remodeling of the baptismal font by Withers is in the Upjohn Collection, Avery Library, Columbia University.
St. Luke's P.E. Church, rectory (1869). *CA,* vignette to Design XI; *BLDGS,* Design 7; drawing in the Avery Library, Columbia University.
St. Luke's P.E. Church, brick schoolhouse (1886). *Building* 5(3 July 1886): 1.

BETHLEHEM, PA.

Garret B. Linderman House, Delaware Ave. (ca. 1870). *BLDGS,* Design 5. The house, which was rebuilt and enlarged in the 1920s, is known today as the Schwab House Apartments.

BRONX, N.Y.

W. S. Duke House, alterations, Palisades Ave. and River Ave. (1880). *DNB*.

Van Schaick Free Reading Room, Westchester Sq. (1882; present Huntington Library). *AABN* 14(20 October 1883).

Helen Irving House, stable, N. River St. (1884). *DNB*.

W. S. Duke House, stable, Palisades Ave. and River Ave. (1886). *DNB*.

City of New York Fordham Reception Hospital, alterations, 2456 Valentine Ave. (Withers and Dickson, 1890–91). *DNB*.

Edwin Kraus House, West 175th St. (Withers and Dickson, 1894). *DNB*.

BROOKLYN, N.Y.

Charles S. Kimball House, Columbia and Clark Sts. (1865; demolished). *BLDGS*, Design 9; *NAD*, 1866, No. 27; drawing in the Karolik Collection, Museum of Fine Arts, Boston.

St. James P.E. Church (1869; never constructed). *CA*, Design XXI; *NAD*, 1871, No. 28; *The New York Sketch-book of Architecture* 2(December 1875).

St. Luke and St. Matthew P.E. Church, Rev. Jacob W. Diller Memorial Reredos (1881). *AABN* 19(9 January 1886).

St. Luke and St. Matthew P.E. Church, Sunday School, alterations to the chancel, and alterations to houses owned by the church on Clinton St. (1881). *ABBN* 9(30 April 1881): v, and notices in the parish records.

James Edwards House, Ocean Parkway (Withers and Dickson, 1890). *DNB*.

George Washington Greene House, alterations, Hancock St. (Withers and Dickson, 1890). *DNB*.

St. Michael's P.E. Church, alterations (1894; demolished). *RG*, 28 April 1894, p. 686.

BURLINGTON, VT.

Richardson and McKillop Stores (Withers and Dickson, 1895). *RG*, 2 March 1895, p. 331.

CENTRAL ISLIP, LONG ISLAND, N.Y.

New York City Asylum for the Insane (Withers and Dickson, 1889). Department of Public Charities and Corrections Annual Report for 1889, pp. 69–78.

CHICAGO, ILL.

St. James P.E. Church, Civil War Memorial (1865–1871). *CA*, vignette to Design XX; *BLDGS*, Design 16.

CLINTON POINT, N.Y.

Messrs. Frost House (1859; demolished). *VC* (1864 edition), Design 28. The house later served as the Gallaudet Home for Deaf-mutes. *NAD*, 1859, No. 17.

CORNWALL-ON-HUDSON, N.Y.

Leonard H. Lee House (in collaboration with Vaux, 1853–1856). *VC*, vignette, p. 256.

DRIFTON, PA.

St. James' Chapel (1883). *AABN* 15(11 August 1883): xii.

GERMANTOWN, PA.

St. Michael's P.E. Church (1858; extant but altered; present Church of God). *CA*, Design VII.

HANOVER, N.H.

St. Thomas P.E. Church (1872). *CA*, Design V; drawing for the Mrs. Walter F. McConnell Memorial Reredos in the Fine Arts Library, University of Pennsylvania.

HARRISBURG, PA.

J. Donald Cameron House, State and Front Sts. (Vaux, Withers and Co., 1868; alterations, ca. 1870). Drawing in the Avery Library, Columbia University.

HARTFORD, CONN.

Church of the Holy Innocents (1867; never constructed). *CA*, Design XII; drawings at the Stowe-Day Foundation, Hartford.

Hartford Retreat, alterations (Vaux, Withers and Co., 1868–70). Hurd, *Institutional Care of the Insane*, vol. 2: p. 88.

James Goodwin House (1871; demolished). Room preserved in the Connecticut Historical Society, Hartford.

Christ P.E. Church, alterations, pulpit, and reredos (1879). Drawings in the Fine Arts Library, University of Pennsylvania.

Christ P.E. Church, rectory and parish hall (1879). *AABN* 8(10 January 1880): 13.

Dr. J. Pierrepont Davis House, Woodland St. (1881; demolished). *AABN* 9(8 June 1881); *L'Architecture Américaine* (1886).

Soldiers and Sailors Monument (1882; never constructed). *AABN* 12(December 1882); drawing in the Connecticut Historical Society, Hartford.

Goodwin Laborer's Cottages (1883). *Building* 3(April 1885).

Bridge, Asylum Ave. (Withers and Dickson, 1886–1900; never constructed). Drawing at the Stowe-Day Foundation, Hartford.

Trinity P.E. Church, chapel, and parish house (1891). *AABN* 33(4 July 1891). Drawings in the Fine Arts Library, University of Pennsylvania.

HIGHLAND FALLS, N.Y.

First Presbyterian Church (1868), *CA*, Design IV; *BLDGS*, Design 6; *NAD*, 1871, No. 5; drawing in the Avery Library, Columbia University.

HUDSON, N.Y.

"Olana," Frederick Church House (consultant to Church with Vaux, 1870–1871). Plans in the possession of the Taconic State Park Commission.
Rev. E. S. Atwill House (1880). *AABN* 7(19 June 1890): 278.

HYDE PARK, N.Y.

James Roosevelt Estate, stable (1886). *Building* 5(3 July 1886): 1.

JERSEY CITY, N.J.

John F. Ward House (1884; present Heppenheimer House). *AABN* 15(19 February 1884).

LOUISVILLE, KY.

Church of the Advent (P.E.) (1887). *The Churchman* 55(19 March 1887); drawings in the Fine Arts Library, University of Pennsylvania.

MEMPHIS, TENN.

Calvary P.E. Church, altar and reredos (1884). Drawings in the Fine Arts Library, University of Pennsylvania.

MIDDLETOWN, CONN.

Berkeley Divinity School Library, Washington St. (1895; demolished). *The Churchman* 66(12 December 1896); drawing in the Fine Arts Library, University of Pennsylvania.

MONMOUTH BEACH, N.J.

"Whitecaps," James Dunbar House, Ocean Avenue (1880; demolished). *AABN* 10(29 October 1881).

MOUNTAIN PARK, N.J. (Llewellyn Park, N.J.)

John W. Burt House (in collaboration with Vaux, 1853–1856; never constructed). *VC*, vignette, p. 314.

NATCHEZ, MISS.

Trinity P.E. Church, parish house (1888). *The Churchman* 56(21 April 1888): 34.

NEW HAVEN, CONN.

Yale University Memorial Chapel (1866; never constructed), *CA*, Design XX; *NAD*, 1867, No. 44.
Yale–New Haven Hospital, Tompkins East Wing (1873).

NEW YORK, N.Y. (Manhattan, Roosevelt [former Blackwells], and Wards/Randalls Islands; see also Bronx and Brooklyn)

John A. C. Gray House, 40 Fifth Ave. (in collaboration with Vaux, 1853–56; demolished). *VC,* Design 29.

Robins Warehouse, 548 Washington St. (in collaboration with Vaux, 1853–56; demolished). *VC,* vignette, p. 170.

Central Park, boat landing (in collaboration with Vaux, 1861). *VC* (1864 edition), vignette, p. 9.

Rev. Henry Field House, 2 West 51st St. (Vaux, Withers and Co., 1866; demolished). *NAD,* 1866, No. 134.

Church of the Holy Trinity (P.E.), Madison Ave. and 42nd St. (1869; never constructed). *CA,* Design XVI.

Church of the Holy Trinity (P.E.), rectory (1869; demolished). *CA,* Design XVII; *BLDGS,* Design 12; drawing in the Avery Library, Columbia University.

Margaret H. Frothingham House, West 57th St. (Vaux, Withers and Co., 1869; demolished). *DNB.*

George B. Grinnell House, stable, West 157th St. (Vaux, Withers and Co., 1869). *DNB*

Central Park, mineral water house (Vaux, Withers and Co., ca. 1869). Cook's *Description of Central Park* (1869), pp. 192–93.

George B. Grinnell House, alterations, 28 West 156th St. (Vaux, Withers and Co., 1870). *DNB.*

Edward Gleason House, West 126th St. (Vaux, Withers and Co., 1871). *DNB.*

Trinity Cemetery, suspension bridge (Vaux, Withers and Co., 1871; demolished). Trinity Church Corporation minutes.

Mrs. A. G. Ullman Cast Iron Store, 448 Broome St. (1871). *DNB; BLDGS,* Design 4.

David Bonner House, alterations, West 140th St. (Vaux, Withers and Co., 1872; demolished). *DNB.*

B. F. Joslin House, alterations, West 29th St. (Vaux, Withers and Co., 1872; demolished). *DNB.*

Third Judicial District Courthouse, Prison and Fire Tower (Jefferson Market Courthouse), Sixth Ave. and West 10th St. (1874; present Jefferson Market Branch, New York Public Library). *BLDGS,* Designs 23 and 24; *NAD,* No. 53.

Jefferson Market, Sixth Ave. and Greenwich Ave. (1874; never constructed).

Study for City Prison and Courts (Vaux and Withers, 1874; never constructed). *The New York Sketch-book of Architecture* 1(April 1874).

Trinity P.E. Church, William Backhouse Astor Memorial Altar and Reredos (1876). *BLDGS,* Design 20; drawing in the Fine Arts Library, University of Pennsylvania.

Trinity P.E. Church, alterations to chancel (1876). *AABN* 3(2 February 1878).

New York City Produce Exchange, Broadway at Beaver St. (1881; never constructed). *AABN* 9(9 April 1881).

John A. C. Gray House, 77th Street and Columbus Ave. (1882; never constructed). In a letter to Olmsted dated 8 June 1882, Withers mentioned that he had prepared preliminary plans for Gray, who may have intended to erect more than one building on the large property he owned across the street from the American Museum of Natural History.

Citizens Bank of New York, alterations, 56–58 Bowery (1883; demolished).

Aaron Wright Store, 9 Bleecker St. (1884). *DNB*.

St. Ann's P.E. Church, alterations to chancel (1886). *Building* 5(10 July 1886).

Christ P.E. Church, Broadway at 71st St. (1886; never constructed). *Building* 5(10 July 1886).

City Mission Society Building, alterations, 38 Bleecker St. (1886; demolished).

Edward Patterson House, alterations, 19 East 45th St. (1887; demolished). *DNB*.

City of New York, insane asylum, alterations, Blackwell's Island (1887). *DNB*.

City of New York, one-story pavilion, Randall's Island (1887). *DNB*.

Chapel of the Good Shepherd (Episcopal Mission Society), Blackwell's Island (1888; present Good Shepherd Community Ecumenical Center). *AABN* 22(20 July 1889); drawing in the Fine Arts Library, University of Pennsylvania.

City of New York, Bellevue Hospital, alterations, East 26th St. (Withers and Dickson, 1888). *DNB*.

City of New York, Bellevue Hospital, alterations (Withers and Dickson, 1888). *DNB*.

City of New York, one-story frame hospital, Blackwell's Island (Withers and Dickson, 1888). *DNB*.

City of New York, brick dormitory, Blackwell's Island (Withers and Dickson, 1888). *DNB*.

City of New York, Bellevue Hospital, chapel, alterations (1888). *DNB*.

City of New York, two- and three-story brick dormitory, Ward's Island (Withers and Dickson, 1888). *DNB*.

City of New York, one-story brick asylum, Randall's Island (Withers and Dickson, 1888). *DNB*.

City of New York, Bellevue Hospital, morgue, alterations (Withers and Dickson, 1888). *DNB*.

St. Agnes Chapel (Trinity Church Corporation) (1889; competitive design, never constructed). *AABN* 25(8 June 1889): 272.

Cathedral of St. John the Divine (1889; competitive design, never constructed). *AABN* 5(2 November 1889).

Alexander MacKay-Smith House, alterations, 772 Madison Ave. (Withers and Dickson, 1889). *DNB.*

City of New York, laundry-kitchen building, alterations, Randall's Island (Withers and Dickson, 1889). *DNB.*

City of New York, one-story brick bath house, Blackwell's Island (Withers and Dickson, 1889). *DNB.*

City of New York, north hospital, alterations, Randall's Island (Withers and Dickson, 1889). *DNB.*

City of New York, gashouse, alterations, Randall's Island (Withers and Dickson, 1889), *DNB.*

City of New York, "The Lodge" lunatic asylum, workshops, alterations, Blackwell's Island (Withers and Dickson, 1889). *DNB.*

City of New York, retreat building, alterations, Blackwell's Island (Withers and Dickson, 1889). *DNB.*

City of New York, two-story brick almshouse, Blackwell's Island (Withers and Dickson, 1889). *DNB.*

City of New York, one-story brick boiler house, Blackwell's Island (Withers and Dickson, 1889). *DNB.*

City of New York, two-story brick hospital, Ward's Island (Withers and Dickson, 1889), *DNB.*

American Bible Society Building (Bible House), alterations, Astor Place (Withers and Dickson, 1889; demolished). *DNB.* Withers had his office in Bible House during the 1880s and 1890s and, for a time, he lived nearby at Colonnade Row.

Harlem Savings Bank, alterations, Third Ave. and 124th St. (Withers and Dickson, 1889). *DNB.*

St. Michael's P.E. Church (1890; competitive design, never constructed). A reproduction of the original drawing is in the Avery Library, Columbia University.

City of New York, Bellevue Hospital, Marquand Pavilion, alterations (Withers and Dickson, 1890). *DNB.*

City of New York, Bellevue Hospital, surgical amphitheatre, alterations (Withers and Dickson, 1890). *DNB.*

City of New York, one-story brick building, Blackwell's Island (Withers and Dickson, 1891; never constructed). *DNB.*

City of New York, bathrooms, alterations, Blackwell's Island (Withers and Dickson, 1891; never constructed). *DNB.*

City of New York, Harlem Hospital, manufactury and workshop (Withers and Dickson, 1891). *DNB.*

City of New York, two-story insane asylum, Blackwell's Island (Withers and Dickson, 1891). *DNB.*

City of New York, Bellevue Hospital, two-story brick building (Withers and Dickson, 1891). *DNB.*

Trinity Chapel (present Serbian Eastern Orthodox Cathedral of St. Sava) Swope Memorial Reredos (1892). Drawing in the Fine Arts Library, University of Pennsylvania.

City of New York, Strecker Memorial Laboratory, Blackwell's Island (Withers and Dickson, 1892). *DNB*. The Strecker Laboratory is one of the few nineteenth-century buildings still standing on Roosevelt Island.

City of New York, Bellevue Hospital, one-story brick kitchen (Withers and Dickson, 1892). *DNB*.

City of New York, Essex Street Prison, alterations (Withers and Dickson, 1893). *DNB*.

City of New York, Department of Public Charities and Corrections Building, alterations, 66 Third Ave. (Withers and Dickson, 1893; demolished). *DNB*.

City of New York, hospital, alterations, Blackwell's Island (Withers and Dickson, 1893). *DNB*.

City of New York, Bellevue Hospital, wall and gates (Withers and Dickson, 1894). *DNB*.

Church of the Transfiguration (P.E.), Zabriske Memorial Altar and Reredos (1895). Drawing in the Fine Arts Library, University of Pennsylvania.

City of New York, Harlem Hospital, alterations (Withers and Dickson, 1895). *DNB*.

City of New York, Harlem Hospital, stable, alterations (Withers and Dickson, 1895). *DNB*.

City of New York, temporary frame shed, Gouvernor St. (Withers and Dickson, 1895). *DNB*.

Church of the Transfiguration, lych-gate (1896). *The Churchman* 74(10 October 1896): 441–42.

City of New York, brick kitchen, Blackwell's Island (Withers and Dickson, 1896). *DNB*.

City of New York Prison ("The Tombs"), Center and Leonard Sts. (1896; demolished). *DNB*.

City of New York, temporary prison, alterations, Center, Thompson, Elm, and Franklin Sts. (Withers and Dickson, 1896). *DNB*.

City of New York, four-story ventilating and water tower, Blackwell's Island (Withers and Dickson, 1896). *DNB*.

City of New York, four-and-a-half-story brick and iron water tower, Blackwell's Island (Withers and Dickson, 1896). *DNB*.

City of New York, Department of Public Charities and Corrections Building, Third Ave. and Eleventh St., office alterations (Withers and Dickson, 1896). *DNB*.

City of New York, Bellevue Hospital, two-story brick boiler and laundry house (Withers and Dickson, 1896). *DNB*.

City of New York, Bellevue Hospital, two-story isolated hospital (Withers and Dickson, 1896). *DNB*.

City of New York, Bellevue Hospital, two-story brick erysipelas hospital (Withers and Dickson, 1896–98). *DNB.*

Trinity Chapel (present Serbian Eastern Orthodox Cathedral of St. Sava), Cotheal Pulpit (1897). *The Churchman* 77(26 February 1898): 317–18.

City of New York, Bellevue Hospital, two-story iron and steel office building (Withers and Dickson, 1897). *DNB.*

City of New York, Bellevue Hospital, drug department building, alterations (Withers and Dickson, 1897). *DNB.*

City of New York, Bellevue Hospital, five-story stone, brick, and terra-cotta stable and ambulance house (Withers and Dickson, 1897; never constructed). *Engineering Record* 37(18 December 1897): 65.

City of New York, temporary prison, alterations, Center, Elm, and Franklin Sts. (Withers and Dickson, 1897; never constructed). *DNB.*

City of New York Bellevue Hospital, one-story morgue (Withers and Dickson, 1897). *DNB.*

City of New York, brick and stone ferry house, Blackwell's Island (Withers and Dickson, 1897). *DNB*

NEWBURGH, N.Y. (see also Balmville, N.Y.)

Daniel Ryan House (in collaboration with Vaux, 1853–56; never constructed). *Harper's,* Design III; *VC,* Design 1.

Rev. Edward J. O'Reilly House, Grand St. (in collaboration with Vaux, 1853–56). *Harper's,* Design IV; *VC,* Design 5.

Halsey Stevens House, Grand St. (in collaboration with Vaux, 1853–56). *VC,* Design 10.

Nathan Reeve House (in collaboration with Vaux, 1853–56; never constructed). *Harper's,* Design XX; *VC,* Design 22.

James Walker Fowler House, Limestone Hill (in collaboration with Vaux, 1854; demolished or never constructed). *VC,* Design 13; drawings and plans in the New York Historical Society.

First Presbyterian Church (1857; present Calvary Presbyterian Church). *CA,* Design XVIII.

St. Paul's P.E. Church (1860; present Seventh Day Adventist Newburgh Tabernacle). This is the first church Withers designed for the parish. It later served as the Sunday School building when the larger edifice was erected in 1864.

George Washington Greene House, Carpenter Ave. (1860). *AMJ* 2(17 March 1860): 191.

Professor G. B. Hackley House, Carpenter Ave. (1860). *AMJ* 2(17 March 1860): 191.

Dr. John Heard House, Carpenter Ave. (1860). *AMJ* 2(17 March 1860): 191.

Rev. Caleb S. Henry House, Carpenter Ave. (1860). *AMJ* 2(17 March 1860): 191.

Capt. James Hooker Strong House, Carpenter Ave. (1860). *AMJ* 2(17
   March 1860): 191.
St. Paul's P.E. Church (1864; present Seventh Day Adventist Newburgh
   Tabernacle). *CA*, Design XV; *NAD*, 1865, No. 128.
Quassaick Bank (1864; never constructed). *NAD*, 1865, No. 124.
Eugene Brewster House, 264 Grand St. (1865). Plans in the possession of
   Oliver Shipp.
Newburgh Savings Bank, Smith and Second Sts. (1866; demolished). *NAD*,
   1867, No. 40.
St. George P.E. Church, proposed remodeling (1885; never carried out).
   AABN 17(2 January 1886).

NEWPORT, R.I.

St. John the Evangelist (Zabriske Memorial) P.E. Church (1893). *AABN*,
   LXXVIII(1 November 1902); drawings and plans in the Fine Arts Library, University of Pennsylvania.

PORTSMOUTH, N.H.

Admiral Enoch G. Parrott Monument, St. John's P.E. Church (1880). *AABN*
   8(10 July 1880): 23.

POUGHKEEPSIE, N.Y.

Hudson River State Hospital (1867). *NAD* 1868, No. 79; *BLDGS*, Design 18.
St. Paul's P.E. Church, schoolhouse (1882). *AABN* 11(24 June 1882).
Vassar Brothers' Hospital (1882). *Building* 3(August 1885).
Frank Hasbrouck House, Market St. (1885). *AABN* 20(2 July 1887).
Hudson River State Hospital, additions (1886). *RG*, 3 November 1886,
   p. 1390.

RIVERSIDE, ILL.

Community Church (1869, extant but altered). *CA*, vignette to Design VII.
Block of Stores (1870). *BLDGS*, Design 1.

ROME, N.Y.

Central New York Institute for Deaf Mutes, alterations (Withers and
   Dickson, 1887). *Sanitary Engineer and Contract Reporter* 16(23 October
   1887): 592.
Central New York Institute for Deaf Mutes, new edifice (Withers and
   Dickson, 1888). *Engineering and Building Record* 17(7 January 1888): 95.

RONDOUT, N.Y.

"Clovertop," J. S. McEntee House, alterations (1874; demolished). Entry in
   the diary of Jervis McEntee, New York Historical Society.

ROSLYN HARBOR, LONG ISLAND, N.Y.

"Clovercroft," Mrs. Fanny B. Godwin House, alterations (Vaux, Withers and Co., 1869). Plans in the Bryant Library, Roslyn, N.Y.

SHREVEPORT, LA.

St. Mark's P.E. Church (1860; demolished). *CA,* Design III.

SUGAR HILL, N.H.

St. Matthew's P.E. Church (1893).

SUMMIT, N.J.

Calvary P.E. Church (1872; demolished). *CA,* Design IX.

TROY, N.Y.

Hall-Rice Building (1871). Plans in the possession of John R. Pattison, Troy.

S. M. Vail Houses, Congress St. (Withers and Dickson, 1888–89). Plans in the library of Russell Sage College, Troy.

WASHINGTON, D.C.

President's House, Gallaudet College (1867). Drawings and plans in the Gallaudet Memorial Library, Gallaudet College.

Professor's House (House No. 1), Gallaudet College (1867). Drawings and plans in the Gallaudet Memorial Library, Gallaudet College.

Chapel Hall, Gallaudet College (1868). *BLDGS,* Design 22; *CA,* Vignette to Design IV; *NAD,* 1869, No. 69; drawings and plans in the Gallaudet Memorial Library, Gallaudet College.

Chapel Hall, terrace, Gallaudet College (1870). Plan in the Gallaudet Memorial Library, Gallaudet College.

Professor's House (House A) (1874). *BLDGS,* Design 15; Bicknell's *Wooden and Brick Buildings,* Design 31; drawings and plans in the Gallaudet Memorial Library, Gallaudet College.

Professor's House (House B), Gallaudet College (1874). Plans in the Gallaudet Memorial Library, Gallaudet College.

College Hall, Gallaudet College (1875). *BLDGS,* Design 21; *NAD,* 1877, No. 72; drawings and plans in the Gallaudet Memorial Library, Gallaudet College.

Gymnasium, Gallaudet College (1880). Drawings and plans in the Gallaudet Memorial Library, Gallaudet College, and the Avery Library, Columbia University.

Commodore J. H. Upshur House, 1416 Rhode Island Ave. (1884; present headquarters of the Society of the Daughters of the War of 1812). *AABN* 15(1 March 1884): 108.

Kendall School, Gallaudet College (1885). Plans in the Gallaudet Memorial Library, Gallaudet College.

WEEHAWKEN, N.J.

Water tower for the Hackensack Water Company (1883). *AABN* 14(8 September 1883): 114.

Gate House for the Hackensack Water Works (1883). *Engineering News and American Contract Journal* 16(6 November 1886): 292.

WILKES-BARRE, PA.

A. T. McClintock House, alterations, 44 South River St. (Vaux, Withers and Co., 1863; present McClintock Hall, Wilkes College). Plans in the Wilkes College Library.

S. Leonard Thurlow House, River and South Sts. (1874; present Kirby Hall, Wilkes College). *BLDGS,* Design 2.

WORCESTER, MASS.

H. H. Chamberlain House, Woodland Ave. (in collaboration with Vaux, 1853–56; demolished). *Harper's,* Design IX; *VC,* Design 19. Prior to its destruction, the house served as the residence of the president of Clark University. Miscellaneous fixtures from the building have been preserved in the Worcester Historical Society and the Smithsonian Institution.

Thomas Earle House (in collaboration with Vaux, 1853–56; demolished). *VC,* Design 28.

YONKERS, N.Y.

J. Foster Jenkins House, High St. (1886). *DNB.* Withers lived here during the last years of his life. Jenkins was his son-in-law.

WORKS FOR WHICH DOCUMENTATION IS INCOMPLETE

Design for a Roomy Country House, Orange County, N.Y. (in collaboration with Vaux, 1853–56). *VC,* vignette, p. 304.

Suburban House with a Curvilinear Roof, Worcester, Mass. (in collaboration with Vaux, 1853–56). *VC,* Design 23.

Study for a Square House (in collaboration with Vaux, 1853–56). *VC,* vignette, p. 268.

Monument for a Mr. Buchanan, Newburgh, N.Y. (in collaboration with Vaux, 1853–56). *VC,* vignette, p. 318. A marker that nearly duplicates the headstone in this design can be found on the grave of Jaspar Cropsey (not the painter) in St. George Cemetery in Newburgh. Cropsey died in 1854.

Study for a Public Museum and Library (Vaux, Withers and Co., 1865). *NAD* 1865, No. 120.

Suggestion for a Park Entrance (1869). *NAD* 1869, No. 79; *The American Builder* 2(July 1869): 138. This may have been intended for Central Park.

Design for a City Church (1875). *The New York Sketch-book of Architecture* 2(April 1875).

House with a Brick and Stone Bay Window (1884). *Building* 3(December 1884).

Design for a Church and Schools (1886). *Building* 5(21 August 1886).

Proposed Church and School House, Connecticut (1888). *Fourth Annual Exhibition of the Architectural League of New York, 1888–1889*, No. 127.

New Spire for an Unidentified Church (Withers and Dickson, ca. 1890). Drawing in the Fine Arts Library, University of Pennsylvania.

Monument for Louisa M. Barker. *CA*, vignette, p. xxii; drawing in the Avery Library, Columbia University.

Unidentified Wooden Villa. Drawing in the Avery Library, Columbia University.

Gordon House, Newburgh, N.Y. Withers's daughter Margaret remembered her father saying that one of his best works was a house in Newburgh belonging to a Mr. Gordon. Old atlases show a large estate in Balmville (to the north of Newburgh) called Stony Wood owned by George Gordon and later by Reginald Gordon. Undoubtedly, this was the property to which Margaret Withers was referring. Today Stony Wood is a neighborhood of modern suburban houses where no trace remains of a nineteenth-century mansion.

BUILDINGS FROM WITHERS'S *CHURCH ARCHITECTURE* THAT CANNOT BE IDENTIFIED

> Design I
> Vignette to Design I
> Design II
> Design VI
> Design VIII
> Vignette to Design VIII
> Design X
> Design XIV
> Design XVII (1859)
> Design XIX
> Vignette to Design XIX, "View of Mission Chapel
>   and Schools"
> Vignette to Design XXII, "View of School-house
>   with Windows in Gables"
> Design XIII, Schoolhouse (1866).

❦BIBLIOGRAPHY❦

THE FOLLOWING BIBLIOGRAPHY, of necessity, is composed primarily of nineteenth-century sources. It contains entries that deal with specific works or furnish biographical information or provide understanding of Withers's place among the architects of his times. Works that may have formed Withers's taste have not been included, but have been referred to in the text and notes.

All buildings mentioned in the titles of articles, unless otherwise noted, are by Withers. Articles in the periodical bibliography have been annotated when the nature of the material they contain about Withers is not evident from the title.

BOOKS, CATALOGS, AND GENERAL WORKS

Addison, Agnes. *Romanticism and the Gothic Revival.* New York: Gordian Press, 1967.

American Architectural Drawings. 5 vols. Philadelphia: Philadelphia Chapter of the American Institute of Architects, 1969.

Andrews, Wayne. *American Gothic: Its Origins, Its Trials, Its Triumphs.* New York: Random House, 1975.

Atwood, Albert W. *Gallaudet College, Its First One Hundred Years.* Washington, D. C.: Gallaudet College, 1964.

Avery Index to Architectural Periodicals. Boston: G. K. Hall, 1963.

Baedeker, Karl. *The United States.* Leipzig: Baedeker, 1893. Withers's Jefferson Market Courthouse received an asterisk, the mark of commendation.

Bicknell, Amos J., comp. *Cottage and Villa Architecture.* New York: A. J. Bicknell, 1878. Withers seems to have maintained a close professional relationship with Bicknell, who published Withers's *Church Architecture* and included examples of the architect's work in his popular architectural anthologies.

———. *Detail, Cottage and Constructive Architecture.* New York: A. J. Bicknell, 1873.

———. *Specimen Book of One Hundred Architectural Designs.* New York: A. J. Bicknell, 1878.

———. *Street, Store and Bank Fronts.* New York: A. J. Bicknell, 1878.

———. *Wooden and Brick Buildings with Details.* 2 vols. New York: A. J. Bicknell, 1875.

Brault, Elie. *Les Architects par leurs oeuvres.* Paris: Librairie Renouard, 1893.

Burdett, Henry C. *Hospitals and Asylums of the World.* 4 vols. London: Churchill, 1893.

Burnham, Alan. *New York Landmarks.* Middletown, Conn.: Wesleyan University Press, 1963.

Burr, Nelson. *Christ Church Parish and Cathedral.* Hartford: Church Missions, 1942.

Cook, Clarence: *Description of the New York Central Park*. New York: D. Huntington, 1869.

Dix, John A., comp., and Lewis, Leicester C., ed. *A History of the Parish of Trinity Church in the City of New York*. New York: Columbia University Press, 1950.

Dixon, Roger, and Muthesius, Stefan. *Victorian Architecture*. New York: Oxford University Press, 1978.

Downing, Andrew Jackson. *Cottage Residences*. Edited by George Harney. New York: G. P. Wiley, 1873.

Early, James. *Romanticism and American Architecture*. New York: A. S. Barnes, 1965.

Eastlake, Charles L. *A History of the Gothic Revival*. London: Murray, 1872. (Reprinted 1975 in Watkins Glen, N.Y. by American Life Foundation.)

Fawcett, Jane, ed. *Seven Victorian Architects*. University Park, Pa.: Pennsylvania State University Press, 1977.

Fergusson, James. *History of the Modern Styles of Architecture*. 3 vols. Revised by Robert Kerr. London: John Murray, 1893. Withers is considered as an important representative of the Gothic Revival in America.

Ferriday, Peter, ed. *Victorian Architecture*. Philadelphia: Lippincott, 1964.

First Presbyterian Church of Newburgh, New York. *Centennial Celebration of the First Presbyterian Church*. Newburgh, N.Y.: Journal Publishing Co., 1884.

Foerster, Bernd. *Architecture Worth Saving in Rensselaer County, New York*. Troy, N.Y.: Rensselaer Polytechnic Institute, 1965.

Garrigan, Kristine O. *Ruskin on Architecture: His Thought and Influence*. Madison: University of Wisconsin Press, 1973.

Germann, Georg. *Gothic Revival in Europe and Britain: Sources, Influences and Ideas*. Translated by Gerald Onn.

Cambridge, Mass.: M.I.T. Press, 1972.

Gillmore, Quincy A. *Official Report of the Siege and Reduction of Fort Pulaski, Georgia, February, March, and April, 1862*. New York: Van Nostrand 1862. Withers's major contribution as a lieutenant in the New York Volunteer Engineers during the Civil War was assisting in the investment of Fort Pulaski.

Girouard, Mark. *Sweetness and Light. The 'Queen Anne' Movement, 1860–1900*. London: Oxford University Press, 1977.

———. *The Victorian Country House*. London: Oxford University Press, 1971.

Gloag, John. *Victorian Taste: Some Social Aspects of Architecture and Industrial Design from 1820–1900*. New York: Harper and Row, 1962.

Hasbrouck, Frank. *The History of Dutchess County, New York*. 2 vols. Poughkeepsie: Mathieu, 1909. Hasbrouck, a friend and patron of Withers, provides information about people and commissions with which Withers was associated in the Hudson Valley.

Henry, Caleb S. *Dr. Oldham at Greystones and His Talk There*. New York: Appleton, 1860.

Hersey, George L. *High Victorian Gothic, a Study in Associationism*. Baltimore: Johns Hopkins University Press, 1972.

History of Real Estate, Building, and Architecture in New York City. New York: Record and Guide, 1898.

Hitchcock, Henry-Russell. *The Architecture of H. H. Richardson and His Times*. Rev. ed. Cambridge, Mass.: M.I.T. Press, 1966.

———. *Architecture of the Nineteenth and Twentieth Centuries*. 4th ed. rev. Baltimore: Penguin Books, 1977.

———. *Early Victorian Architecture in Britain*. 2 vols. New Haven, Conn.: Yale University Press, 1954.

———. *Modern Architecture, Romanticism and Re-integration.* New York: Payson and Clarke, 1929.

———. *Richardson as a Victorian Architect.* Northampton, Mass.: Smith College Press, 1967.

House, H. H., comp. *The Sherborne Register, 1823–1892.* London: Clowes, 1893. Withers attended King Edward's School, Sherborne, from 1839 through 1843.

Hurd, Thomas. *Institutional Care of the Insane.* 4 vols. Baltimore: Johns Hopkins University Press, 1919. Hurd deals especially well with Withers's Hudson River State Hospital.

In Memorium, Joseph Howland, 1834–1886. New York: Privately printed, 1886. Howland was a friend and patron of Withers, who named one of his sons after him.

Jordan, James Furneaux. *Victorian Architecture.* London: Penguin Books, 1966.

Karolik Collection of American Water Colors and Drawings, 1800–1975. Boston: Museum of Fine Arts, 1962. Withers was an accomplished watercolorist. His perspective view of the Kimball House is in the Karolik Collection.

King, Moses. *King's Handbook of New York City.* New York: Moses King, 1892.

Landau, Sarah B. *Edward T. and William A. Potter, American Victorian Architects.* New York: Garland Publishing, Inc., 1978.

Leiby, Adrian C. *The Hackensack Water Company, 1869–1969.* New York: Rudge, 1969.

Lewis, Arnold, and Morgan, Keith, eds. *American Victorian Architecture: A Survey of the 70's and 80's in Contemporary Photographs.* New York: Dover, 1975. A modern reprint of *L'Architecture Américaine.* Paris: André, Daly fils Cie, 1886.

Linstrum, Derek. *The Wyatt Family.* Farnborough, Hampshire: Gregg International, 1974.

Loth, Calder, and Sadler, Julius Trousdale, Jr. *The Only Proper Style: Gothic Architecture in America.* Boston: New York Graphic Society, 1975.

Lynes, Russell. *The Tastemakers.* New York: Grosset and Dunlop, 1972.

Maas, John. *The Victorian Home in America.* New York: Hawthorne, 1972.

McLaughlin, Charles, and Beveridge, Charles, eds. *The Papers of Frederick Law Olmsted: The Formative Years, 1822–1852.* Vol. 1. The Papers of Frederick Law Olmsted. Baltimore: Johns Hopkins University Press, 1977.

Morgan, Thisbe. *St. Mark's Protestant Episcopal Church. Shreveport, Louisiana.* Shreveport: Castle, 1957.

Mumford, Lewis. *The Brown Decades.* New York: Harcourt Brace and Co., 1931.

National Academy of Design. *Winter Exhibition Catalogues, 1862–1877.* New York: By the Academy. Withers was one of the small group of architects who exhibited regularly at the National Academy of Design.

National Register of Historic Places. Washington, D.C.: U.S. Department of Interior, 1969.

New York City. *Proceedings of the Board of Aldermen.* Vol. 144 (1876). Reports troubles surrounding the construction of the Jefferson Market Courthouse.

New York City Department of Public Charities and Corrections. *Annual Report of the New York City Asylum for the Insane for the Year 1889.* New York: By the Department, 1894. Discusses the Central Islip, Long Island, asylum.

New York Historical Society. *National Academy of Design Exhibition Record, 1826–1860.* 2 vols. New York: By the Society, 1943.

New York Illustrated. New York: Appleton, 1881.

Nutt, John J. *Newburgh: Institutions, Indus-*

tries and Leading Citizens. Newburgh: Ritchie and Hull, 1891. The most complete history of the city where Withers worked from 1852 until 1863, this work contains valuable information about several of his commissions.

O'Gorman, James. *The Architecture of Frank Furness.* Philadelphia: Pennsylvania Academy of Fine Arts, 1973.

Olmsted, Frederick Law, Jr., and Kimball, Theodora, eds. *Frederick Law Olmsted, Landscape Architect, 1822–1903.* 2 vols. New York: G. P. Putnam and Sons, 1922.

Pierson, William H., Jr. *Technology and the Picturesque, The Corporate and Early Gothic Styles.* Vol. 2, pt. 1. *American Buildings and Their Architects.* New York: Doubleday, 1978.

Riverside Improvement Company. *Riverside.* Riverside, Ill.: By the Company, 1871. Withers designed the community church and store block, later known as the Hetty Green Block.

Roe, Mary A. *Edward Payson Roe: Reminiscences of His Life.* New York: Dodd, Mead, and Co., 1899. Withers designed the Rev. Roe's First Presbyterian Church in Highland Falls, N.Y., a building the minister-author sentimentally included in his novel *Barriers Burned Away.*

Roper, Laura Wood. *FLO: A Biography of Frederick Law Olmsted.* Baltimore: Johns Hopkins University Press, 1973.

Ross, Isabel. *Through the Lich Gate.* New York: Payson, 1931.

Ruttenber, Edward M. *The History of the County of Orange, New York.* Newburgh, N.Y.: Ruttenber, 1875. Another work containing information about patrons and projects in the Newburgh area.

St. Luke's Episcopal Church, Altoona, Pennsylvania. *Centennial Yearbook 1856–1956.* Altoona: By the Church, 1956.

Salmagundi Club and American Black and White Society. *Illustrated Catalogue Eighth Annual Black and White Exhibition.* New York: Privately printed, 1886. Withers exhibited several drawings, including renderings of the Jefferson Market Courthouse, the Hartford Soldiers and Sailors Monument, and the Weehawken Water Tower.

Schuyler, Montgomery. *American Architecture and Other Writings by Montgomery Schuyler.* Edited by William H. Jordy and Ralph Coe. 2 vols. Cambridge, Mass.: Harvard University Press, Belknap Press, 1961.

Shepherd, Massey H. *History of St. James Episcopal Church.* Chicago: By the Church, 1934.

Shinn, George W. *Notable Episcopal Churches.* New York: Moses King, 1889. Shinn included Withers's St. Thomas P.E. Church, Hanover, N.H.

Silver, Nathan. *Lost New York.* New York: Schocken, 1971.

Soule, Sherrod. *Francis Goodwin of Hartford.* Hartford, Conn.: Privately printed, 1939. Goodwin, an enthusiast of Gothic architecture who had a high opinion of Withers, was largely responsible for having him design Trinity P.E. Church in Hartford.

Stanton, Phoebe. *The Gothic Revival and American Church Architecture, An Episode in Taste, 1840–1856.* Baltimore: Johns Hopkins University Press, 1968.

———. *Pugin.* New York: Viking, 1971.

Stevenson, Elizabeth. *Park Maker: A Life of Frederick Law Olmsted.* New York: Macmillan Co., 1977.

Stuart, Suzette G. *Illustrated Guide Book with Historical Sketch of the Little Church Around the Corner.* New York:

Church of the Transfiguration, 1963.

Unrau, John. *Looking at Architecture with Ruskin,* Toronto: University of Toronto Press, 1978.

Upjohn, Everard M. *Richard Upjohn, Architect and Churchman.* New York: Columbia University Press, 1939. Reprint. New York: Da Capo Press, 1968.

Van Brunt, Henry. *Architecture and Society: Selected Essays of Henry Van Brunt.* Edited by W. A. Coles. Cambridge, Mass.: Harvard University Press, Belknap Press, 1969.

Van Zanten, David. *The Architectural Polychromy of the 1830s.* New York: Garland Publishing, 1977

Vaux, Calvert. *Villas and Cottages: A Series of Designs Prepared for Execution in the United States.* New York: Harper and Brothers, 1857. Revised edition appeared in 1864 with later printing in 1867, 1872, and 1874. (Reprinted in 1968 and 1970: New York: Da Capo Press and Dover Publications, respectively.)

Waite, Diana S. *New York City Architecture: Selections from the Historic American Buildings Survey, Number Seven.* Washington, D.C.: National Park Service, 1969.

White, James F. *The Cambridge Movement: The Ecclesiologists and the Gothic Revival.* Cambridge: Cambridge University Press, 1962.

White, Norvel, and Willensky, Elliott, eds. *American Institute of Architects Guide to New York City.* 2d ed. revised. New York: Macmillan Co., 1978.

Withers, Frederick C. *Buildings Erected from the Designs of F. C. Withers, Architect, New York.* New York: G. P. Putnam and Sons, 1877. This collection of perspective drawings is one of the most valuable documents for reconstructing Withers's career. The only copy known to exist is in the American Architectural Archive, Greenwich, Conn.

————. *Church Architecture.* New York: A. J. Bicknell, 1873.

Wodehouse, Lawrence. *American Architects from the Civil War to the First World War.* Detroit: Gale Research Company, 1976.

Wright, F. A., ed. *Architectural Studies.* New York: Comstock, 1886.

Wright, John. *Some Notable Altars in the Church of England and the American Episcopal Church.* New York: Macmillan Co., 1908.

PERIODICALS

A.K.H.B. "Concerning Villas and Cottages." *Frazer's Magazine* 58(December 1858): 689–705. A British writer's view of American domestic architecture as represented by the works in *Villas and Cottages.*

"Altar and Reredos, St. Luke's Episcopal Church, Brooklyn, New York, Mr. F. C. Withers, Architect." *The American Architect and Building News,* 19(9 January 1886): 8 (ill.).

"Altar and Reredos, Trinity Church, New York." *The Building News* 31(22 September 1876): 24.

"Alterations in Trinity Church, New York." *The American Architect and Building News* 3(2 February 1878): 42 (ill.).

"American Architecture." *The Architect* 4(6 August 1870): 72–73. An English view of American architecture at the peak of Withers's career.

"Architectural Competition for a Church and Adjoining Buildings." *Engineering and Building Record* 18(28 July 1888): 49. Notice of the competition design for St. Agnes Chapel, New York City.

"Architectural Designs in the Academy."

The New Path 2(July 1865): 114–15. The Tioronda School, built for Joseph Howland, is reviewed.

"Architectural Drawings in the National Academy of Design." *Architects' and Mechanics' Journal* 2(2 June 1860): 81. Discusses Withers's drawings of the Dutch Reformed Church, Beacon, N.Y., and the F. Deming House, Newburgh, N.Y.

"Architectural Drawings in the National Academy of Design." *Architects' and Mechanics' Journal* 2(16 June 1860): 101. Discusses St. Michael's P.E. Church, Germantown, and Tioronda, Joseph Howland's house in Beacon, N.Y.

"Astor Memorial." *The American Builder* 7(July 1877): 150.

"Best Ten Buildings in the United States." *The American Architect and Building News* 17(13 June 1885): 282.

"Best Ten Buildings in This Country." *The American Architect and Building News* 17(11 April 1885): 178–79. In a national poll of architects, Withers's Jefferson Market Courthouse placed fifth.

Bloor, Alfred Janson. "Address to the Tenth Annual Convention of the American Institute of Architects. Philadelphia, October, 1876." *The American Architect and Building News* 2(24 March 1877): supplement. Bloor comments on the Jefferson Market Courthouse.

"Board of Aldermen." *The New York Times,* 19 December 1876, p. 2. Contains information about the Jefferson Market Courthouse.

"Brick and Stone Bay Window with Wooden Gable Over. Drawn from the Working Drawings. F. C. Withers, Architect, New York." *Building* 3(December 1884): ill.

"Brooklyn." *Record and Guide,* 20 December 1890, p. 837. Notice of the James Edwards House.

Brumbaugh, Richard I. "The American House in the Victorian Period." *Journal of the Society of Architectural Historians* 2(January 1942): 27–42. Discusses *Villas and Cottages.*

"Builders. Brooklyn." *Record and Guide,* 28 April 1894, p. 686. Notice of alterations to St. Michael's P.E. Church.

"Building Intelligence." *The American Architect and Building News* 2(23 June 1877); v. Contains information about the Jefferson Market Courthouse.

"Building Intelligence." *The American Architect and Building News* 7(19 June 1880): 278. Contains information about the Reverend Atwill House, Hudson, N.Y.

"Building Intelligence." *The American Architect and Building News* 7(10 July 1880): 23. Contains information about the Admiral Parrott monument in Portsmouth, N.H.

"Building Intelligence." *The American Architect and Building News* 15(1 March 1884): 108. Contains information about the Commodore J. H. Upshur House in Washington, D.C.

"Building Intelligence." *Engineering and Building Record* 17(7 January 1888): 95. Notice of the new building for the Central New York Institute for Deaf Mutes, Rome, N.Y.

"Building Intelligence." *Engineering Record* 37(18 December 1897): 65. Notice of the proposed stable and ambulance house for Bellevue Hospital.

"Building Intelligence." *Sanitary Engineer and Contract Reporter* 16(22 October 1887): 592. Notice of alterations to the Central New York Institute for Deaf Mutes, Rome, N.Y.

"Building News: Hudson River Insane Hospital." *The American Builder* 2(April 1869): 91–92.

"Building News Supplement." *Building* 5(3 July 1886): 1. Mentions the James Roosevelt stable at Hyde Park, the J. Foster Jenkins House, Yonkers. Jenkins was Withers's son-in-law.

"Building Progress." *The Architects' and Mechanics' Journal* 2(17 March 1869): 191–92. A valuable reference for Withers's early career in Newburgh.

"Building Projected." *Record and Guide,* 30 May 1891, p. 889.

"Chapel of the Good Shepherd, Blackwell's Island, New York." *The Churchman* 57(2 June 1888): 678.

"Chapel of the Good Shepherd, Blackwell's Island, New York, Mr. F. C. Withers, Architect." *The American Architect and Building News* 26(20 July 1889): 27 (ill.).

"Charges Against Mr. Porter." *The New York Times,* 20 December 1876, p. 8. Concerns the construction of the Jefferson Market Courthouse.

"Chetwood." "Correspondence: Christ Church." *The American Architect and Building News* 6(13 September 1879): 85. Concerns Withers's remodeling of Christ Church, Hartford, Conn.

————. "Correspondence: Christ Church." *The American Architect and Building News* 8(10 January 1880): 13.

————. "Correspondence: Church Alterations." *The American Architect and Building News* 5(8 March 1879): 78. Concerns the Christ Church, Hartford, Conn., project.

"Church Architecture in America." *The Building News* 25(5 September 1873): 245. An unfavorable British review of Withers's *Church Architecture.*

"Church of the Advent, Louisville, Kentucky." *The Churchman* 55(19 March 1887): 311 (ill.).

"Church of the Transfiguration, New York City: Recent Additions and Improvements." *The Churchman* 74 (10 October 1896): 441–42.

Columbia Institution for the Deaf and Dumb. Annual Reports to the Secretary of the Interior, 1866–1886.

Washington, D.C.: U.S. Government Printing Office. The annual reports contain building descriptions, accounts of construction progress, and other information about the structures Withers designed for Edward Miner Gallaudet.

"Columbia Institution for the Deaf and Dumb, Washington, D.C." *The Building News* 31(28 July 1876): 74 (ill.). Deals with College Hall.

"Columbia Institution for the Deaf and Dumb, Washington, D.C., Mr. F. C. Withers, Architect." *The American Architect and Building News* 1(18 March 1876): 93 (ill). Gives information about College Hall.

"Competitive Design for the Cathedral of St. John the Divine, New York, Mr. F. C. Withers ('Patmos'), Architect," *The American Architect and Building News* 26 (2 November 1889): 206 (ills.).

"Competitive Design for a City Church." *The New York Sketch-book of Architecture* 2(December 1875). This design, prepared for St. James P.E. Church in Brooklyn, Withers considered one of his best.

"Competitive Design for Church, Clergy-House and Schools for Trinity Corporation, New York, N.Y., Mr. F. C. Withers, Architect, N.Y." *The American Architect and Building News* 25(8 June 1889): 272 (ill.). This was the design for St. Agnes Chapel.

"Competitive Design for the New York Produce Exchange, Mr. F. C. Withers, Architect." *The American Architect and Building News* 9(9 April 1881): 174 (ill.).

"Connecticut: Christ Church." *The Churchman* 40(3 January 1880): 9.

"Conversazione of the New York Chapter A.I.A." *The American Architect and Building News* 2(3 March 1877): 70. Contains comments about the Jefferson Market Courthouse.

Cook, Clarence. "Architecture in America." *The North American Review* 135(November 1882): 243–53. This article helps to assess Withers's position following the decline of the Victorian Gothic style.

"Correspondence: The Astor Reredos." *The American Architect and Building News* 2(7 July 1877): 218.

"Correspondence: An Audacious Claim for Extras." *The American Architect and Building News* 5(1 February 1879): 37–38. Concerns the Jefferson Market Courthouse scandals.

"Correspondence: New Churches." *The American Architect and Building News* 2(22 June 1877): 198. Gives information about the Astor Reredos in Trinity Church.

"Correspondence: New York." *The American Architect and Building News* 1(26 August 1876): 279. Gives information about the Astor Reredos.

"Correspondence: New York." *The American Architect and Building News* 2(27 January 1877): 29–30. Contains comments about the Jefferson Market Courthouse.

"Correspondence: The Third District Court-house Investigations." *The American Architect and Building News* 2(10 February 1877): 45.

"Correspondence: The Trinity Church Reredos." *The American Architect and Building News* 2(8 June 1877): 182.

"Costly Courthouse," *The New York Herald,* 8 May 1877, p. 5. Comments on the high cost of the Jefferson Market Courthouse.

"Courthouse, Bell Tower, and Prison: Third Judicial District, New York, U.S.A." *The Building News* 29(9 July 1875): 36 (ills.).

"Courthouse, Bell Tower, and Prison, Third Judicial District, New York, Messrs. F. C. Withers and C. Vaux, Architects." *The New York Sketch-book of Architecture* 2(June 1875). A slightly revised version of the Jefferson Market Courthouse appears

here from the illustration published in *The Sketch-book* in July 1874.

"Description of a Country House Designed by F. C. Withers, Architect, Newburgh, on the Hudson," *The Horticulturist* 12(May 1857): 230–32. An account of the D. M. Clarkson residence, Balmville.

"Design for Church and Schools. F. C. Withers, Architect." *Building* 5 (21 August 1886): 91. Probably Withers design for Christ P.E. Church, New York City.

"Design for a City Church, Mr. F. C. Withers, Architect." *The New York Sketch-book of Architecture* 2(April 1875).

"Design for Court House, Third Judicial District, New York." *The New York Sketch-book of Architecture* 1(July 1874). This is the first published account and drawing of the Jefferson Market Courthouse.

"Design for St. George Church and Tower, Newburgh, New York, Mr. F. C. Withers, Architect." *The American Architect and Building News* 19(2 January 1886): 6 (ill.).

"Design for Soldiers' Monument, Hartford, Connecticut, Mr. F. C. Withers, Architect." *The American Architect and Building News* 12(9 December 1882): 279 (ill.). Presented is a proposed design for a Gothic triumphal arch that proved too costly to erect.

"Design for Yale College Memorial Chapel." *The American Builder* 2 (April 1870): 859 and frontispiece.

"Diocesan News." *The Churchman* 57(14 April 1888): 443. Announces the construction of the Chapel of the Good Shepherd on Blackwell's Island, New York City.

"Diocesan News." *The Churchman* 71(22 June 1895): 901–903. Describes Withers's reredos for Calvary P.E. Church, Memphis, Tenn.

Donnell, Edna. "A. J. Davis and the

Gothic Revival." *Metropolitan Museum Studies* 5(September 1936): 183–233.

Downs, Arthur C. "America's First Medieval Churches." *Historical Magazine of the Protestant Episcopal Church* 45(June 1976): 166–76.

———. "Downing's Newburgh Villa." *Bulletin of the Association for Preservation Technology* 4(1972): 1–113.

———. "Victorian Premonitions of Wright's Prairie House in Downing and Scott." *Nineteenth Century* 2 (Summer 1976): 35–39.

First Annual Report of the Managers of the Hudson River State Hospital for the Insane for the Year Ending November 30, 1867. Contains a detailed account of Withers's plan for the hospital.

"First Presbyterian Church, Newburgh, New York." *The Architects' and Mechanics' Journal* 1(17 March 1860): 194–95.

"First Presbyterian Church, Newburgh, New York." *The Crayon* 6(February 1859): 49.

"First Presbyterian Church, Newburgh, New York." *The Ecclesiologist* 2(April 1859): 142.

Gallaudet, Edward M. "A History of the Columbia Institution for the Deaf and Dumb." *Records of the Columbia Historical Society of Washington, D.C.* 15(1912): 1–22.

"Gallaudet Home for Deaf Mutes." *The Churchman* 124(26 December 1896): 869–70. Gives information and an illustration for the house Withers designed originally for the Frost brothers at Clinton Point, N.Y.

"Grant Memorial." *Record and Guide,* 28 June 1886, pp. 112–13. An interview with Withers who framed the letter concerning the competition for the Grant monument that appeared in *Building* 3(October 1885): 147.

"Hartford: Christ Church—Semi-Centennial Anniversary." *The Churchman* 41(3 January 1880); 9.

"Hartford Monument." *The American Architect and Building News* 10(10 December 1881): 283.

Hitchcock, Henry-Russell. "Ruskin and American Architecture or Regeneration Long Delayed." in *Concerning Architecture,* edited by John Summerson. London: Penguin Books, 1968.

"House for Mr. Frank Hasbrouck, Market Street, Poughkeepsie, New York. Mr. F. C. Withers, Architect." *The American Architect and Building News* 22(2 July 1887): 7 (ill.).

"Hudson River Hospital for the Insane." *The New York Times,* 15 February 1867, p. 8.

"Hudson River State Hospital, Poughkeepsie, N.Y. Mr. F. C. Withers, Architect." *The American Architect and Building News* 3(30 March 1878): 110 (ill.).

"Hudson River State Hospital, Poughkeepsie, New York, Mr. F. C. Withers, Architect." *The American Architect and Building News* 3(24 August 1878): 65 (ill.).

"Huntington's Generous Gift." *The New York Times,* 10 January 1891, p. 5. Gives an account of the Huntington Library, Bronx, N.Y., which Withers originally designed for the Van Schaick family.

"Impressive Ceremonial." *The New York Times,* 30 June 1877, p. 2. Describes the dedication ceremonies for the Astor Reredos, Trinity Church, New York City.

Jacobus, Melancthon W. "The Soldiers and Sailors Memorial in Hartford." *Bulletin of the Connecticut Historical Society* 34(April 1969): 33–42.

"Jefferson Market." *Record and Guide,* 15 September 1883, pp. 683–84. The article describes Douglas Smyth's market and compares it to Withers's proposed design.

"Jefferson Market and the New Courthouse." *The New York Times,* 4 February 1874, p. 4.

"Jefferson Market Courthouse, Mr. F. C. Withers, Architect." *The American Architect and Building News* 18(25 July 1885): 42 (ill.).

"Jefferson Market Monument." *The New York Times,* 9 May 1877, p. 4. Deals with the high cost of the Jefferson Market Courthouse.

Kornwolf, James D. "High Victorian Gothic: Or the Dilemma of Style in Modern Architecture." *Journal of the Society of Architectural Historians* 34(March 1975): 37–48.

Kowsky, Francis R. "The Architecture of Frederick Clarke Withers (1828–1901)." *Journal of the Society of Architectural Historians* 35(May 1976): 83–109.

———. "Gallaudet College: A High Victorian Campus." *Records of the Columbia Historical Society of Washington, D.C., 1971–1972.* Washington, D.C.: By the Society, 1973, pp. 439–67.

———. "The Van Schaick Free Reading Room and the Huntington Memorial Library." *Journal of the Bronx County Historical Society* 7(January 1970): 1–7.

Lang, S. "The Principles of the Gothic Revival in England." *Journal of the Society of Architectural Historians* 25(December 1966): 37–46.

"Late George Bliss and the Church on Blackwell's Island." *The Churchman* 63(4 April 1896): 440–41. Details Withers's relationship with Bliss, the donor of the Chapel of the Good Shepherd.

L.F. "Notes from New York." *The Architect* 3(26 February 1870): 99–100. A brief review of the New York architectural scene.

"Local Miscellany: Charges Against Commissioner Porter." *The New York Times,* 9 February 1877, p. 8. Reports details of the Jefferson Market Courthouse troubles.

"Local Miscellany: Common Council Deliberations." *The New York Times,* 9 February 1877, p. 5. Reports details of the Jefferson Market Courthouse troubles.

"Local Miscellany: Third District Courthouse." *The New York Times,* 28 December 1876, p. 2.

"Local Miscellany" Third District Courthouse." *The New York Times,* 23 January 1877, p. 8.

"Memorial Church of St. John the Evangelist, Newport, R.I." *The Churchman* 68 (9 September 1893): 309–10. The church was a memorial to Sarah Zabriske.

"Memorial to William B. Astor." *The New York Times,* 2 July 1876, p. 2.

"Men and Things." *Record and Guide,* 3 August 1887, p. 1075. Notice of a two-story brick asylum for Blackwell's Island.

"Miscellaneous Notes." *The American Builder* 13(August 1877): 191–92. Gives an account of the relationship between Withers and Roland Plumbe, FRIBA, who in the 1850s was an assistant in Withers's Newburgh office.

"Municipal Extravagence." *The New York Times,* 8 May 1877, p. 2. Deals with the Jefferson Market Courthouse troubles.

"National Deaf-mute College at Washington." *Old and New Magazine* 6(October 1872): 492–97.

"New Churches: Holy Innocents, Hartford, Connecticut." *The Ecclesiologist* 18(April 1867): 185. The article reviews Withers's proposed design for a memorial to the Colt children.

"New Hampshire: Hanover, St. Thomas Church." *The Churchman* 41(15 May 1880): 539–40.

"New Jefferson Market Prison." *The New York Times,* 4 April 1878, p. 2.

"New Library Building for the Berkeley Divinity School." *The Churchman* 73(25 January 1896): 125–26.

"New Pulpit in Trinity Chapel, New

York." *The Churchman* 77(26 February 1898): 317–18.

"New Reredos in the Church of the Transfiguration." *The Churchman* 71(8 June 1895): 808.

"New Reredos in Trinity Church." *The Churchman*, 36(30 June 1877): 19, and 36(28 July 1877): 7.

"New Tombs Prison." *The New York Times*, 1 December 1898, p. 6.

"New York City: Church of the Transfiguration." *The Churchman* 71(1 June 1895): 774. Describes the reredos Withers designed for the church.

"New York: Memorial Altar and Reredos." *The Churchman* 34(29 July 1876): 91–92. Describes the Astor Reredos, Trinity Church, New York City.

"New York: The New Altar and Reredos in Trinity Church." *The Churchman* 35(30 June 1877): 726–27.

"News at the Building Trade." *Record and Guide*, 28 July 1894, p. 128. Notice of work for the Church of the Transfiguration, New York City.

"News of the Building Trade Beyond the Metropolitan District." *Record and Guide*, 2 March 1895, p. 331. Notice of the Richardson and McKillop store in Burlington, Vt.

Norton, Charles Elliott. "The Harvard and Yale Memorial Buildings." *The Nation* 5(11 July 1867): 34–35. Norton compares the design of Ware and Van Brunt's Memorial Hall for Harvard with Withers's plan for the Yale memorial chapel.

"Notes and Clippings." *The American Architect and Building News* 1(15 July 1876): 232. Contains comments on the Astor Reredos, Trinity Church, New York City.

"Notes on Current Topics." *The American Builder* 11(April 1875): 223. Contains information about the Jefferson Market Courthouse.

"Notes and Answers to Correspondents:

Secular Gothic Works in the United States." *The Ecclesiologist* 28(April 1867): 187. Offers brief comments on Withers's secular architecture.

"Oak Pulpit, Christ Church, Hartford, Conn. F. C. Withers, Architect." *Building* 2(September 1884): 136 (ill.).

"Observer." "Hartford Soldiers Monument." *The American Architect and Building News* 11(20 May 1882): 238.

"Old Trinity Renovated." *The New York Times*, 17 June 1877, p. 2.

Olmsted, Frederick L., Jr. "Riverside, Illinois." *Landscape Architecture* 21(July 1931): 256–91.

"Opening of the Library of the Berkeley Divinity School." *The Churchman* 74(12 December 1896): 794–95.

"Our New York Letter." *The American Builder* 1(October 1868): 14–16. Withers's name appears among the group of most promising young architects in New York City.

"Our New York Letter." *The American Builder* 2(July 1869): 137–39. Contains comments on Withers's design for a large park entryway.

"Out Among the Builders." *Record and Guide*, 3 July 1886, p. 860. Notice of the remodeling of St. Ann's Church, New York City, and the proposed design for Christ Church, also in New York City.

"Out Among the Builders." *Record and Guide*, 19 October 1889, p. 1409. Notice of a new hospital for Ward's Island.

"Out Among the Builders." *Record and Guide*, 28 June 1890, p. 949. Notice of the alterations to the G. W. Greene House, Brooklyn, N.Y.

"Out Among the Builders." *Record and Guide*, 26 October 1892, p. 473. Notice of a new kitchen building for Bellevue Hospital.

"Out Among the Builders." *Record and Guide*, 28 April 1894, p. 665. Notice of a wall and gates for Bellevue Hospital.

"Out of Town." *Record and Guide,* 24 July 1886, p. 948. Notice of a school house for St. Luke's Church, Beacon, N.Y.

"Out of Town." *Record and Guide,* 13 November 1886, p. 1390. Notice of additions to the Hudson River State Hospital, Poughkeepsie, N.Y.

"Out of Town." *Record and Guide,* 19 February 1887, p. 234. Notice of the Church of the Advent, Louisville, Ky.

"Out of Town." *Record and Guide,* 17 March 1891, p. 436. Notice of the alterations of the Cathedral of the Immaculate Conception, Albany, N.Y.

"Out of Town." *Record and Guide,* 15 April 1893, p. 581. An announcement of Mrs. Zabriske's intention to build a memorial church to her mother.

"Plans to Change the Tombs." *The New York Times,* 5 June 1896, p. 12.

"Presbyterian Church, Newburgh, N.Y." *Architects' and Mechanics' Journal* 1 (17 March 1860): 194–95.

"Proposed New Market." *The American Architect and Building News* 1(18 March 1876): 96. Deals with the market adjacent to the Jefferson Market Courthouse.

"Reredos in Trinity Chapel, New York." *The Churchman* 66(31 December 1892): 900–901.

"Reredos (of Caen Stone) and Altar (of Oak), Christ Church, Hartford, Conn., F. C. Withers, Architect, New York." *Building* 2(May 1884): 92 (ill.).

"Residence, Jersey City, N.J., for Mr. John F. Ward. Mr. F. C. Withers, Architect." *The American Architect and Building News* 15(19 February 1884): 77 (ill.).

"Residence of Dr. Pierrepont Davis, Hartford, Connecticut, Mr. F. C. Withers, Architect." *The American Architect and Building News* 9(18 June 1881): 296 (ill.).

"Return of Old Jeff." *Progressive Architecture,* October 1967, pp. 175–78. Discusses the modern renovation of the Jefferson Market Courthouse.

Review of *Church Architecture* by Frederick C. Withers. *The American Builder* 9(November 1873): 284.

"Riverside." *The American Builder* 2(December 1869): 228–29.

"Roofer's Tricks." *The American Architect and Building News* 3(16 February 1878): 56. Concerns the Jefferson Market Courthouse.

"St. George Church, Newburgh, New York." *The American Architect and Building News* 18(2 January 1886).

"St. Helen, Little Cawthorpe, Lincolnshire." *The Ecclesiologist* 20(April 1859): 287.

"St. Luke's Church, Altoona, Pennsylvania." *Building* 2(January 1884): 44.

"St. Michael's Church and Parsonage." *The Building News* 5(4 November 1859): 1000. Discusses Withers's design for St. Michael's, Germantown, Pa.

"St. Michael's, Germantown, Pennsylvania, U.S." *The Ecclesiologist* 21(August 1860): 215–16.

"St. Thomas, Hanover, N.H. Mr. F. C. Withers, Architect." *The New York Sketch-book of Architecture* 1(February 1874).

"St. Thomas Church, Hanover, N.H., Mr. Frederick C. Withers, Architect, New York." *The American Architect and Building News* 3(11 May 1878): 165 (ill.).

Schuyler, Montgomery. "Concerning Queen Anne, Recent Building in New York." *Harper's Magazine* 67 (September 1883): 557–78.

———. "The Third District Court House of New York." Reprinted from *The*

New York World in *The American Architect and Building News,* 2(21 April 1877): 127.

————. "Trinity's Architecture." *The Architectural Record* 25(June 1909): 411–25.

"Secular Towers, Modern." *The American Architect and Building News* 18(17 October 1885): ill.

"Semi-Detached Laborers' Cottages, Hartford, Conn., for J. J. and F. Goodwin. Frederick C. Withers, Architect, New York." *Building* 3(April 1885): 78 (ill.).

"Silent Schools of Kendall Green." *Harper's Magazine* 69(July 1884): 96–104. A description of Gallaudet College.

"South East View of Proposed Church and School-house, Conn., F. C. Withers." *Fourth Annual Exhibition of the Architectural League of New York, 1888–1889,* p. 37, No. 127 (ill.).

Spingarn, J. E. "Henry Winthrop Sargent and the Early History of Landscape Gardening and Ornamental Horticulture in Dutchess County, New York." In *Yearbook of the Dutchess County Historical Society for 1937.* Vol. 22, pp. 36–70. Spingarn gives an account of Sargent's connection with Withers's St. Luke's Church, Beacon, N.Y.

"Study for City Prison and Courts, New York, Mr. F. C. Withers, Architect." *The New York Sketch-book of Architecture* 1(April 1874).

Sturgis, Russell. "Modern Architecture." *The North American Review* 112 (January 1871): 160–77, and 112 (April 1871): 370–91.

"Swope Memorial Reredos." *The Churchman* 66(31 December 1892): 900–901. Discusses the reredos Withers designed for Trinity Chapel, New York City.

"Ten Most Noted Buildings in the Country." *The American Architect and Building News* 17(7 March 1885): 109. The list included the Jefferson Market Courthouse. See "Best Ten Buildings."

"Third District Court-house." *The New York Times,* 30 December 1876, p. 2.

"Third District Court-house." *The New York Times,* 30 January 1877, p. 8.

"Third District Court-house, Bell Tower, and Prison." *The American Architect and Building News* 3(15 June 1878): 209–10.

"Third District Courthouse in New York: Bills of Quantities." *The American Architect and Building News* 2(10 February 1877): 41.

"Tombs Prison Muddle." *The New York Times,* 16 February 1897, p. 8. Charges of corruption surrounding the construction of the New York City Prison are discussed.

"Tombs Prison Muddle." *The New York Times,* 4 December 1898, p. 8.

"Trinity Church, Chapel, and Parish House, Hartford, Connecticut, Mr. F. C. Withers, Architect." *The American Architect and Building News* 33(4 July 1891): 14.

"Trinity Church: Dedication of the Altar and Reredos." *The Churchman* 36 (14 July 1877): 36.

"Trinity Church Extension." *The American Architect and Building News* 1(19 August 1876): 270.

"Trinity Parish Building, Natchez, Mississippi." *The Churchman* 57(21 April 1888): 475.

"Troy's Rice Building." *The Troy* (New York) *Record,* 2 November 1968, p. 7.

"Van Schaick Free Reading Room." *The American Architect and Building News* 8 (5 September 1885): 110.

"Van Schaick Free Reading Room, Westchester, New York, Mr. F. C. Withers, Architect." *The American Architect and Building News* 14(20 October 1883): 298 (ill.).

"Vassar Brothers Hospital, Poughkeepsie, New York, Mr. F. C. Withers, Architect, New York." *Building* 3(August 1885): 126 (ill.).

Vaux, Calvert. "American Architecture." *The Horticulturist* 8(April 1853): 168–72.

———. "Hints for Country House Builders." *Harper's New Monthly Magazine* 11(November 1855): 763–78.

Verplank, Mrs. Samuel. "Historical Notes of the Reformed Dutch Church of Fishkill Landing." In *Centennial of the Reformed Dutch Church of Beacon, New York, 1813–1913* (1913), pp. 32–42.

"Villa Residence, Wilkes Barre, Pennsylvania, Mr. F. C. Withers, Architect." *The American Architect and Building News* 1(9 December 1876): 397 (ill.). The house was built for S. L. Thurlow.

Ware, William R. "On the Condition of Architecture and Architectural Education in the United States." *Sessional Papers of the Royal Institute of British Architects* (1867), pp. 81–90. Withers is called an important young architect.

"Watertower for the Hackensack Water Company, Mr. F. C. Withers, Architect." *The American Architect and Building News* 14(8 September 1883): 114 (ill.).

"Weehawken Water Tower." *Engineering News and American Contract Journal* 16(6 November 1886): 292–93.

West, Edward. "Rethinking Need Means Rethought Plan." *Cathedral News,* May 1967, pp. 1–10. Reviews the competition for the Cathedral of St. John the Divine.

"Westchester Refuses a Gift." *The New York Times,* 29 August 1885, p. 5. Concerns the Van Schaick Free Reading Room.

"Whitecaps: Marine Villa of James M. Dunbar, Monmouth Beach, New Jersey, Mr. F. C. Withers, Architect."
The American Architect and Building News 10(29 October 1881): 207 (ill.).

"Whitehall." "The Produce Exchange." *The New York Times,* 3 March 1881, p. 8.

Wilbur, H. B. "Buildings for the Management and Treatment of the Insane." *Proceedings of the National Conference of Charities and Correction, September, 1877,* pp. 134–38. Contains comments on the Hudson River State Hospital.

Wilson, Richard. "American Architecture and the Search for a National Style in the 1870's." *Nineteenth Century* 3(Autumn 1977): 74.

Withers, Frederick C. "The Astor Memorial." In *The Yearbook and Register of Trinity Church, New York, 1878,* Appendix 1.

———. "A Few Hints on Church Building." *The Horticulturist* 13(July 1858): 348–52.

"Work on the Tombs Stops." *The New York Times,* 20 November 1898, p. 2.

"Yale College Memorial Chapel, New Haven, Connecticut, U.S." *The Builder* 25(12 October 1867): 747 (ill. and plan).

"Yale Memorial Chapel." *The American Builder* 2(April 1870): 85.

"Zabriske Memorial Church, Newport, Rhode Island, Mr. F. C. Withers, Architect." *The American Architect and Building News* 77(1 November 1902): 39 (ill.).

"Zabriske Memorial Church of St. John the Evangelist, Newport, Rhode Island." *The Churchman* 77(13 July 1895): 48–49.

UNPUBLISHED MATERIAL

American Architectural Archive. Greenwich, Connecticut. A collection of miscellaneous personal and professional documents of Withers. The Archive also possesses notes from interviews conducted by Alan Burnham in 1958 with Margaret Withers, the architect's last surviving child.

Diaries of Alfred Janson Bloor (1828–1917), New York Historical Society.

Diaries of the Reverend Dr. Morgan Dix, manuscript collection, Trinity P.E. Church, New York City.

Diaries and miscellaneous papers of Edward Miner Gallaudet, Gallaudet Memorial Library, Gallaudet College, Washington, D.C., and the Library of Congress, manuscript division.

Kramer, Ellen W. "The Domestic Architecture of Detlef Lienau, a Conservative Victorian." Ph.D. diss., New York University, 1958.

National Archives, Washington, D.C. Miscellaneous documents related to Withers's service in the Union army during the Civil War.

New York Historical Society. A collection of miscellaneous documents and letters relating to Withers's career.

Olmsted, Frederick Law. Papers in the Library of Congress, manuscript division.

Sigle, John D. "Calvert Vaux, an American Architect." Master's thesis, School of Architecture, University of Virginia, 1967.

Tatum, George B. "Andrew Jackson Downing, Arbiter of American Taste." Ph.D. diss., Princeton University, 1952.

Vaux, Calvert. Correspondence and miscellaneous papers in the New York Public Library, manuscript division.

Withers, F. C. Drawings and miscellaneous papers in the Avery Library, Columbia University.

<h1>❦INDEX❦</h1>

Numbers in *italics* refer to pages on which illustrations appear. References to the Notes are indicated by the page followed by the number of the note in parentheses. Buildings are listed by name; for an inventory by location of Withers's projects, see the List of Works.